CONFLICTING WORLDS

New Dimensions of the American Civil War

T. Michael Parrish, EDITOR

Fort Pillow,
a Civil War Massacre, and Public Memory

John Cimprich

John Cimprich (signature)

Louisiana State University Press ✺ *Baton Rouge*

Designer: Amanda McDonald Scallan
Typeface: Baskerville BE
Typesetter G&S Typesetters, Inc.
Printer and binder: Edwards Brothers, Inc.

Library of Congress Cataloging-in-Publication Data

Cimprich, John, 1949–
    Fort Pillow, a Civil War massacre, and public memory / John Cimprich.
        p.   cm.   –   (Conflicting worlds)
    Includes bibliographical references (p.   ) and index.
    ISBN 0-8071-3110-5 (cloth : alk. paper)
    1. Fort Pillow, Battle of, Tenn., 1864.   2. Fort Pillow (Tenn.)–History.   3. Memory–Social aspects–
Southern States.   4. Memory–Social aspects–United States.   5. United States–History–Civil War,
1861–1865–Social aspects.   I. Title: Fort Pillow.   II. Title.   III. Series.
E476.17.c56   2005
973.7′36–dc22

                                                                                      2005002839

Contents

Preface

A high bluff in the Fort Pillow State Historic Area gives visitors a panoramic view of the Mississippi River, but thick forest sharply limits the area visible in much of the park. Most of the time only bird calls and the breeze swishing through the foliage break the silence, for the site lays off the beaten path and does not draw many visitors. The location's isolation and natural beauty impress tourists today, much as they did military men during the Civil War. Still, we cannot entirely recapture their experience of the place. Since 1865, trees have returned to man-made clearings, the river has shifted westward, and the landscape has undergone much erosion.

The fort's fame rests upon a massacre, the occurrence of which has been questioned. Anyone who does not think that some men on both sides of the Civil War were capable of atrocities will not find this work useful. The unnecessary killing of noncombatants or of surrendering soldiers has often occurred in the past, and the United States' history has its share. A few of the more prominent ones are of Creeks at Horseshoe Bend in 1814, of Mexicans in a Mexico City neighborhood in 1848, of Cheyennes at the Washita River in 1868, of some German prisoners during the Normandy campaign in 1944, and of Vietnamese at My Lai in 1968.[1] To say that such things occurred is not to condemn all American soldiers, for the great majority had enough idealism or discipline not to participate in massacres. Still, the troubling events exist. The Fort Pillow incident in 1864 stands out as the most famous atrocity of the nation's bloodiest war.

Events preceding the massacre at the fort provide a context for better understanding the controversial incident. Moreover, the full history of the fort offers a panoramic view of several major themes of the American Civil War: the gradual shift from the awkward warfare of the armies' amateur enlistees to the efficient efforts of veterans, the many challenges of military life, the ongoing struggle between Federal dominance and secessionist resistance in occupied areas, the conflicts over changing race relations, the difficulties faced by Southern unionists in dealing with both sides, and the controversy over rules in a new type of war. This study will illuminate the war's formative aspects, which helped to shape events at the site beyond the massacre. In addition, the concluding chapter will examine the role stories about the massacre played in the evolving public memory of the Civil War.

This book approaches the story of Fort Pillow and the sources about it afresh. Some common statements in earlier histories proved wanting upon examination, and I even caught minor errors in my own earlier publications. The primary sources, especially those for the 1862 naval battle and the 1864 massacre, contain many contradictions. Following professional standards, this work generally gives the most weight to evidence close in time and location to events, but it also scrutinizes all the authors' purposes and reliability.[2] Comments on analytic method may seem unnecessary, but some preceding writers have not abided by such guidelines. Amateur historians have written many of the most controversial works on the subject. Still, the major events at Fort Pillow are unavoidably controversial, for they poke the sensitive nerves of American racial and sectional differences.

A number of individuals and institutions generously assisted this project during its long development. The Phi Alpha Theta National Honor Society in History, the Thomas More College Faculty Relations Committee, and the Southeast Missouri State University Grants and Research Funding Committee financed portions of the work. Tim Burke, Jim Cunningham, Roy Finklebine, Mark Grimsley, Ken Heger, the late Sarah Dunlap Jackson, Joe Mannard, Mike Musick, Michael Parrish, the late Tom Shouse, John Y. Simon, and Marion Smith aided me in the research. Steve Ash, Vickie Cimprich, Merton Dillon, Richard Lowe, Malcolm Muir, James Ramage, and Donald Yacavone thoughtfully critiqued chapter drafts. Some passages from *Black Soldiers in Blue: African American Troops in the Civil War Era,* edited by John David Smith (copyright © 2002 by the University of North Carolina Press) were used by permission of the publisher.

I profited from the assistance of numerous librarians and archivists, especially those at the National Archives, the Library of Congress, Tennessee State Library and Archives, Fort Pillow State Historic Area Museum, Alabama Division of Archives and History, Illinois State Historical Library, Indiana State Library, Indiana Historical Society, State Historical Society of Iowa, Missouri Historical Society, Historical Society of Pennsylvania, Rush County (Indiana) Archives, Duke University Library, University of North Carolina Library, Dartmouth College Library, University of Tennessee Library, University of Memphis Library, University of Cincinnati

Library, Southeastern Missouri State University Library, Thomas More College Library, Greensburg (Indiana) Public Library, Public Library of Cincinnati and Hamilton County, Kenton County (Kentucky) Public Library, Lawrenceburg (Indiana) Public Library, Mason City (Iowa) Public Library, Memphis and Shelby County Public Library, Story City (Iowa) Public Library, and Vigo County (Indiana) Public Library.

I would like to dedicate this book to my wife, Vickie Hucker Cimprich. She consistently encouraged the effort during the many years the work took.

Fort Pillow,

a Civil War Massacre, and Public Memory

ILLINOIS

Cape Girardeau

Ohio River

Mound City
Cairo

Paducah

MISSOURI

Tennessee River

Cumberland River

Belmont   Columbus

KENTUCKY

New Madrid

FT. HENRY

Island No. 10   Union City

FT. DONELSON

Mississippi River

MEMPHIS AND OHIO RAIL ROAD

Obion River

Forked Deer River

North Fork

South Fork

Eaton

Plum Bend

Key Corner

Craighead
Point   Ripley   Woodville

Osceola

TENNESSEE

Island No. 30   FT. PILLOW   Durhamville   Poplar
                 Fulton   Corner

Island No. 34   Brownsville

Covington   Jackson

Randolph   Bloomington

MOBILE AND OHIO RAIL ROAD

Hatchie River

Denmark

Mason

Bolivar

Memphis

Pittsburg Landing

MEMPHIS AND CHARLESTON RAIL ROAD

Moscow   LaGrange

Corinth

Wolf River

MISSISSIPPI

Mid-Mississippi Valley

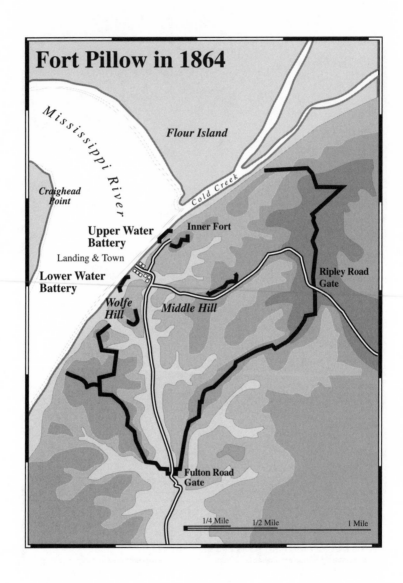

Fort Pillow in 1864

Mississippi River

Flour Island

Craighead Point

Cold Creek

Upper Water Battery

Inner Fort

Landing & Town

Lower Water Battery

Wolfe Hill

Middle Hill

Ripley Road Gate

Fulton Road Gate

1/4 Mile   1/2 Mile   1 Mile

Chapter One

The Fort's Beginnings

B EFORE the Civil War, Gideon Pillow ranked as Tennessee's best known war veteran. Pompously, he often reminded listeners about his extensive combat experience in the Mexican War as a major general, a position gained solely through political connections. After that war he earned great wealth as a lawyer, planter, and entrepreneur. By 1861 and the age of fifty-four, the hair and beard of this short, stout leader had gone partly gray. The presidential election of Abraham Lincoln, an anti-slavery Republican, had convinced him that the South must secede and fight to preserve its way of life, especially white supremacy and slavery. Consequently, he helped Governor Isham G. Harris activate militia units in West Tennessee during a long and contentious referendum campaign on separation from the United States and alliance with the new Southern Confederacy.[1]

Fearing a swift Federal invasion down the broad highway of the Mississippi, the governor authorized militiamen to construct two large earthen forts along the river. The poorly located Fort Harris sat in bottomlands a little north of Memphis. Upriver, another structure, called both Fort Randolph after a nearby village and Fort Wright after a militia commander, occupied a strong position on the Second Chickasaw Bluff. After the Civil War started in April, the issuance by Kentucky's governor of a proclamation of neutrality encouraged Harris to continue concentrating his efforts on West Tennessee, rather than on the long border with that neighboring state. The self-promoting and excessively ambitious Pillow used his military reputation and political ties first to secure responsibility from Governor Harris for river fortifications and then to win command of the Provisional Army of Tennessee. Sharing Harris's fear of an invasion, he entered into his new duties with great energy and organizational skill.[2]

Lacking military training, Pillow in some ways remained an amateur general. He had only begun to learn from his Mexican War experiences when that conflict ended, and a quick return to civilian life had left whatever knowledge he had acquired to rust during the years before secession. But that was still better than most of the 3 million men who served in the Civil War with no military background whatsoever. The majority were twenty-five years old or younger when they enlisted.[3] So, to a large degree the war began as a conflict of amateurs.

On June 6, 1861, Colonel Patrick Cleburne, an immigrant with experience in the British army, led a small force of Arkansans upstream from Fort Randolph to build a battery at an advanced "post of honor," according to a Memphis newspaper. After Arkansas's secession, its governor had loaned these troops to Pillow, who owned much land in that state. Fort Randolph's commander had encouraged Cleburne to move upriver because the post suffered from unhealthy overcrowding and false alarms of surprise attacks.[4] Cleburne chose a site on the high First Chickasaw Bluff two miles above Fulton. Local secessionists warmly welcomed the troops, and grateful Memphis women sent up an embroidered flag for one unit. The troops began digging what they called Fort Cleburne on forested land owned by two sawyers from the North and a businessman from Missouri. A lightly populated agricultural area surrounded the new fort. Although the farmers concentrated on cotton and tobacco, the area contained much unimproved land.[5]

On June 8, Tennessee officially left the Union, and on July 4 Pillow and his forces in West Tennessee entered the Confederate army as part of Major General Leonidas Polk's Western Department. Polk, an Episcopal bishop from Louisiana, had much zeal and a West Point education but practically no military experience. His first general order exhorted his troops "to resist the invasion at all hazards and to the last extremity." By then Cleburne, who would later win fame for his combat skills, had returned home with his force.[6]

Pillow decided to expand Cleburne's battery into a huge fortification. Captain Montgomery Lynch, a Memphis sappers and miners unit (specialists in earthwork construction), a small group of hired slave laborers, and several Tennessee regiments moved upriver for the project after having worked on Fort Randolph. During the next nine months, Lynch, a former civil engineer with a military school education, would design and direct construction of what he called Fort Pillow.[7] The garrison would undergo frequent changes of commanders and size (see Tables 1 and 2).

While at Fort Randolph, the infantrymen had quickly tired of manual labor and had asked that slaves replace them. Pillow had appealed to area slaveholders, who spared but few bondsmen during spring planting. General Pillow, "fond of the good opinion of his men," according to Private William G. Stevenson, now agreed to let the Fort Pillow troops, other than the sappers and miners, focus on drilling instead of digging. On July 15, the 4th Tennessee Infantry passed glowing resolutions thanking Pillow for contributing to their "wellbeing, health, and comfort," as well as for saving the state from invasion.[8] By August, General Polk had appointed a group of slave hirers to operate in West Tennessee as well as several neighboring states. Since many masters feared that the army would overwork slaves and disregard their welfare, Polk encouraged owners to send along overseers, and fairly soon fifteen days became the standard work period. Polk sent army steamers for the slaves but expected them to bring tools, blankets, and food for the trip. He threatened to impress slaves into service if planters did not provide enough laborers voluntarily.[9]

The Mississippi River Valley south of the fort held a large slave population, which in these unsettled times had prompted several slave insurrection panics and the creation of home guard units. In Lauderdale County, where Fort Pillow sat, slaves made up 38 percent of the population, and most belonged to owners possessing ten or more. The county court created a home guard in May but disbanded it in July, possibly from a sense of security created by the fort.[10]

Army steamers brought numerous slaves to the fort during the late summer. These workers built a half-mile-long series of batteries on the bank where the river first flowed under the bluff. Pillow also had a heavy chain, which he had used to block the river at Fort Randolph, moved up to Fort Pillow. While the records do not specify when the workers installed the chain, by October it ran across the river on flatboats anchored one hundred feet apart. This barrier would halt enemy ships in front of the riverbank artillery, called the water batteries, which would easily pummel them since the channel ran close to the east shore. The use of this tactic on the Hudson River during the American Revolution may have inspired the idea. Work crews also built a military road from the water batteries to the top of the bluff, where they established a mortar battery. Hardly had these efforts begun when Polk and Pillow decided to initiate fortifications upriver at New Madrid, Missouri, and nearby Island Number 10.[11] This move reduced Fort Pillow to the second line of defense.

In late August, Pillow met Polk at the fort to make plans. Humiliated by the Confederacy's decisions to place Polk over him and to issue him a lower rank than he had held in the Mexican War, Brigadier General Pillow developed a fervent desire to launch an offensive operation in the hope of promoting his career. Polk agreed to an invasion of Missouri, but several days later Pillow won approval to substitute a movement to occupy the high bluff at Columbus, Kentucky, where he would build another huge fort. This action, however, stirred up much trouble for the Confederacy by ending Kentucky's neutrality. The Confederate government quickly sent General Albert Sidney Johnston, a highly experienced professional soldier, to command the entire western war theater. Johnston emphasized a defensive strategy, since the end of Kentucky's neutrality forced him to stretch his forces over a long northern line of fortifications.[12]

Numerous new construction sites competed for the limited pool of slave laborers, artillery, and troops. The Confederates, therefore, abandoned Fort Harris and shipped its cannons to Fort Pillow, which in turn forwarded some artillery to more advanced positions. Forts Columbus and Pillow, the largest fortifications, each had elaborate batteries on the riverbank, in the face of the bluff, and on the bluff top, plus extensive earthworks on the landed side. The fortifications of Fort Donelson on the Cumberland River and of Fort Randolph had most of the same features. Pillow and Polk clearly intended these works to be invincible. Perhaps the success of early recruiting had fooled them into thinking that they would have no trouble filling huge bastions with troops.[13] Great enthusiasm for the cause still predominated in the Confederacy; the war had not yet caused much suffering.

The anticipated Federal invasion of Tennessee would not come in 1861, although rumors and false alarms persisted. In the fall of 1861 Fort Pillow had a garrison too small to man all the earthworks.[14] Descriptions of the works began to appear in Northern newspapers. Several months after an official complained that spies easily lurked around the fort because of the disbanding of the Lauderdale County home guard, the county court reinstated the guards. At the same time, Captain Lynch complained that a stricter picket line interfered with construction. Communication improved, though, with telegraphic connection to Memphis.[15]

Riverboat traffic decreased as Northern-owned ships withdrew, many Southern crewmen enlisted, and Pillow banned shipments to the North. Polk ordered the garrison to halt and inspect all nonlocal boats coming downriver. Rivermen saw this as a great nuisance and sometimes tried to slip past the inspectors. One escaped altogether when a green officer, preparing a warning shot, mistakenly ordered a cannonball loaded before ammunition. Much to the amusement of onlookers, no explosion occurred when the artillerymen tried to fire. In another case, a steamer refused to stop, even after the firing of warning shots. Soldiers boarded an army steamboat for pursuit but did not catch up with the mystery ship until they found it docked at Memphis with no one aboard. The commander at Memphis took over the investigation and sent the troops back to the fort without any answers.[16] Since Pillow's chain barrier did not interfere with commercial traffic, it apparently remained slack. In October, rising waters broke the chain and thereby provoked jokes among the troops about "Pillow's trot-line" floating loose in the river.[17]

Most construction at the fort during the fall of 1861 focused on entrenchments along the irregular terrain of the landed side. Essentially, the First Chickasaw Bluff is a huge, well-eroded pile of loess or fine silt on the West Tennessee plain. The engineers surveyed a three-and-a-half-mile line for the earthworks to follow, atop ridges wherever possible. The enclosed area consisted of three hills divided by a Y-shaped ravine system. The Y's leg, a short central ravine, started at the Mississippi below a waterline battery. A dirt road ran up it and out the Y's right arm toward Fulton. At the exit point, a low spot in the fort's southeast corner, the earthwork rose higher and had a square indentation to aid defense. Another road branched off the Fulton Road near the Y's junction point, crossed the middle hill, and ran out a gate toward Ripley.[18]

The engineers relied upon Irish immigrant workers for tasks requiring the most skill. When the army failed to pay these men for several months, the engineers had to head off repeated strike threats and to loan money to workers needing to feed families. Slave laborers did the bulk of the heavy work, which at this time mostly involved digging a ditch eight to twelve feet deep and wide, and piling up the dirt immediately behind the ditch in an embankment of the same proportions. In places where a slope dropped off in front, they dug a wide and shallow trench behind the embankment to obtain enough dirt. Slaves lined the inside part of the earthwork with planks. Within the enclosure they cleared some areas and left the rest wooded. In October the slave crew probably reached its highest number at fifteen hundred.[19]

Planter resistance to slave-hiring increased as Confederate agents approached some for a second time and as harvesting began. John H. Bills, who sent four slaves, labeled Polk's plea for help "a most villainous call, one he has no right to make and is the beginning of a despotism worse than any European Monarchy." Numbers of slave laborers fell off sharply in November. A very disgusted official discovered that General Pillow himself refused to hire out slaves from his Arkansas plantations and that the general's neighbors followed his example.[20]

At that time, Pillow's military reputation crested (despite his uneven performance) with the repulsion of Brigadier General Ulysses S. Grant's advance toward Columbus in the Battle of Belmont, Missouri, on November 7, 1861. Because the Federal menace had finally shown its face, a Memphis newspaper published a call for three thousand more slaves "urgently needed" to finish fortifications at Fort Pillow and other upriver sites. Polk soon rated construction of Fort Pillow as "substantially accomplished" and ordered most of the slave laborers there to New Madrid. The sappers and miners unit followed in December. That month, Fort Pillow's armament probably reached its high point with fifty-eight cannons mounted, but some were soon shipped with surplus construction tools to upriver posts.[21]

At Fort Pillow the newly recruited troops often found their lives monotonously centered on drilling, which most officers had to learn from books or from the few experienced colleagues before teaching their men.[22] In 1861, Confederate camps had many civilian visitors, such as the sprightly young woman who found the fort a "wild & romantic . . . charming spot." Guests encouraged the novice soldiers during awkward military exercises.[23]

A lack of weapons limited training in many of the earliest Confederate regiments. When the 39th Tennessee Infantry had no rifles, its colonel ordered wooden copies cut to enable his men to practice the manual of arms. He begged Confederate officials repeatedly for weapons before receiving any.[24] Since the seceding states had little time to prepare for war in 1861, officials often outfitted regiments with a miscellany of mostly old weapons collected from civilians. The 39th Tennessee eventually received a shipment including display pieces with silver mountings, outdated flint and steel muskets, shotguns, and antique Belgian rifles. Many lacked parts or needed repairs. A common response to the multiplicity of weapons was to rebore them to the same caliber and thereby simplify the distribution of ammunition. The process took so long for the 11th Arkansas Infantry as to leave most of the men unarmed throughout their stay at Fort Pillow. The 39th Tennessee Infantry discovered that 30 percent of its rebored rifles burst when first used. Ammunition was another necessity sometimes in short supply at the fort in 1861. Once, in the fall, artillerists discovered all the cannon powder to be damaged beyond use; a fresh supply took nearly two months to arrive.[25]

Because of militia tradition, the selection of the officers to respond to these challenges unfortunately rested upon elections. These popularity contests put egos on the line. Captain Joe Barbiere resentfully but quietly endured deep humiliation when the men selected his competitors as regimental field officers. But Captain John L. Logan refused to accept defeat. First, he convinced a group of peers to demand a new election, but the winners took an adamant stand and eventually forced apologies from the protesters. Undeterred, Logan claimed his company wanted to switch to a new unit and even secured permission to leave to help raise the new unit. He returned when he also lost the field officer elections in the new regiment; by then his old colonel had learned that the company held mixed views about leaving.[26]

Early in 1862, Polk concentrated most of his troops at Columbus, New Madrid, and Island Number 10. Both garrison size and construction activity decreased during the winter at Fort Pillow. Captain Lynch drove piles into the Mississippi to narrow the channel and tried again to run the chain across the river. The still-rising waters and a need for the chain's flatboats at Columbus terminated these projects. At the north end of the fort, slave laborers graded a road from Cold Creek to run along the inside of the outer earthworks. When cold, rainy weather impaired digging and harmed the laborers' health, the army started providing medical care for them, but worried owners increasingly refused to hire out their slaves. The hirers in turn pressured planters by requesting a 50 percent quota of able-bodied male slaves and by recording the names of those who refused. This tactic and collecting slaves in new areas farther downriver worked to raise a crew of over five hundred slaves in early February.[27]

That month a grave military danger arose in Tennessee when General Grant bypassed Columbus, Kentucky, to puncture the Confederate front line with the capture of Forts Henry and Donelson. Gideon Pillow ruined his reputation by resigning command of Fort Donelson and saving himself by flight shortly before the fort's surrender. Governor Harris's government fled Nashville, the state capital, and soon became ineffective. Grant soon advanced up the Tennessee River to Pittsburg Landing. To the west another Federal force, under Brigadier General John Pope, marched overland to besiege New Madrid, Missouri. These threats made Confederate general

Albert Sidney Johnston pull his troops back. While Johnston oversaw a concentration of forces east of the Tennessee River, he sent General P. G. T. Beauregard, his second-in-command, to manage matters to the west.[28]

Beauregard had a West Point education like Polk and Johnston, much military experience like Johnston, and a big ego like Pillow. He had already won fame for his role in the capture of Fort Sumter and the Battle of First Bull Run. Now he quickly decided to evacuate Columbus for fear that Grant's army would trap and capture another large garrison. Beauregard saw Island No. 10 as a place at which a smaller force than that at Columbus could block Federal progress down the Mississippi. Immediately after Pope arrived outside New Madrid, the Confederate army shipped all of Fort Pillow's slave and Irish laborers there for a week to participate in a desperate effort to finish fortifications. Some troops from the downriver fort also headed to these defenses. Seeing Fort Pillow as the backup to Island No. 10, Beauregard subsequently ordered more artillery, ammunition, supplies, and troops shipped to Fort Pillow. He sent rat-tail files (the type with narrow, pointed extensions for handles) to both fortifications for spiking cannons, in case the garrisons should have to withdraw. His numerous military messages showed great attention to detail and to controlling subordinates, as well as a mind sometimes very changeable.[29]

Obviously, Beauregard wanted the engineers to "hurry with the defenses" at Fort Pillow. In early March, heavy rains made the ground very slippery and eventually created areas of knee-deep muck, which rendered dirt roads almost impassable. Still, slave laborers completed cutting down the trees for at least three hundred yards outside the rear earthworks and arranging the felled wood as abatis, an entangling obstacle to hinder attackers. The crews also had to rebuild some earthworks damaged by the downpours. After receiving reports describing Lynch's work, Beauregard, a very experienced military engineer, judged some of it inadequate. Lynch, who lacked prior military service, had thoughtlessly built several ammunition magazines into battery walls. Beauregard directed that the captain rebuild all magazines as detached structures and that he add solid walls or traverses between every set of three cannons in the water batteries. When the river inundated those batteries, the general wanted them moved uphill. Beauregard also mandated the construction of an inner defensive line on the land side to enable a small garrison to defend the fort. Just when Lynch had thought the fort nearly done, he found himself with more work than he could easily finish.[30]

On March 13, the Confederates abandoned New Madrid but left a force on Island No. 10. Beauregard reassigned most of the evacuated troops to Corinth, Mississippi, and sent all the slave laborers to Fort Pillow. Expecting the loss of Island No. 10 and then an attack on Fort Pillow, the army issued another urgent call for more slave workers to finish the fortification; it even asked small-scale owners to volunteer their bondsmen.[31] Several of the Western Department's top-ranking engineers with West Point training visited Fort Pillow to direct Lynch on final preparations. Sometime in April, Lynch would find himself reassigned to Corinth.[32]

At Fort Pillow the situation required a skillful commander. Beauregard twice appointed and removed generals about whom he had second thoughts. Then he agreed to try Brigadier General John B. Villepigue, recommended by Major General Braxton Bragg as an officer who "would never be stampeded." A young West Pointer and professional soldier from South Carolina, the new commander had already earned a reputation for coolness, determination, and skill in combat. By March 26, Villepigue had arrived at the fort, which he would command throughout the upcoming campaign.[33]

Villepigue undertook the task with great energy. He asked for field artillery and cavalry to help protect the fort's land side; he sought more ordnance for the riverfront batteries, too, because a number of the fort's cannons had gone to other sites. The fort ended up with forty-two pieces of artillery. Villepigue also had to beg for pay for his disgruntled Irish laborers, whom he could not afford to lose. Following up on a concern of Beauregard's, he finished repairs on a road running southeast to Mason, the closest depot on the Memphis and Ohio Railroad.[34]

In the Battle of Pittsburg Landing (or Shiloh) on April 6 and 7, the main Confederate army attacked Major General Grant in the war's first extremely bloody battle. Johnston was killed, Beauregard succeeded him, and Grant–after losing much ground–finally forced a Confederate withdrawal. Refusing to admit defeat, Beauregard tried to encourage Villepigue: "Be of good cheer. I hope and expect to whip the enemy once more." Yet, on April 8, the Confederates at and near Island No. 10 surrendered. Fort Pillow then became the next line of defense on the Mississippi.[35]

A nervous Beauregard decided to replace Villepigue with an older and more experienced general but quickly reversed himself. Meanwhile, the Western Department's commander sent reinforcements to the fort through Brownsville, the first railroad depot north of the Hatchie River, in order to avoid a problematic ferry on the newly repaired route from Mason. Other troops, who had escaped capture in the New Madrid area, came to the fort in a very discouraged condition. Unfortunately for the post, at this time the enlistment term for one of the garrison's regiments, the 12th Louisiana Infantry, expired, and the men demanded furloughs as the price of reenlistment. Beauregard approved two hundred thirty-day furloughs grudgingly, since "this is no time for men to be leaving their Standard." He required the furloughed men to leave their guns with the regiment's unarmed, newer recruits. The worried general also called upon local civilians to arm themselves for the defense of the fort.[36]

Retreating to Fort Pillow from New Madrid, Captain George N. Hollins brought a fleet of six wooden gunboats, converted from river steamers. In the belief that his force stood no chance against the innovative ironclads in the Federals' river squadron, he wanted to take his fleet to New Orleans, which was threatened by a wooden flotilla. When the Navy Department refused Hollins's request, he stubbornly headed south on the *Ivy* after turning five gunboats over temporarily to Captain Thomas B. Huger. Hollins left orders for Commander Robert F. Pinkney to assume the command upon returning from a leave but to send the flagship *McRea* to New Orleans.[37]

At the same time, a Memphis shipyard neared the end of work on two rams. James E. Montgomery, a steamboatman critical of the Confederate navy, had convinced the army to finance the refitting of some riverboats into rams in the belief that they could sink Federal ironclads. He had started the conversion process in New Orleans with heavy oak for planking, compressed cotton in the bulkheads, and one-inch iron plating on the bows. Commanding the upriver portion of this ram fleet as an army captain, he sent each of the eight rams when ready to Memphis for finishing with iron reinforcements and/or stern cannons. On April 12, *General Sterling Price* and *General Earl Van Dorn,* the first rams completed at Memphis, proceeded to Fort Pillow. That evening *Price* escorted a steamer on a foraging expedition to Island No. 25, to which the navy gunboats had advanced. *Price* scouted a little farther and discovered enemy ships at the mouth of the Obion River. During the night the Confederate gunboats' commander also learned about the Federals' presence from a civilian.[38] The front lines would soon arrive at Fort Pillow.

Virtually none of the Confederates assigned to defend the fort had prior military experience. Amateurs by definition lack a professional's discipline and training. Their judgment is often poor, as is shown by the construction of overly large forts. They tend to miss the mark with either excessive fear (e.g., frequent invasion rumors) or rash boldness (e.g., the seizure of Columbus, Kentucky). Besides facing great difficulties obtaining and allocating the materials of war, the newborn Confederacy suffered an unbroken string of defeats on the western front that winter and spring. The once glorious namesake of Fort Pillow had fallen into disrepute, as noted in General Bragg's comment that "The name of the place is unfortunate—Fort Pillow." Still, with the fort's numerous batteries, a soldier could write home, "I never felt so perfectly safe." [39] The defenders had some grounds to feel confident, though it was partly the confidence of the unknowing.

Chapter Two

The Federal Attack

C APTAIN Andrew H. Foote, the career navy man who commanded the Federal Mississippi fleet as its flag officer, worried about the strength of Fort Pillow, as described in fairly accurate reports from spies. Furthermore, the recent death of a son had depressed the spirits of the emotional fifty-five-year-old man with a weathered face, dark hair, and cropped beard. He had lost much of his original enthusiasm for the experimental ironclads composing most of his command, when in battle at Fort Donelson they suffered a bad battering and he received a foot injury requiring the use of crutches. Afterward he informed his wife that the clash "was a bad fight. . . . I won't run into the fire so again, as a burnt child dreads it." [1] This veteran officer's newfound reluctance to take risks would set the tone for an operation that involved mostly amateur military men.

Foote could not help but find ironclads and river warfare a challenge, since his long service had mostly involved wooden vessels and saltwater combat. All of the fleet for the Fort Pillow campaign, except for the *Conestoga,* a wooden steamer refitted as a gunboat, consisted of ironclads constructed by St. Louis engineer and businessman James Eads. The seven ironclads had three levels: a hurricane deck with a pilot house, a gun deck with angled sides, and living quarters below water. Two and a half inches of iron plating covered the gunboats above the waterline. Two paddle wheels sat side by side in a recessed position toward the stern. Six of the ships (*Cairo, Carondelet, Cincinnati, Mound City, Pittsburg,* and *St. Louis*) were identical, with thirteen cannons each. The flagship *Benton,* a rebuilt salvage ship, differed only in having a larger size and sixteen cannons. Acting much like floating batteries, the ironclads moved slowly. [2]

Foote's great wariness in the campaign against Island No. 10 had created some tension in his relations with Major General John Pope, an ambitious army professional. Now Foote wanted to move on Fort Pillow "before the rebels recover from their panic, and then we are on to Memphis." Irritated on April 12, 1862, by the protracted boarding of Pope's twenty thousand troops on twenty-two transports at New Madrid, he left at noon with most of the ironclads. The flag officer decided to clear the path of Confederate vessels, though he suspected the unarmored enemy would avoid his ironclads, as they had done so far.[3]

The ships headed south on a river swollen by spring rains. After an uneventful day, Foote's gunboats anchored at the mouth of the Obion River. A tug reconnoitered the area as a precaution. At nightfall the ironclad *Cairo* arrived with steamers towing sixteen mortar boats. The unstreamlined shape of the 25 by 60–foot mortar boats had slowed their movement.[4]

Late that night the captain of the Confederate ram *Price* and Captain Thomas Huger, commander of five gunboats (*Livingston, Maurepas, McRae, Polk,* and *Pontchartrain*), agreed upon an attack. At dawn, Federal lookouts spotted the Confederates' smoke, as the first Federal troop transports arrived from New Madrid. Six ironclads advanced in a battle formation, led by the *Benton*. The opening shots from both sides fell short. Having realized the number of ironclads present, Huger quickly decided that he had no chance and retreated. Foote tried to pursue, but the ironclads' weight prevented them from gaining on the enemy's much lighter wooden vessels. He soon sent orders back for the rest of the flotilla to join him.[5]

The sluggish parade composed "a scene never to be forgotten . . . filling the river for miles," according to Federal private Augustus G. Sinks. After the ironclads came various supporting ships, steamboats towing the mortar boats, the *Conestoga,* those transports which had caught up with the fleet–the last ones had left the New Madrid area only that morning–and finally riverboats towing coal and blacksmith barges. During that clear and mild day a sailor noted that "our trip down the river was very pleasant indeed. . . . The islands, covered with willow and poplar to the water's edge, form some very picturesque scenes." On the transports crammed with troops, wagons, horses, equipment, and supplies, an Indianan writing his hometown newspaper observed that "anticipation of service kept the men in good spirits." Unionists, silenced after the secession of Arkansas and Tennessee, cheered the flotilla from the shore; secessionists watched it glumly.[6] The expansion of Federal power southward would reignite political conflict within Southern society.

As the *Benton* rounded a bend about 11:00 A.M., Fort Pillow suddenly came into sight, and the procession turned back to anchor upstream in Plum Bend. That afternoon Foote and Assistant Secretary of War Thomas Scott, who had accompanied the fleet, took *Benton* and three ironclads on a brief reconnaissance of the fort. General John Villepigue's batteries opened fire but overshot the ships. Symmes Browne, an uninitiated sailor, noted the "very unusual" experience of seeing a ball pass within twenty-five feet of him. Immediately after returning to safety, Scott and Foote conferred with Pope. As Fort Pillow clearly exceeded the strength of Fort Donelson, Foote feared that a naval attack would result in the destruction of his fleet. He convinced the others to let the mortar boats start a bombardment under gunboat protection the next day, while Pope's forces went upstream in search of a landing site from which to mount an assault on the fort's rear.[7]

Meanwhile, the last transports arrived at the anchorage. After the long trip on packed ships, the troops briefly disembarked. Excited by reaching their destination, many of the youths noisily frolicked by racing, wrestling, or playing leapfrog. A false rumor ran through the 2nd Iowa Cavalry that the fort had surrendered. To cap off the excitement, a tugboat caught on fire. A reporter quipped that "She spun around in the river like a pyrotechnic grasshopper," endangering other ships. Several steamers managed to rescue the crew and tow the remains into shallow water.[8]

The next afternoon seven Federal mortar boats, after being towed downstream, opened fire with short intervals between rounds. Starting on the day after the Federals began, Confederate artillery would respond occasionally to the mortars. Due to the distance and the trees, neither side's gunners could see their targets. Both forces would keep their ships beyond range of the bombardment. The Confederates tied up at Fulton, Tennessee, while the Federals anchored a little below Osceola, Arkansas.[9]

When Pope returned from exploring the Tennessee shore, he reported that the flooded river offered no safe landing spots. He proposed to seek a route for cutting a canal through the Arkansas lowlands. At New Madrid, this labor-intensive tactic had aided him in supplying his troops. At Fort Pillow he hoped to use it to get his forces somewhere below the fort for crossing the Mississippi. Foote did not mind the delay, as his foot injury had become inflamed. In coming days it would cause a swelling of his entire leg, fevers, disrupted sleep, reduced appetite, and a generally "depressing effect" on him. His noisy, smelly, hot, dark quarters on the *Benton* did not help.[10]

Pope and some of his troops disembarked on April 14 at Georgia McGavock's plantation on the wide bottom of Craighead Point, the spit of land south of Plum Bend and across the river from the fort. The widowed mistress had moved further south with most of her slaves before the Federals arrived. Pope made his headquarters in her mansion, a comfortable but plain one with a portico supported by cypress posts, and cavalrymen corralled their horses on the plantation. A few regiments camped there, but, due to flooding, most spent the days ashore and slept on ships at night. As the 10th Illinois Infantry's transport pulled up to land, an explosion occurred. A soldier had lifted the lid of a mess chest while holding a candle, and a spark touched off an opened gunpowder can he had carelessly stored there. The man suffered facial burns as a result.[11]

Once ashore, Captain Aden G. Cavins found the area "delightful," with its many wildflowers and birds. Since secessionists seemed more likely than unionists to abandon farms in the Federals' path, some of Pope's troops felt free to partake of the bounty on McGavock's model farm. Men detailed to chop wood for boat fuel simply cut up fence rails. Yet, at this point in the war most Federals still respected private property in the belief that a conciliatory policy would help undermine a Confederate war effort supposedly instigated by a few leaders against the wishes of the masses.[12]

While some of the Federal troops had experienced combat at New Madrid, all had to get accustomed to the irregular Confederate shelling. Captain Cavins bragged: "Our boys pay no more attention to the occasional cannonading here than they would to the hammering around a town. We feel confident that in some way Fort Pillow will fall into our hands before ten days." A journalist on the scene, however, wrote: "We stand in breathless silence to hear the screaming in the air. We are interested to know where the shot will fall. Every sense is quickened. We live fast for ten or twenty seconds. The shot falls short. We breathe again and laugh at the enemy." Although enemy artillery never hit the Federals during the "siege," rumors about daily casualties soon circulated.

The men began to steel themselves for battle. Hugh Johnson noted that his family remained in a "land of peace & plenty & where they have not to sleep with their revolvers fitted on & their saber at their feet where they can get them in a moment." He believed himself "ready & willing for a fight . . . in defense of liberty." Captain Bernard Schermerhorn wrote his wife that the war "must be fought out to the bitter end," lest successful secession cause the nation's political and economic ruin.[13]

The outnumbered Confederates, many of them raw recruits, tried to buttress their morale, too. Lieutenant Mark Lyons wrote his sweetheart back home that "Too much sympathy cannot be expressed for the poor soldier. . . . My prospects are very good to be killed, wounded, or taken prisoner." After a shell ripped through a tent, Lyons's unit moved its camp a half-mile back. Soon all the campgrounds lay out of the mortars' range.[14]

On the day the Federals had arrived, Brigadier General Albert Rust brought Confederate reinforcements to a camp outside the fort. General Beauregard had created this independent field army to counter any moves by Pope's men. He anticipated possible Federal maneuvers up the South Forked Deer River toward the fort's rear or across the Arkansas lowlands toward the river below the fort. Rust's patrols watched those areas and also started burning cotton, lest it fall into enemy hands.[15]

The weather now entered a rainy period, especially hard on the soldiers living in tents and on Pope's scouts toiling unsuccessfully to find the de-sired canal route across the flooded lowlands. They did catch three enemy scouts at the Lanier plantation across the base of Craighead Point. In a swampy area above the fort Federals also caught a Confederate mail car-rier. Confederate deserters, probably including some undercover agents, started to show up at the Federal camp.[16]

During the evening of April 16, Pope received an order to remove most of his force to Pittsburg Landing, Tennessee, from which Major General Henry W. Halleck, the Federal commander of this war theater, planned to march on Beauregard's camp at Corinth, Mississippi. The next morning, Pope, Scott, and the bulk of the troops steamed away. The fame-seeking Pope in a few months would secure a larger command in Virginia, where he would suffer a major defeat in the Second Battle of Bull Run. At Plum Bend he left behind the 43rd and 46th Indiana Infantry, about twelve hun-dred men, under Colonel Graham N. Fitch with orders to cooperate with Foote in trying to bypass the fort with a canal.[17]

Shortly before Pope departed, Foote, upon the advice of the fleet doc-tors, had applied for a leave in order to recuperate from his injury. Foote considered letting Captain Seth L. Phelps, the young and very ambitious commander of the *Benton,* serve as temporary commander of the fleet but sensed that it would create an unhealthy jealousy among the ship captains. So he requested that an old friend, Captain Charles H. Davis, come to replace him, and the Navy agreed. As it would take Davis some time to reach the fleet, the flag officer, who could barely move even with crutches, would have to endure the wait. Foote felt that Pope's withdrawal "left us in quite a forlorn condition" without enough men for the task. Believing some Confederate deserters' exaggerations about the enemy's strength, he demanded of the secretary of the navy that "if disaster comes you will vindicate my memory." He especially feared that Confederate ironclads under construction at New Orleans and Memphis would appear, destroy his ships, and charge up the Mississippi with nothing to stop them.[18]

Learning of Pope's exit within one day, Beauregard soon called General Rust's force to Corinth. When Robert W. Haywood sought to raise an independent company in the area for guerrilla operations under the Confederacy's newly passed Partisan Ranger Act, Beauregard prohibited it and urged recruits to join the fort's garrison. Although the fort's garrison of some thirty-six hundred men now outnumbered the Federals, Villepigue remained alertly on the defensive. He maintained a camp of scouts at the Lanier plantation for observing enemy activity. On the Tennessee side, he had cavalry patrol the area near Ripley to watch for a Federal movement on the fort's rear. The rain-soaked terrain and numerous insects plagued the troops, especially the horsemen.[19]

Inside the fort, the Confederates adjusted to life under bombardment. Sergeant Hiram T. Holt at first wrote his wife that the men had "lots of fun dodging the Yank's shells" but soon admitted it made him "a little skittish." He slept little during nighttime shelling and once saw a bomb blow a hole in the ground as large as his room at home. Worse yet, "a shell struck a fellow & literally tore him into fragments, you could find pieces of him scattered all around." He worried to his wife that "I may never see you . . . more but this is with God to decide." A Memphis newspaper reported that a slave laborer fled for his owner's plantation after an encounter with a shell, which he called "a large ball of fire, nearly as big as the moon."[20] Villepigue tried to serve as a model for the men by maintaining his headquarters on the river bluff, the most dangerous area, and acting unbothered by the bombardment. Brigadier General Meriwether "Jeff" Thompson judged that Villepigue was "either the bravest man I ever saw, or he had better control over his nerves." As occurred in other bombarded forts, each soldier gradually became "quite an expert dodger," as Lieutenant Lyons put it. The explosions killed two Confederates during the first weeks, but none thereafter.[21]

Villepigue soon finished construction at the fort. Records contain no references to the fort's Irish workers after the Federals' arrival and none to the slave laborers after early May. The completed outer embankment at its northern end had zigzag entrenchments up the bluff from Cold Creek. A broken inner line of defenses included an earthwork a short distance back from the bluff in the fort's southern end, rifle pits at unknown locations, a crescent battery on the middle wedge of land between the two large ravines, and a similar battery on the northern bluff above the mouth of Cold Creek. Workers constructed several additional riverfront works, including a second waterline battery. Part of the way downhill, in ravines cutting through the bluff, one battery had a heavy Columbiad cannon in a casemate or roofed enclosure, while others contained a single Columbiad without a casemate. A sunken pit held six heavy siege guns. All batteries had protective walls with embrasure openings as well as wood plank floors for the cannons. Workers made the walls from sandbags, rammed earth, timber, and iron rails. Most batteries at the bluff had furnaces for heating shot (to cause fires on ships), plus ammunition magazines and crew shelters made of earth and timber. A few additional cannons sat on the bluff between the fort and Fulton.[22] In its final form Fort Pillow appeared very menacing to the Federals.

The offensive efforts of the Federal fleet now settled into a daily routine. A naval official observed that the expedition seemed "condemned to only keep watch and ward on Fort Pillow until the army moves [against Corinth]." After Pope's departure, Foote sharply decreased the number of mortar boats in use, and the daily firing rates varied widely. Most mornings, except during rain, which made the mortars slip dangerously, tugs towed one or two mortar boats to a spot a little above the tip of Craighead Point. When a mortar fired in a high arc, the recoil put so much downward pressure on its barge that the seams opened and admitted water, which the crew had to pump out after every two or three shots. Observers of the dramatic bombardment saw smoke, heard the explosion, and felt everything shake. At night they could see the burning fuses streak across the dark sky. George R. Yost, a powder boy on the *Cairo,* retained a vivid image of "the commingling of clear starlit southern skies; bombs flying through the air[;] . . . the black masses of the gunboats floating quietly upon the river's bosom, lined on either bank with a heavy growth of forest trees."[23]

By the fort's fall, the mortars had fired 1,448 shells. Federal officers used periodic reconnaissances to evaluate the bombardment's effectiveness and to make aiming adjustments, and the Confederates probably did likewise. After the Federals learned that many shells stuck in the silt bluff, they tried to hit the campgrounds farther east instead. A Cincinnati journalist suspected correctly that hitting a target had "little more probability than that the enemy should be struck with lightning." A *New York Tribune* reporter took a stronger stand: "Mortar firing amounts to . . . make-believe warfare, at least as we conduct it; and when we reflect that every discharge costs

$25, the practice seems rather a reckless expenditure of money." Captain Henry Maynadier, commander of the mortar boats and a member of the regular army, would later admit that the mortars' "services have not been near equal to their costs."[24]

Guarding the mortar boats fell within the infantry's duties. Because of the flood, pickets often had to stand in water, sometimes two feet deep. Scouting expeditions depended on use of the navy's rowboats, but at its crest the muddy brown water's speed made returning upriver and avoiding accidents difficult. Federal patrols started to confiscate cotton in order to prevent Confederates from burning it. Periodically the expeditions and camp pickets exchanged fire with Confederate scouts. Fitch unsuccessfully tried to run the enemy off Craighead Point by cutting the levee there.[25]

As the days passed, gunboat captains regularly held inspections, artillery practices, Sunday services, and laundry days, but the river had risen high enough to keep troops from drilling. Some of the 43rd Indiana lived in the McGavock plantation's slave huts, but most soldiers now remained aboard two transport ships. One wrote his hometown newspaper that "Each day here is just like the preceding one—all excessively dull—monotonous beyond conception." In an earlier letter he had exaggerated a bit to claim that the troops had "not done much but eat, sleep, and fight mosquitoes."[26]

Living by the flooded river, the Federals especially suffered from mosquitoes, whose propagation the flood facilitated. Worst at night, the attacking insects made sleep difficult and left the men with swollen faces. Journalist Junius H. Browne claimed that "the countless mosquitos . . . must have had strong Secession sympathies." A St. Louis reporter commented that "they will not be 'put off' with less than their 'pound' of blood." Mosquito-borne malaria infected a large number of Federal soldiers and sailors. Only smoky fires helped to keep these parasites away.[27]

Another insect, previously unknown to the Midwesterners, attacked livestock in both armies. The buffalo gnat stayed active longer than its normal two-week period that spring. Fitch moved his horses and mules to the Tennessee shore, where the gnats seemed less numerous. The caretakers tried keeping the animals in swamp water up to their necks and covering their heads with axle grease. Still, most of the horses died from either buffalo gnat bites or from eating green cane in the swamp. Again, only smoky fires helped.[28]

Other developments followed from the Federals' presence. Since secessionists claimed that Northerners intended to destroy slavery and since slaves had fled to Federal lines almost from the beginning of the war, some planters moved slaves away when the Federals approached. Confederate rams helped Felix Lanier and a neighbor relocate their slaves soon after the enemy's arrival. Some of the slaves, though, decided that an opportunity for their liberation had come and escaped to the Federals. Other slaves slipped away from their work at the fort. One Confederate officer there had warned his body servant that the Federals' leader was a cyclops with eight arms, a tail, and a penchant for eating blacks. This common tactic for retaining slaves by trying to make them afraid of monstrous Federals rarely worked. Instead, the runaways sought protection from the Federals in return for aiding the Union cause. They received the popular label "contrabands" because property used to aid an enemy's war effort was confiscatable contraband of war.[29]

However, both Foote and General Halleck, Fitch's superior, adhered to a conciliatory policy that required Federals to avoid harming slavery in order to help revive loyalty to the United States. While Congress had prohibited the army from returning runaway slaves, Foote, Halleck, and some other Federal commanders issued orders to exclude runaways from the lines except for those who had worked directly for the Confederate army and those who provided military intelligence. Many contrabands around Fort Pillow qualified and so entered service as servants, laborers, or scouts for the Federals. Furthermore, not all navy and army officers strictly followed the exclusion rules. Fitch seems to have grown lax about it over time. Several contrabands found work on dispatch steamers and left the area before someone questioned their status. One who stayed as a servant on a commissary steamer had nightmares about recapture. Not trusting Federals to protect her, she firmly told a *Cincinnati Gazette* reporter, "I doesn't want to go Souf again." A male fugitive slave successfully used a club to beat off those trying to capture his family. Fitch ordered that owners could retrieve runaways only through persuasion, not by the use of force or the jail at Osceola, Arkansas.[30]

Federal policy, though, required some protection for unionists' property rights. When a Tennessee unionist claimed three runaways working on *Benton*, Captain Phelps wanted Brigadier General Andrew Johnson, the state's military governor, to order their return. Johnson merely sent a request for cooperation, and the fleet commander then intervened to prohibit the African Americans' delivery as violating a congressional directive against the military's return of slaves, a law that curbed the conciliatory policy.[31]

Unionists greatly aided the Federals by bringing in military information. To reward the area's unionist minority, Fitch gave them permission to ship out cotton and to bring in trade goods. However, he had to argue with navy officials to get space on a government vessel for such shipments. Then, the army commander at Cairo, Illinois, the depot at the junction of the Mississippi and Ohio Rivers, banned all trade with occupied areas and seized the unionists' shipments. When Fitch tried holding an enlistment rally after unionists expressed great concern about the Confederacy's new Conscription Act, he had no success, and many of his men doubted the commitment of Southern white loyalists.[32] Distrust and friction quickly crept into relations between Federals and unionists.

Complicating matters further, some secessionists cloaked themselves in a false unionism for subterfuge. Federal sailors recognized a civilian selling them chickens as a Southern steamboat captain and arrested him as a spy. Deserters gave such varying reports about the forces at the fort that the Federals eventually suspected that some were Confederate operatives trying to pass false information. While historians today can easily use hindsight in distinguishing between the accurate and untrue reports, Foote could not. The more frightening stories usually sounded persuasive to him.[33]

Both sides easily obtained their opponents' newspapers. Because the *Chicago Times* had revealed Pope's use of a canal at New Madrid, Foote banned newspapermen from the flagship and from talking to civilians. Of the dozen or so journalists who originally accompanied the flotilla, only six remained by late April for lack of news. Except when they could catch a rowboat ride to talk to military personnel, they stayed stuck aboard *J. H. Dickey,* the commissary boat where they had quarters.[34]

One newspaper report infuriated Foote by merely stating that he wanted a leave because of an injury. The flag officer wrote the secretary of the navy: "I would far rather die in the harness from sickness or a shot, than to leave my post in face of the enemy on personal grounds." In a rare moment his letter asked Gideon Welles to "excuse my egotism," a trait that filled his tormented correspondence at this time. The pain in his foot now mostly confined him to his cabin. Colonel Fitch, a doctor before the war, took a look at the injury but only worsened Foote's mental state by judging incorrectly that it would likely result in permanent damage or loss of the foot. Having abandoned the canal plan as unworkable, Fitch energetically sought alternatives, but a scheme to build a battery on Craighead Point near the fort came to nothing. A related plan to take control of the Point through use of howitzer rafts had practical difficulties. Mostly the Federal expedition waited.[35]

Meanwhile, six Confederate army rams had joined the two already at the fort. The daring and inexperienced Captain James Montgomery, commander of the ram fleet, joined forces with the flamboyant Brigadier General Meriwether "Jeff" Thompson. Thompson's independent force of Missouri militiamen, who had participated in a few skirmishes, would serve as snipers and artillerymen on the rams. Even though Thompson found most of the rams too slow, he agreed with Montgomery that the best way of defending the river was to join with the navy gunboats and mount an attack.[36]

However, Commander Robert F. Pinkney, who had recently returned from leave to lead the Confederate naval fleet, concurred with his predecessors' belief that the wooden gunboats could not withstand the Federal ironclads and refused to participate in an attack. The reaction from Montgomery's crewmen and a Memphis newspaper caused Lieutenant Charles W. Read, a gunboat officer, later to note that "ridicule . . . was so great and general, that I was really ashamed." Following Hollins's orders, Pinkney reduced his force by sending the *McRae* to New Orleans. Naval authorities soon reassigned the *Maurepas* and *Pontchartrain* to the White River in Arkansas, so that only *Livingston* and *Polk* remained. On Beauregard's urging, Pinckney moved his men and cannons into Fort Randolph. Montgomery and Thompson persisted in preparing for an offensive by regularly scouting the positions of Federal ships.[37]

On April 28, the Federals heard multiple reports from deserters and contrabands that the Confederates planned an assault by land and water. Foote ordered the whole fleet several miles upriver. During the process Mortar Boat No. 12 came untied and floated down near the fort before its crew could secure it to shore and destroy all the ammunition they could not carry. A Federal tug successfully retrieved the mortar boat early the next morning. Meanwhile, the ironclads tied up sterns at new moorings so that bows would face an assault from downstream. All Union troops boarded transports for two nights and then once again after an interval of several days. No attack came.[38]

A Federal scout made the major discovery that flooding had rendered the fort's water batteries unusable. Because of this situation and news of David G. Farragut's successful run past Confederate forts to capture New Orleans, bored reporters began to use their columns to lobby for action, just as they had done when the naval advance had stalled at Island No. 10. Foote weighed the possibility, wavered on the matter, and ultimately rejected it. He feared that the fort's artillery, especially pieces high on the bluff, could still do great harm to the fleet, that the current would prevent disabled ships from escaping, and that "if disaster should occur to us, the rebel gunboats would have complete possession of the river or rivers above us."[39]

In early May, when the Mississippi finally started to drop, some of the 46th Indiana established a campground at the McGavock plantation. Once enough land for a parade ground had dried, drilling started to occupy a large part of the troops' day. Through a direct appeal to Indiana's governor, Fitch obtained better rifles for his brigade. Still hoping for some action, he had a tug outfitted with a navy howitzer and sent it on reconnaissances.[40]

An initiative would come instead from the Confederate side. In early May, Beauregard shifted most of the Fort Pillow troops to his camp at Corinth, Mississippi, to brace it against Halleck's huge approaching force. Beauregard advised Villepigue to retreat whenever it seemed prudent, but the post commander decided to obstruct the Federals as long as possible. This required the out-manned garrison to maintain an image of strength while avoiding excessive risks. Under the dark cloud of a Confederate fleet's defeat at New Orleans, Montgomery and Thompson settled upon a plan of action. Before 5:00 A.M. on May 8, *General Sumter, General Bragg,* and *General Earl Van Dorn* moved to attack the mortar boats, but arrived before those vessels reached their usual firing spot. The alert spread through the Federal fleet, and several ironclads opened fire from a distance before the rams fled. That afternoon Foote initiated a new practice of sending an ironclad to guard the mortar boats during shelling. After taking that precaution, the Federals seem to have expected no further trouble. In the words of a Cincinnati reporter, "The rebels had so often made menaces of attack upon the national flotilla that no one believed they had any idea of putting their threat into execution."[41]

On the evening of May 8, Captain Charles H. Davis, a man the same age as Foote but with a long, fanciful mustache and partly silvery chin whiskers, finally arrived to take acting command of the Union fleet. As Foote felt great relief, and Davis found Foote's bad health shocking, the two old friends cried upon meeting. The flag officer explained his views about the dangers downriver and asked his protege, Captain Phelps, to discuss this further with Davis later. Foote left his cooking and bedding equipment, including an invaluable mosquito net, for Davis to use. The next morning an emotional farewell speech by Foote raised three cheers from the flagship's men. Although his foot injury would eventually heal after the proper diagnosis and treatment of a broken bone, he would die from Brights Disease while en route to his next command in 1863.[42]

The evening after Foote left, a Confederate war council took place on the flagship ram *Little Rebel*. Montgomery, Thompson, and the ram captains decided to attack the ironclad guarding the mortar boat early the next morning. Thompson liked a May 10 offensive because it would come as revenge on the first anniversary of the Camp Jackson incident, in which Federals had fired on a civilian crowd in his home state of Missouri. Neither the riverboat captains commanding the rams nor any of the men aboard had engaged in naval combat before this. The captains, not trusting their facility in understanding naval signaling, drew up detailed plans for various contingencies. Afterward, the "bravest passed a restless, and some a sleepless night," according to Thompson.[43]

On the morning of May 10 the Confederates ate a hurried breakfast. At 6:00 A.M., just as Mortar Boat No. 16 started shelling the fort, *General Bragg*, the fastest ram, led out a line ordered by speed: *General Sumter, General Sterling Price, General Earl Van Dorn, General Beauregard, Colonel Lovell, General M. Jeff Thompson*, and *Little Rebel*. Upon rounding Craighead Point, the leading rams accelerated to top speed toward the mortar boat and *Cincinnati*, the ironclad on guard duty that morning.[44]

The mortar crew quickly made adjustments to get their shells to explode above the rams, though without much effect. The ironclad's sailors halted morning activities and scrambled into action. The *Cincinnati*'s crew built up the ship's head of steam, discharged the four stern cannons, and untied mooring lines. While the current swung the *Cincinnati*'s bow around, the *Bragg* rammed the ship's side at an angle and punched a hole in the unarmored area below the waterline. The *Bragg*'s starboard paddle wheel climbed up the *Cincinnati*'s deck, but the *Cincinnati*'s motion and a close broadside from it shoved the *Bragg* off before Captain Roger Stembel could get a Federal boarding party on the ram. Water rushed into the *Cincinnati*'s ammunition room through a six by twelve–foot hole. The ironclad's broadside had ignited a fire on *Bragg*, forcing its sailors to focus on dousing the flames. Simultaneously, a tiller rope problem caused the ram to drift downstream.[45]

The other rams kept advancing. Thompson's sharpshooters, stationed behind cotton bales on the ships' decks, fired ineffectively at the mortar boat's iron sides. *Van Dorn* put two cannonballs harmlessly through the upper walls of the mortar boat. At about the time that *Price* and then *Sumter* rammed the *Cincinnati*'s stern on either side of its rudder, a Confederate sniper brought down Captain Stembel with a nonmortal neck wound that paralyzed him from the waist down. Meanwhile, the Federal ship's stern guns did some damage to the *Price*'s hull and steam pipes. Shortly thereafter, the ironclad shook and sank. With only the pilot house above water, the crewmen "perched [on it] like so many turkeys on a corn crib, . . . spectators of the exciting and magnificent scene around us," according to sailor Eliot Callender.[46]

Because of the battle's noise, infantrymen about a mile upriver on the transports "left their beds with commendable promptitude," according to one regimental history. Private Augustus G. Sinks remembered the sight of the battle as "magnificent at the commencement . . . but in a few minutes the Smoke and fog completely obscured the scene." Morning fog hampered communication between Federal ships. The alert passed quickly between ships on the Tennessee shore. On the Arkansas side just *Mound City* got underway. With cannons blazing, *Mound City* reached the battle scene first, only to be rammed on the starboard bow by *Van Dorn*. The impact spun *Mound City* completely around and thrust *Van Dorn* into the Arkansas shore. The Confederate ship backed off the bank and fruitlessly tried to ram *Mound City* again. With water pouring in the hole, *Mound City* headed upstream for a sand bar. *Van Dorn* escaped with just a little damage to its upper works.[47]

Steaming forward, *Carondelet, Pittsburg, Benton,* and *Cairo* bombarded the enemy. In the process, *Pittsburg* accidentally hit *Carondelet* with some grapeshot. With the ironclads closing in on the rams, Montgomery ordered a retreat. The rams at the end of the line discharged several shots from stern cannons as they fled. One cannonball hit a bow porthole on the *Cairo* at an angle and merely bounced off. Having clocked the Battle of Plum Bend at thirty-two minutes, General Thompson commented that "it seemed like an age to those who had never been under fire."[48]

Once back at Fulton, the temperamental and theatrical Thompson found that his men had survived with nothing more than slight wounds: "My heart could hold up no longer, between the Joy and reaction. I sank down and choked up with tears, and had the surgeon not been at hand to give me a stimulant, I would have either fainted or burst out crying, both of which [are] unsoldierly acts." He ordered the daily grog ration issued and then dashed off a note to the *Memphis Appeal* touting the battle as a great victory and a boost for Confederate morale.[49]

Both sides claimed a victory and thought they had done significant damage to the other, but the minor skirmish of Plum Bend deserves the rating of a draw. The Confederates lost two noncombatant cooks, one Federal died from wounds, and each side had a handful of wounded survivors. Neither fleet gained any more control of the river from the battle. The Confederates refurbished their rams in one day, while the Federals needed more time to repair the greater damage their ships had suffered. A crew easily refloated *Mound City*. Raising the *Cincinnati* took a little longer because it lay within Confederate cannon range and the task required use of a submarine bell. This experimental equipment was dangerous enough that, even though they only worked twenty feet underwater, one volunteer died and two became ill. *Cincinnati* and *Mound City* underwent repairs at Cairo and would return to active duty in the near future.[50] Evaluating the skirmish's outcome, the Southern Lieutenant Lyons observed, "our boats fought well, but theirs proved invulnerable. . . . They are vastly superior to ours." Thomas W. Knox, a Northern journalist, later commented that "neither fleet had much to boast of."[51] Neither side had caused any permanent damage to the other.

The Confederates, though, may have won a psychological victory, which halted the Federal advance down the river for another month. The shock of the surprise attack, shortly after Davis took command, definitely encouraged cautiousness. Even without the attack Davis may have acted the same, since his long career as a naval bureaucrat and scientist had allowed him very little combat experience. Foote and Phelps certainly tried to influence him toward wariness. Whatever the cause, he soon started expressing exactly the same fears as had Foote. Davis especially worried about the enemy's effort to build an ironclad at Memphis (Confederates had moved the second unfinished ship downriver). The captain begged for more warships and refused Halleck's request that the fleet try to run the fort in order to capture supplies at Memphis before they could reach Beauregard at Corinth.[52]

Confederate rams never again succeeded in mounting a surprise attack but repeatedly raised alarms in the Union fleet. On May 11 at 10:00 P.M., probably because of an inaccurate intelligence report, Davis's flagship fired a rocket calling all hands in the fleet to quarters. Noting the response time for each ship, Davis observed that the *Cairo* set a record at four minutes, while the other gunboats took between seven and ten minutes. Davis kept the crews on alert all that night and even halted the bombardment for the next week. Upon Captain Phelps's suggestion, the commander had a skirt of chained logs attached below the waterline of each ironclad to protect the unarmored area. Because that interfered too much with mobility, he replaced the bow and stern portions with chained railroad iron. Davis also secured another Eads ironclad, *Louisville,* as a temporary replacement for the two damaged ships. When the mortar boats returned to shelling, the guarding gunboat had to move about periodically because Confederate shells now landed closer.[53]

On the Confederate side, nothing except a brief morale boost followed from the naval skirmish. Thompson unhappily saw the "monotony of ordinary duties[,] . . . drills, & and now boat races" occupy his men in succeeding days. As Farragut's Federal fleet steamed upriver, a nervous Beauregard urged Montgomery to send several rams down to defend Vicksburg but backed down when the captain objected. After Fitch conducted explorations up the South Forked Deer River, Villepigue placed the 12th Louisiana Infantry near Ripley to watch for a movement on the fort's rear.[54]

Two new Confederate policies directly affected the fort. In an effort to improve officer quality, the Confederacy decided to accept the election of commissioned officers in militia units only if they passed oral tests. Despite the enemy's presence, Villepigue had to convene a board and examine officers. The new Conscription Act enabled him to expand the garrison by forcing civilians into military service, but many of them quickly deserted to the Federals.[55]

Behind Federal lines, some secessionist civilians formed guerrilla bands. Prewar Southern literature had romanticized and popularized guerrilla warfare. Often during the Civil War, groups with a deep commitment to the cause and limited military capability turned to this tactic in an effort to reinstate some Confederate authority. Upriver from Fort Pillow, partisans began sniping at Federal steamers and at unionists. Their threats joined with Confederate conscription to send a stream of unionists into Federal lines.[56]

So many refugees hailed Federal dispatch boats for help that Captain Davis ordered several steamers to collect them, and Fitch assigned some troops to go along in an effort to overawe guerrillas. On one trip a Federal officer forced a wealthy secessionist to act as security for a unionist's store.

Refugees plus increasing numbers of deserters swelled the crowd at Fitch's camp. After some guerrillas slipped into the crowd and took potshots at Federals, Fitch banned all civilians from his lines except those processed into a refugee camp. Then, after some haggling to gain the navy's approval, he began shipping them upriver.[57]

On May 19, two hundred Confederate war prisoners came downriver as part of an exchange agreement. When their transport ship arrived, Davis perfunctorily sent them on under a flag of truce without a second thought, but one Northern reporter noticed that a few captives were sick. Villepigue quickly penned Davis an indignant note demanding that he take back three men who had the dreaded disease of smallpox. Davis refused but offered to allow their placement in a camp between the armies. Rejecting this alternative, Villepigue and Beauregard filed formal protests. Villepigue wound up placing the ill men in a quarantined camp near the fort.[58]

On the day after the Confederate prisoners' transfer, Brigadier General Isaac F. Quinby, the Federal district commander, brought down a small flotilla carrying about twenty-five hundred men in the hope of quickly taking the fort. Quinby first had his cavalry scout Craighead Point. Near the Lanier plantation a newspaperman's horse came unhitched and ran with two pursuing Federals into a Confederate party. The scouts and reporter abandoned the horse to escape amidst a hail of enemy bullets.[59] After the scouts' return, Quinby decided to place a battery of heavy siege guns on a levee across Craighead Point. During the night, using fencing from the McGavock plantation, troops began building a plank road for the artillery. Then a picket in an inexperienced regiment shot and killed a comrade who failed to give the password. The noise prompted Villepigue to send over a force, which beat the Federal workers back, discovered the road, and then evacuated under fire from *St. Louis.*[60]

After daybreak both sides sent more men into Craighead Point. Private Aurelius Voorhis of the 46th Indiana Infantry later remembered that "I felt somewhat afraid but still was willing to go wherever ordered. . . . We went plunging around in the mud and through the bushes." After a brief clash, the outnumbered Confederates withdrew a second time under a cannonade from the *St. Louis.* The Federals, some having gone twenty-four hours without food, then left the swamp, too. Two Federals had died in the skirmishes, while no record of Confederate losses has survived. Knowing that surprise was lost and incorrectly fearing that a large Confederate force had flanked him to the northeast, Quinby on May 24 took his expedition back upriver.[61] Isaac McMillan, one of the expedition's infantrymen, wrote: "We have been mutch disappointed. It is a mistery to me . . . we had quite a ride at Uncle Sam's expense." A few observers blamed Colonel Fitch for carelessness during this operation, but several novice soldiers had made mistakes.[62]

Although Villepigue moved carefully, he too had trouble from men fresh to the soldier's life. The Quinby expedition had had little difficulty from enemy artillery, not only because the water battery remained too muddy for use but also because a group of artillerists refused to do any more work due to late pay. For three days Villepigue placed them on a bread and water diet while having them tied up by the thumbs (a common Civil War punishment in serious cases) until "they begged most piteously to be allowed to return to duty," according to Lieutenant Lyons.[63] They had threatened the fort's survival, given the small size of its garrison and the large enemy force facing it.

During Quinby's campaign, six Federal rams, an odd independent army force similar to Captain Montgomery's command, arrived. Colonel Charles Ellet, a famous civil engineer and longtime proponent of rams, headed it. His ideas had not interested the navy, but, when the Confederate ironclad ram *Virginia* destroyed two Federal warships near Newport News, the army had agreed to commission him and finance the experimental conversion of several riverboats into rams. *Horner, Lancaster, Lioness, Mingo, Monarch,* and *Switzerland* could deliver a more powerful punch than Montgomery's rams because they had oak-filled prows and bow-to-stern oak bulkheads braced with ironwork. Unlike the Montgomery rams, they carried neither cannons nor compressed cotton, furnishings that improved security but reduced speed. They also had the steam machinery safely located in the hold, rather than above on the deck. Unwisely, Ellet hired civilian ship crews and had few infantrymen aboard. As was the case in Montgomery's force, none of Ellet's officers had prior naval experience. A journalist ridiculed the fleet of rams as "an old ewe and five lambs." Davis also judged them as "not good for much in reality." [64]

Due to an accident, Ellet's flagship, *Queen of the West,* did not arrive until after Quinby's departure. On May 27 the headstrong Colonel Ellet visited Captain Davis to urge that their combined fleets run past the fort and attack the Confederate ships. Ellet also asked if his rams could guard the firing mortar boats. Davis agreed to think about Ellet's proposals, although he viewed both as risky.[65]

The river's flood stage had passed. Federal William Harper noted that it left "drowned hogs and cattle by the hundreds . . . the most disgusting smell that I ever smelt." Scouting parties discovered that the Confederates were repairing the now dry water battery and bringing large steamboats up to the Lanier plantation. Fitch interpreted the steamboats to be transports carrying reinforcements for a major assault.[66]

Actually, Beauregard, having decided to abandon Corinth, ordered Villepigue on May 28 to prepare for withdrawal to Grenada, Mississippi.[67] Once Beauregard retreated south, Halleck's superior force could easily send a detachment westward to capture Memphis and Fort Pillow. The steamboats, unmentioned in Confederate records, may have come to facilitate a withdrawal. Villepigue decided to take about a week in order to mask his evacuation carefully. Meanwhile, the Federals had gone on alert, expecting a battle. Fitch cancelled all furloughs, borrowed another howitzer from the navy, and boarded his men on transports to withdraw upriver, where they spent most of the next two days. The ironclads conducted several reconnaissances near the fort, and Ellet's rams constantly kept up a head of steam to be ready for action. On May 28, Davis advised Ellet that he preferred that the rams stay out of the fort's range because it would be a "great mortification" if any Federal ship was hit "without the means of retaliation." As long as the rams avoided being hit, they could help guard the mortar boats. Davis added that in a battle the rams should play a secondary role. Following the gunboats on the rear and flanks, they should watch for ramming opportunities, aid damaged Federal vessels, and capture disabled Confederate ships.[68]

An offended Ellet, who was also having problems with sleep and digestion, took a tug around the bend to study the enemy's positions. The fact that the Confederates only fired one shot at the unarmed vessel convinced him that he could easily run the fort. He concluded that his rams should attack independently: "I must carry out my plans, and not lie here in a vain and useless enterprise." Ellet's men began to build angled roofs for several coal barges. The inventor planned to fill the barges with driftwood and then lash them to the port side of the rams as protection from the fort's guns. Hot weather and constantly hot engines made his men very uncomfortable; merely walking barefoot across a deck could blister feet. The ships could only keep cool during the day by cruising around. During this time of vigilance for Confederate night attacks, one lookout roused a crew, only to find a wandering cow rustling the underbrush, a common error for an inexperienced picket.[69]

On June 1, infantrymen at the fort started a long circuitous march to Randolph to board transports. When an impressment of farmers' wagons yielded only one per company, the troops had to leave much equipment behind. Given six inches of mud from a rainstorm and his unit's lack of marching experience, Captain Evander Graham observed: "[It] used us up. My feet were one solid blister and many of the boys could hardly drag one foot after the other the next day." A cavalry regiment screened the fort's rear and burned as much cotton as it could before withdrawing southward. Only the artillerymen and ram crews remained at the fort. Departing before the evacuation order came, Thompson spoke in Memphis at a rally, which resolved that all able-bodied men should defend the city by reporting for service at Fort Pillow. Confederate authorities observed that the call aroused little enthusiasm.[70]

Also on June 1, Ellet sent one of his supporting steamers close to the fort to try to induce an attack from a Confederate ram. Several of his rams lay hidden just around Craighead Point to surprise any enemy ship lured upriver. Smoke plumes may have revealed their presence, and in any case the scheme did not work. Ellet then decided that he would run the fort on June 3. He pleaded with Davis to let at least one ironclad support him and to allow veteran sailors to volunteer to join his inexperienced crews. Davis refused and asked to see Ellet's orders from the War Department. Ellet sent a reply "regretting sincerely your indisposition" since he believed the Confederates were "lying within easy reach." He asserted he would help Davis whenever needed, since Secretary of War Edwin Stanton had ordered him to cooperate with the navy and to do nothing endangering the campaign. Contending that he planned nothing rash, Ellet sent Stanton a self-righteous message asserting that "An exaggerated view of the powers of these rebel rams has spread among my fleet from the gunboats, and I feel the necessity of doing something to check the extension of the contagion." When Stanton required Ellet to obtain Davis's approval before attacking, Davis responded that "your mode of warfare is novel . . . and under the circumstances of the case I willingly defer to your judgment and enterprise."[71]

Despite winning permission for the attack, Ellet encountered resistance from some of his hired civilian boatmen. The captain, engineers, some pilots, and most of the crew of one ram refused to go. After chiding them as cowards and traitors, he took down all their names and fired two individuals. A few returned to duty and some crewmen from the rams' tender ships volunteered to replace the others. Ellet concluded that he would just take *Queen of the West* and *Monarch* to attack the Confederate ram *General M. Jeff*

Thompson, which lay beside the fort. He assigned *Lioness* to lag behind as a reserve force.[72]

The rams headed downriver on June 3 during an evening rainstorm. After Confederate batteries opened fire and the outnumbered *Thompson* fled, Ellet ordered a retreat. As his ships did so, a group of Confederate rams appeared at a distance and pursued Ellet. When the enemy rams came around Craighead Point, shots from *Cairo* and *Mound City,* which were guarding the mortar boats that day, sent them back downstream. Montgomery, believing that he had driven Ellet off, calmly proceeded to load materials from the fort onto his rams. The expedition convinced Captain Phelps of the *Benton* that Ellet was a foolhardy coward. The vain Ellet later boasted that his attack forced the fort's evacuation.[73]

Unknown to Ellet, his attack had disrupted a secret operation that Colonel Fitch had under way. The rapid fall of the river had made it feasible to land on the Tennessee shore and attack the fort by crossing Cold Creek. The colonel had sent several companies to prepare an approach route and to build a moveable pontoon bridge in the river channel behind Flour Island. The forest hid this operation from the fort's troops. Unaware that the ram expedition had provoked the burst of artillery fire, the workers fled, believing that the enemy had discovered them.[74]

On the same day, Federal scouts found Confederates loading ice onto *General Beauregard* from the Lanier plantation's ice house. A Federal attack captured seven of the foe before the rest fled to the ram, which opened fire with grapeshot. The scouts escaped on horseback with their captives riding behind them. Even though these prisoners, like deserters over several preceding days, reported the evacuation of the fort, Federal leaders remained unconvinced.[75] That night during a lightning storm Confederate artillerymen set fire to buildings and to some supplies. The next morning the gunboats and rams left for Memphis. Most of the artillerymen departed on steamers. Villepigue kept a small group behind to fire cannons periodically in response to the Federal mortars. The impending abandonment of the artillery caused Confederates between shots to try either bursting cannons with an overcharge set off by a fire underneath or jamming and breaking the narrow end of rat-tail files in cannon touchholes, an operation called spiking. For lack of experience, they had little success. Some spikes were too loose and therefore removable. At least one cannon's wooden carriage burnt, and its collapse threw the overloaded cannon out of the fire. That evening the crew gave up and walked to Fulton to board the last steamer.[76]

The *Memphis Avalanche* crowed: "We held it [the fort] as long as we wanted to hold it, and when we got ready we left it in our own way and in our own good time." Actually, Villepigue had wanted to hold it longer so that he could evacuate all supplies and dismantle the telegraph line. He did not, due to his understandable but misplaced fear that the Federals "of course knew everything" after the capture of the men at the Lanier plantation. Thompson, shocked to learn of the fort's evacuation, begged a superior "for God's sake, order the River Defense Fleet to . . . dispute every mile of river."[77]

The Federals did not notice the fires at Fort Pillow until the late afternoon of June 4, and even then some suspected a trick. Captain Phelps and Colonel Ellet separately conducted reconnaissances and concluded that the Confederates had genuinely withdrawn. Because ammunition was exploding, Davis delayed an advance until the next day. Fitch called back infantrymen finishing the pontoon bridge near Cold Creek, and the Federals spent the evening watching the show as "a glow like a flame tinted the clouds above, giving them a very beautiful appearance," according to an Illinois newspaper correspondent. Clouds of black smoke poured from the fort. At nightfall the explosions rivaled the lightning during another thunderstorm.[78]

At 4:00 A.M. on the cloudy and cool morning of June 5, Davis ordered his fleet forward. A race resulted, and an Ellet ram probably reached the fort first, as his men raised the United States' flag there. Fitch's tug likely arrived next, followed by the *Benton*. Sailors, soldiers, and reporters debarked from the ships to tour the impressive fortifications. After discovering that most bluff cannons could not be lowered enough to hit close-range targets, Captain Phelps admitted that, when the water battery remained unusable and the river had fallen, "our boats could have hugged the shore and passed under their fire."[79] A journalist for the *St. Louis Missouri Democrat* sarcastically editorialized that *"Our Commanding officers do not afflict themselves with regrets that they did not attack it sooner."* On the other hand, emphasizing the amount of supplies and equipment left behind, Captain Davis preferred to conclude that "it must have cost the poor devils some pangs of mortification to abandon."[80]

Fitch quickly got down to business by sending out a patrol to confiscate Confederate rations, tents, and tools taken by local civilians. He also assigned one company and a transport to stay for a few days at the fort. The infantrymen enjoyed a celebratory dinner including infrequently seen items such as lettuce, radishes, dried apples, molasses, and pie.[81]

After Davis detailed the *Pittsburg* to remain at the site and *Mound City* to guard the troop transports, the other gunboats and rams departed at noon to pursue the Confederates. Fitch's infantry followed at 3:00 P.M. At Fulton the navy confiscated two undamaged cannons, but nothing useful seemed left at Fort Randolph. Nearby a gunboat picked up two Northern pilots, who several days earlier had volunteered to go by dugout canoe to seek contact with Farragut's fleet but had found the way blocked by the evacuating enemy. The sailors observed many cotton bales floating in the river and at Island No. 37 captured a Confederate steamer used by a cotton-burning crew. On the way to an anchorage several miles above Memphis, Federals observed that slaves along the banks enthusiastically greeted them.[82]

On June 6, the two naval forces fought a climactic battle at Memphis. Federal ships sank or captured all the rams except *General Earl Van Dorn*. It fled along with Pinckney's two disarmed gunboats southward to the mouth of the Yazoo River, where sailors burnt them to prevent capture. Before the battle, Confederate authorities at Memphis had destroyed the unfinished ironclad *Tennessee*.[83]

Colonel Ellet died from wounds received during the battle, and Colonel Fitch soon resigned his command to return to civilian life. Before the year's end the navy would transfer Davis back to a desk job. On the Confederate side, Beauregard soon found himself reassigned to another command, something that happened repeatedly to him during the war. Thompson won much fame in later campaigns as a guerrilla leader in Missouri. Unfortunately for the Confederacy, Villepigue would die from illness later in 1862.[84]

As part of the Federal campaign to split the Confederacy, the fort's capture opened the Mississippi River down to Memphis, but the effort required time, expense, and trouble. The Confederacy lost some valuable supplies and equipment, but not another garrison. Beauregard justly praised Villepigue for conducting his defense with great "skill, vigor, and intrepidity."[85] Except for a period in late April, the Federals had outnumbered the defenders. While the fort's strong position aided Villepigue, he benefitted the most from the cautiousness of Foote and Davis. The two professional naval officers did not realize that the innovative ironclads probably could have run the fort. On the other hand, Ellet, Fitch, Montgomery, and Thompson, as relatively inexperienced commanders, had advanced some risky plans. Their superiors' conservative strategies limited both the damage done to the enemy and their own losses.

The soldiers and sailors on both sides suffered from shelling, bad weather, and mosquitoes, all challenges of military life. Neither this nor wartime rhetoric had yet fostered much hostility toward the enemy. Except for a sneer by Lieutenant Lyons about "negro worshipers," the diaries and letters consulted for this study strikingly lack angry references to the enemy. Many soldiers retained a civilian mentality in uniform: very cautious about combat and naive about the dangers. Thoughtless accidents killed several men, such as the mortar crew member who strode around with a lit cigar while carrying a leaky bag of gunpowder.[86] Only a handful of casualties seem to have resulted from the brief skirmishes.

The campaign initiated the area's Federal occupation, which in turn started several other processes. Since unionists and many of the slaves did not share their neighbors' Confederate identity, a number of both went to the Federals seeking refuge or offering to help. Meanwhile, offended masters and secessionists sometimes turned to violence to preserve their power in the face of Federal military might. The Federals' arrival created multi-layered social conflicts, challenges for their military rule in the future.

Chapter Three

Military Life at the Fort

O NE of the first Confederates stationed at Fort Pillow wrote that it sat on the Chickasaw Bluff "so high that I have thought many of us would never get nearer to heaven." The site offered a pleasant campground and beautiful vistas during the warmer part of the year. During winter, though, Private James M. Williams from Alabama called the brown landscape "bleak and cheerless." In that season troops encountered a penetrating wind, which whipped over the hills, as well as what an Iowan described as "snow & rain & mud in superabundance." [1]

During the year of Confederate presence and the two years of Federal occupation, military units stayed at or near Fort Pillow for periods ranging from a few days to sixteen months (see Tables 3 and 4). Soldiers from both sides commented, like Confederate Captain Evander Graham, that the fort was a "very much out of the way place." Wilderness areas in the river bottoms had an amazing abundance of wetlands wildlife.[2] Like that environment, military life also must have seemed exotic to many in the fort's garrisons. Since the difficulties played an important role in affecting events there, the challenges of everyday military life deserve examination.

In general, the Federal government provided better for its forces than the Confederacy did. The United States' logistical systems for the army and navy had long been in place and could draw upon the more diversified Northern economy. Nevertheless, newly created Confederate military structures supplied the fort's garrison with ample food for the most part in 1861. In addition, during warm weather local farmers either sold produce at low prices or gave it away.[3] During April and May 1862, all of General Beauregard's command had to endure a beef shortage. Although surviving records are silent about it, soldiers at the fort could have obtained meat then by hunting, foraging, or stealing. They did build ovens at the fort to bake their own bread. Confederates operating in the area after the fort's fall fed themselves with donated, purchased, or appropriated supplies.[4]

During the campaign against the fort, the Federals regularly had plenty of rations shipped downriver. They also procured fresh meat by hunting and by foraging. After establishing a garrison at the fort in the fall of 1862, they relied mostly upon foraging for basic foods. An Iowan wrote his hometown paper that "whatever we find in the country that we need, we feel it our duty to take. The boys enjoy the feasting."[5]

Meat came mainly from Arkansas, especially from the Lanier and McGavock herds, which grazed in Craighead Point's swampy canebrakes. Archaeological work at the fort has uncovered many bones of butchered domestic animals. From December 1862 through July 1863, the post bene-fitted from the services of a government steamer, first the *Davenport* and later the *O'Brien*. Foraging parties would surround an area and drive the cattle toward the steamboat's ramp. As Captain Franklin Moore noted, "We loaded it pretty heavily down."[6] When lacking a steamer, Federals used gunboats and light craft to bring smaller quantities of butchered meat across the river, and they foraged more on the Tennessee side. A company stationed briefly at Fulton in the fall of 1862 did much fishing with long trot lines.[7]

For the variety and challenge, some soldiers liked to steal animals. Be-cause of the need to speed and hide depredations, looters preferred chick-ens and hogs. One day on a march back from an unsuccessful raid, a cav-alry captain, lenient but concerned about Confederate pursuers, banned all shooting yet advised his men to kill "anything that has'nt taken the oath [of loyalty to the United States]" by quietly using rifle butts as clubs. Pri-vate Albert Trask remembered: "By the time we reached the [Mississippi] river it was very evident that poultry, at least, had'nt taken the oath worth a cent." Since the army strictly banned unauthorized foraging of this sort, the looters had to sneak the goods into the fort. Two mounted soldiers once slipped away from a march and, after waiting for the column to get out of hearing, killed a hog. They wrapped the butchered meat in blankets, which they placed under their saddles when passing the fort's pickets. While this sort of activity provided great satisfaction to adventuresome young sol-diers, it harmed relations with civilians.[8]

Both governments tried to provide clothing for their troops, but the Confederacy always had trouble producing enough. The Tennessee sap-pers and miners unit that helped to build the fort suffered from worn-out clothes, as did some of the succeeding garrison units. Fearing future short-ages, a number of recruits went barefoot in the summer of 1861 to save their shoes for the coming winter. A youngster who joined the 13th Ar-kansas Infantry at the fort got to pick pieces of his uniform out of a pile of remnants from which few items fit him well. Many enlisted men had to rely on homemade clothes, while officers purchased handsome, even flamboyant outfits from tailors.[9] Captain Joe Barbiere's huge hat plume prompted sharp enough ridicule from the post commander to induce the owner to stop wearing it. Surgeon Lunsford P. Yandell, meanwhile, enjoyed creating a "sensation" by wearing a scarlet flannel jacket trimmed in green with his white pantaloons and high boots.[10]

Like the Confederates, the Federal government had difficulty producing uniforms quickly enough early in the war. Furthermore, uniforms tended to wear out within a year. In early May 1862, the 43rd Indiana Infantry held a dress parade in clothes that had "passed the ragged state," according to a hometown paper. One soldier actually marched in underwear! To the troops' great relief a shipment of new clothes and shoes arrived the next day. Colonel Graham Fitch had obtained these supplies only by appealing directly to Indiana's governor.[11]

Most troops began encampments at the fort with tents for shelter. The commander of a battalion from the 6th U.S. Colored Heavy Artillery had his men lay plank floors under their tents because many of his men had grown ill after sleeping on damp ground. However, troops who lived on the windblown bluff during winter months needed better quarters. In their first winter at the site, the Confederates lacked enough lumber for many structures. So, some just constructed mud and stick chimneys for their tents. Others excavated square holes into the sides of hills and covered them with tent canvas for a partially insulated shelter. These improvisations appeared in many of the Confederate army's winter camps. But Civil War soldiers staying put for a winter preferred to build cabins, as garrisons from both armies eventually did at the fort. One Federal, who built upon the remains of a Confederate building, praised his predecessors' structure as exceptionally well made.[12]

The first Federal troops at the fort camped in a ravine, which provided some protection from the wind. After remodeling or rebuilding surviving Confederate cabins, they erected more by disassembling vacant buildings in Osceola.[13] When the 32nd Iowa Infantry arrived on the *Davenport,* the men used the steamer to haul in more wood from Osceola's houses and from the Lanier plantation's slave cabins for reconstruction as barracks and post headquarters. Each of the new cabins measured about twenty by twenty by ten feet and had a brick chimney foundation. Tents sufficed as roofs until replaced by either split-wood shakes or sticks and mud. Private Will Kennedy referred to his as a "snug little room."[14]

Officers tended to have the best housing. Confederate captain William M. Mobley, who had a cot and mattress in a large floored tent shared with another officer, reported: "All in all I live very well." Builders dressed up the house of the Federal post commander with windows and doors taken from the Lanier mansion. Furthermore, officers more likely benefitted from the labor of either slaves or contraband servants who performed housework for them.[15]

Water came from springs within the fort. A Northern reporter claimed the fort had several good springs, although a garrison member's map labeled one near the mouth of Cold Creek as a "sulphur spring." The commander of the 178th New York Infantry complained only about his need for wagons and teams to haul water from a distant spring to his campground.[16]

During the first two years of the war no one recorded the presence of sewage facilities at the site. Soldiers, as was common practice in military camps then, seem to have relieved themselves wherever they wished. In 1863, the Federals dug a set of sinks, communal trench toilets with shovels for covering feces with dirt. They may have located the sinks in the southwestern part of the fort at a place marked on the folk map with a row of dots labeled "burnt meat."[17]

The sailors on the gunboats stationed at the fort lived in self-contained, compactly designed quarters aboard ship. Officers and men had separate quarters, as those in the fort had separate cabins. The officers had toilets and showers, using water drawn by collection buckets on the paddle wheels. Hammocks came out only at night, so that space was clear for cooking, eating, and other activities in the daytime. Federal sailor Symmes Browne complained about living so closely with noisy colleagues. Yet, one professional naval officer who visited the Federal commander of Fort Pillow bragged that he had not been on land more than two days at a time in twelve years. Ships contained everything necessary for daily life in some form.[18]

The necessity least adequately supplied at the fort was medical care. Illness plagued both armies at a time when science knew nothing about the role of microbes. Early in the war, numerous cases of diarrhea and dysentery among Confederates arose from a lack of sanitary precautions. Loose bowel problems formed the most common of the many illnesses suffered by soldiers during the war. Exposure to winter weather could facilitate pneumonia and severe colds. In 1861, two Confederate regiments at the fort each reported around two hundred cases of measles, which was highly contagious among the many rural recruits without previous exposure. The Confederates laid out two graveyards in the northern part of the fort.[19]

Federal soldiers and sailors at the fort suffered most often from fevers, another major killer of the time. Several officers suspected a connection to sluggish streams and stagnant pools but blamed bad vapors, rather than the lush breeding sites for malaria-carrying mosquitoes.[20] Diarrhea and dysentery decreased after the Federal garrison initiated the use of sinks and took more care with sanitation.[21] During the harsh winters of 1862–1864, the Federals lost small groups of men who froze to death or suffered from severe colds. In early 1863, the 32nd Iowa saw less illness after it replaced pup tents with cabins.[22] As gunboat sailors ate in a common mess, the men of the *St. Louis* shared a round of botulism, probably from badly canned food, and the *Benton*'s crew had an outbreak of scurvy from a diet lacking in vitamin C. Federals who died of disease received burial in two of their own cemeteries on the hill north of the central ravine.[23]

Both armies probably started care for the severely ill in separate tents. The Confederate 11th Arkansas Infantry built the first hospital cabin at the site. The Federal garrison also constructed small hospital cabins. When smallpox broke out in the 52nd Indiana during late 1862, the surgeon successfully contained it by quarantining the ill in the northeastern corner of the fort, far from the main campground.[24] Gunboats had sick bays aboard. Fitch's "besieging" force used the McGavock mansion and an abandoned wharf boat as field hospitals. Confederate cavalry operating in the area probably had some covered wagons designated for the ill. Both armies had larger, better-equipped general hospitals behind the lines to which they could move some of the most serious cases.[25]

Because of the painfulness and ineffectiveness of many medical treatments in the 1860s, doctors could be unpopular. Surgeon Yandell reciprocated hostility directed toward him by his fellow Confederates by declaring that "Our men when sick, are like spoiled children." Medical science had advanced more in the area of surgery, but most American doctors had no training in it. In 1861, the chief surgeon of the Confederate 4th Tennessee Infantry refused to perform surgery at the fort because of his ignorance and squeamishness about it. Military doctors eventually had to learn surgery to retain their positions, although combat wounds killed fewer Civil War soldiers than disease.[26]

While inadequate medical care, clothes, or shelter threatened the lives of some, boredom ranked as the most common complaint about garrison life. Soldiers and sailors spent much of their noncombat time on drilling, guard duty, and other tasks.[27] Both military forces followed roughly the same daily routine. One winter schedule had the Federals rising at 6:00 A.M. and having breakfast at 7:00. Morning drill started at 9:00 and was followed by lunch at noon. Afternoon drill at 1:30 led to dress parade at 4:30, supper at 5:00, and bedtime at 8:30. A typical day on the Federal gunboat *Silver Cloud* opened at 5:30 A.M., followed by breakfast at 6:00, scrubbing the decks at 6:45, and inspection plus drill at 9:30. Then came a work assignment, lunch at noon, more work, supper at 5:00 P.M., stringing up hammocks at 7:00, and bedtime at 9:00.[28]

Military work involved a wide variety of activities. The grave demands and dangers of combat consumed the least time. Training, target practice, guarding the post, maintaining equipment, caring for horses, and other labor duties were more common. Constructing buildings, strengthening defenses, and moving supplies could exhaust the men. Black laborers at the fort lightened the load somewhat for soldiers, especially those in Confederate garrisons. Guard duty and forced marches, especially in bad weather, prompted complaints.[29]

In their spare time the soldiers and sailors turned to a variety of activities. Informal prayer services occurred in both armies, although Confederate records mention them more frequently. The Confederate Junius Bragg participated in nightly services because he believed that camp life easily corrupted morals.[30] Much spare time in both armies went into card games. When the *Silver Cloud*'s captain banned cards, the sailors substituted checkers, chess, and backgammon. Other common recreations were reading and music, sometimes by regimental bands. Sailors often developed a fondness for woodcarving.[31] A naval doctor with a scientific bent took sailors out to collect specimens of insects, worms, and lizards, while a surgeon in Fitch's brigade organized a lodge of Masons and had a navy blacksmith make pins for the members. Some Irish recruits in the Confederate garrison entertained themselves by picking fights. Despite orders forbidding it, mounted Federals conducted horse races. Corporal Addison Sleeth even raced a slow old horse against a crippled mule. Many young men enjoyed playing pranks. Sleeth remembered that within his veteran unit "things were continually happening in camp and on the march and served to break up the monotony and revive the spirits of the boys."[32]

The presence of the wide Mississippi created special leisure time opportunities. Tempted in the summer of 1861 to try swimming the river, Augustus Kean, a Confederate, realized midstream that he did not have enough strength to finish. Carried by the strong current, he barely regained the shore two miles downriver and had to make a long walk naked back to his clothes. Confederate infantry assigned to the ram fleet held rowboat races in the river. Watching the river was a quiet pastime, although on one occasion Sleeth and a crowd of comrades grew very excited while watching a dog successfully paddle across it.[33] The Federals left no record of swimming, possibly because increased steamboat traffic made it too dangerous.

The intensity of communal life created challenges for garrisons. The officers' personal pride, especially among the Southerners, who emphasized individual honor, caused many difficulties. As shown in previous chapters, officer elections and promotions provoked several disputes. Exercising power, like obtaining it, also caused conflict. Lieutenant Mark Lyons of the 2nd Alabama Infantry wrote: "the life of a soldier does not suit me, merely from the fact that I have always controlled my own actions but in my present circumstances I am only a piece of mechanism moved by the will of others." Lieutenant Colonel Otto F. Strahe took the position of post commander for himself by charging his colonel with drunkenness over a month after the incident occurred. When chief engineer Montgomery Lynch and post commander Lawrence O'Banion feuded and gave conflicting orders, General P. G. T. Beauregard had to remind them that "for the sake of cause and country, harmony must prevail."[34]

Federal officers also had many egotistic squabbles over power. Colonel Edward H. Wolfe and his lieutenant colonel filed charges against each other without result during a dispute over a soldier's promotion. In another instance, a lieutenant in Wolfe's regiment ineffectually produced a list of countercharges against his accuser on the day of his court martial. He and several other officers in the units received dismissals for being absent without or beyond leave.[35] Post commander Wolfe's dismissal of the 32nd Iowa's chaplain, due to an excessively long absence to collect reading materials and delicacies for the ill, left Colonel John Scott of the Iowans disgruntled. Soon after another disagreement over policy, Wolfe reported Scott for issuing unauthorized furloughs and forced Scott to recall them. Lieutenant Baxter K. Logan got into disciplinary trouble for refusing to obey Wolfe and publicly calling his superiors "*a set of Asses.*" In the worst clash between a commander and a subordinate officer at the post, Major William F. Bradford killed Lieutenant John F. Gregory because the latter drew a gun while resisting arrest.[36]

When not squabbling, officers kept very active working with the troops. Confederate lieutenant colonel William T. Avery wrote his wife: "You have no idea how much work writing[,] drilling[,] granting furloughs[,] settling little camp troubles[,] and a thousand other little annoyances and big ones too a Col. has to contend with." He also noted that it took him two to three hours to perform a daily inspection when in charge of the camp.[37]

Leadership styles varied. The most foolish officers promoted trouble by participating in it. Federal captain John McCowick, according to Corporal Sleeth, opened and shared a captured barrel of whiskey with his men, so that "long before we reached the Fort we were gloriously light." Sleeth's memoir, correctly or symbolically, linked this incident with some violent insubordination toward McCowick. At the other extreme, some officers emphasized their power and privileges. During a long march without canteens on a hot summer night, Federal major William T. Strickland refused to allow a water break until 2:00 A.M. When Private Bill Butler broke from the ranks to get himself water, Strickland drew his sword. Butler responded by aiming his rifle at the major and soon found himself under arrest, though his service in a subsequent guerrilla hunt won him a reprieve. When on another march Federal officers rode in an enclosed ambulance to hide their consumption of medicinal alcohol, discontented enlisted men arranged for the wagon to slip off a ferry and into the Obion River. The best officers, like Confederate lieutenant Mark Lyons, minimized disciplinary problems through leading by good example and showing concern for the troops' welfare. As John Ryan, a Federal cavalryman, remembered, "The great officers were not tyrants. The best Company and regimental Commanders were loved and respected by the men under them."[38]

Given the youth of most enlisted men, it is unsurprising that many acted immaturely at times. Surviving Confederate accounts say little about major disciplinary difficulties at the fort, while Federal records contain much detail. A court martial sentenced a soldier who shot at Captain McCowick's cabin door to three years at hard labor plus a walk through camp wearing a "mutineer" sign while a band played the "Rogue's March." Major Seldon Hetzel of the 178th New York Infantry received dismissal from the service for mismanaging a deceased soldier's effects and for using disloyal speech in publicly condemning the Emancipation Proclamation. In the worst robbery case, which involved the theft of $1,800 from a secessionist, the group's leader went to prison for a year and two others earned shorter terms at hard labor. Caught Federal deserters drew one or more years of imprisonment, while those who returned to duty only lost pay for the time absent.[39]

Lesser disciplinary problems among the Confederates involved drinking, bullying, brawling, and bringing prostitutes into camp. Philip Stephens, an underaged enlistee, observed "an old man, bent, decrepit, wicked, coming up to the camp from the back country with his daughter every day or so! The boys used to call him 'Silver Heels.' What did he bring his daughter for? He sold eggs and things—ostensibly—but! My boyish mind did not take hold of things then. I was innocent and modest."[40]

Federal sources record gambling, leaving the fort without a pass, unauthorized firing of guns, disobedience of orders, insubordinate talk, and especially drunkenness as the most common infractions.[41] Although General Grant forbade liquor to his troops through early 1864, it never disappeared. Archaeological investigations at the site have found bottles for liquor and highly alcoholic patent medicines at a Federal campground. Liquor came into the fort through smuggling, as when a supposed shipment of canned peaches actually contained whiskey. Enforcement of the alcohol ban and other rules lay largely in the hands of the post provost marshal and his guard, which acted as military police.[42]

The Federal navy had a reputation for particularly strict discipline. On *Silver Lake,* late completion of morning dressing and hammock storage meant marching on the hurricane deck while carrying the hammock for half of the day. Inadequate personal cleanliness resulted in a forced scrubbing with soap, sand, and hickory brushes. For additional humiliation to white sailors, some officers had blacks administer the punishment.[43]

Occasionally, individuals resolved disciplinary conflicts through compromise. When one company of Confederate Missourians refused to obey orders because of an incompetent captain, General M. "Jeff" Thompson managed both to pressure them back to duty and to secure the captain's resignation. When a picket duty assignment infuriated Corporal Sleeth after thirty-six hours of continuous service, he negotiated permission to share the shift with two trusted colleagues so that he could get some sleep.[44]

Disciplinary difficulties multiplied when morale declined, and enlisted men had much about which to grumble. New soldiers especially had trouble adjusting to drilling, guard duty, inactivity, or deaths of colleagues. Suffering from exhaustion could make a veteran, like Sleeth, blow up at a superior. The defeats of one's army elsewhere also lowered hopes. Lieutenant Colonel William T. Avery noticed that the Confederate loss at Logan's Crossroads, Kentucky, in early 1862 "cast a gloom upon this part of the army." Of course, problems with food, shelter, clothing, or medical care raised complaints and depressed spirits as well.[45]

The repeatedly late arrival of pay often caused bad feelings, not to mention real harm to families. As the Confederacy struggled to create a new government and military organization, it probably had more administrative failures than the Federal side. The Confederate army's failure to send pay and enlistment bounties motivated a company of the 4th Tennessee Infantry to stack arms in protest rather than drill on one summer morning at the fort. Colonel Joseph Knox Walker galloped over and ordered them to drill. When they still balked, he scorned them for insufficient patriotism. An antagonized soldier responded that "officers could afford to be very patriotic, as they drew their pay regularly." Walker ordered the man arrested, but no one would perform the deed. The colonel then declared all the other commissioned officers under arrest for their lack of cooperation but allowed the regiment to go off duty until paid two days later.[46]

Lesser aggravations involved amenities. The periodic unavailability of newspapers limited the Confederate garrison's knowledge of war news. The lack of razors forced Lieutenant Mark Lyons to grow a beard. The Federal garrison, while well supplied by sutlers and stores, eventually faced high costs "amounting almost to *extortion*" for local produce, which led to price regulation by the post commander in 1863.[47]

Letters from home sometimes challenged morale. A sweetheart's letter that seemed too distant in tone disturbed Lieutenant Lyons so much that he violated lights-out time to write her a reprimand, which gained him a reassuring reply. Touched deeply by his wife's letters, Lieutenant Colonel Avery admitted to her that "I would give anything in this world almost . . . if this war was over. I never wanted to see you all half as bad in my life." Some men deserted because a wife became ill or neared childbirth.[48]

Low morale, together with the common problem of homesickness, formed a volatile combination. Some commanders relieved the tension by issuing many furloughs to visit home, but sometimes the homesick found leaves nearly impossible to obtain. The first desertion from the fort came shortly after the Confederates arrived at the site in 1861. Authorities quickly caught the deserter at his home in Arkansas and returned him. Another homesick Confederate took the safer but more demanding route of acting as if severe rheumatism made him barely able to walk. After gaining a discharge, he had no trouble hiking seven miles to catch a steamboat home.

Bradford's cavalry battalion of Tennessee unionists had a particularly high number of desertions, partly because of the financial suffering endured by many of the men's families.[49]

Morale generally rose when matters of subsistence, leadership, comradeship, furloughs, and pay went well. After recording complaints about late pay, one angry letter-writer changed his tone when the paymaster paid a surprise visit before the document's completion. News of victories by one's army, of course, especially helped. So did treats shipped from home. A company of Iowans wrote a tender note of thanks when their hometown Soldiers' Aid Society pampered them with a variety of goods rarely seen in camp: onions, butter, dried fruit, dried meat, cakes, horse radish, maple molasses, pumpkin butter, and tomatoes (dried, canned, and preserved). Occasionally wives, especially of officers, came to visit, and some refugees who enlisted in the Federal army kept their families at the fort.[50]

Most Civil War soldiers had to depend upon mail for contact with loved ones. Both armies generally received frequent mail at the fort via steamers. Federal private Will Kennedy joked that "I get letters about every mail. I think I am greatly slighted if I do not." But many a soldier felt that his letters did not come often enough. Long gaps between letters caused Hiram Holt "a painful suspense," and another Confederate wrote, "Oh father! you do not know how letters and messages from home touch the tender chords of the young soldier's heart, or you would write to me oftener than you do."[51] Soldiers far from home welcomed reassurance that the family was managing well. In addition, patriotic missives could reaffirm their commitment to the cause. When one such letter was read at a Federal dress parade, the men broke into loud cheering. Support from the home community, plus a reciprocal commitment to it, helped military men endure their trials.[52]

Garrison life at Fort Pillow and elsewhere during the Civil War included both pleasant and painful times. Green soldiers were the most vulnerable to the challenges of military life. Veterans more likely would seize food or shelter, if needed. Length of service generally made veterans grow tougher and more stoic, yet even their morale and self-discipline could wear thin under pressure.[53] The difficulty of military life was one of many factors that influenced events at the fort for both Confederate and Federal garrisons.

Chapter Four

The First Federal Garrison

A SUCCESSION of individual gunboats maintained a weak Federal presence at Fort Pillow during the summer of 1862. After the Confederate evacuation, civilians worried about what the change of government would entail. Secessionists insisted that the populace avoid contact with Federals on the grounds that the conquerors would harm all Southerners and their way of life; the most determined secessionists had already formed guerrilla bands in an effort to preserve some local control. Masters generally worried that slaves expected freedom and might gain it from the Federals. Nonetheless, the reappointment of either home guards or slave patrols disappeared from the agenda of the cautious Lauderdale County Court in July 1862. Wary slaves remained at home, while bold ones sought Federal protection, just as unionists and Confederate deserters did. For lack of facilities, naval officers advised runaway slaves to return home and paroled enemy deserters. They tried to reassure civilians of the new government's benevolence but simultaneously collected information on secessionists' activities from unionists.[1] The Federal sailors represented a limited but potent danger to the status quo.

While the *Pittsburg*'s captain thought that "To occupy their works [at Fort Pillow] will tend much to avoid annoyance to our transports, give an asylum to those that love the Union, and keep the back country quiet," the army at first showed no interest in garrisoning the site. The sailors, therefore, conducted a variety of activities, such as removing repairable cannons from Forts Pillow and Randolph. Gunboats twice went to the aid of disabled ships. On one such run the crew picked up some stranded provisions and Confederate prisoners of war. While guarding another disabled ship from the guerrillas who menaced it during repairs, sailors provided care for ill and wounded Federals aboard it. Guerrilla attacks on transports and small scouting parties grew more frequent in July when farmers began bringing cotton to landings at the fort and Fulton for shipping. With newly built protective walls around its boilers, the *Cairo* periodically searched for cotton-burning guerrillas who sought to nullify the efforts of the Northern buyers now permitted to operate in the area. The navy also seized a small steamer and a large rowboat from hiding places before guerrillas could use them. While sailors watched for smugglers and guerrillas, there simply were not enough of them to patrol much on land around Fort Pillow.[2]

By the late summer of 1862, the war had become longer and bloodier than Americans had originally expected. Many Federals interpreted Congress's passage of a major confiscation law in July as a sign that troops could get tougher with an unrelenting enemy society. The law provided for the seizure of secessionists' property, including slaves who would eventually be freed. General Grant, the regional commander as head of the new Department of the Tennessee, stopped excluding contrabands from Federal lines, and the navy did likewise a little later. As the conciliatory policy toward secessionist civilians faded, a new hard policy replaced it. In early August, Union cavalrymen, showing little respect for slavery or other forms of property, may have used Fort Pillow as a temporary base during operations in the area.[3]

These expeditions came searching for partisan ranger cavalry under formation by Confederate captains William W. Faulkner and Robert W. Haywood. The Confederate Congress, through the Partisan Ranger Act, sought to channel guerrilla warfare behind Federal lines into a new form. Partisan rangers would conduct operations similar to civilian guerrillas but, unlike them, would operate in larger numbers, mostly stay in encampments, and come under army regulations. Typically, the ranger units grew slowly as a core of original recruits collected additional volunteers and conscripts. The Federals' adoption of a harsher war policy probably aided their recruitment efforts. While the Federal army generally considered guerrilla tactics a violation of civilized warfare, it eventually designated rangers as legitimate soldiers and irregulars lacking proof of Confederate enlistment as outlaws. Since Federals generally referred to both groups as "guerrillas," their records often leave an individual's status unclear.[4] Some bands seeming to be civilian guerrillas may have represented partisan ranger units just beginning recruitment.

Across the occupied South, the Federals' hard war policy included similar counterinsurgency tactics. Usually, the first technique used involved sending a large force to sweep guerrillas out of an area. On August 22, 1862, a company from the 52nd Indiana Infantry, a battle-tested regiment, came by steamer from Memphis to Fort Pillow for such a patrol. At the time the army hoped to pacify all of West Tennessee so as to allow railroads to reopen.[5]

The *Cairo* escorted the Indianans to Fulton, where they learned that the enemy had removed southward to Covington. The Federals marched during the night to that town but, finding themselves outnumbered, retreated while repeatedly and bloodlessly skirmishing with mounted but inexperienced rangers. The Union soldiers reembarked for Memphis to obtain reinforcements. The next day most of the regiment steamed upriver. Landings en route led to several arrests as well as the capture of arms, ammunition, and supplies. At Fulton a thorough search of boats turned up a shipment of quinine and brandy, probably intended as medical supplies for the Confederate army. One column undertook a night march to Covington via Randolph, and another took a longer route through Bloomington. Besides appropriating foodstuffs, the men rounded up some wagons, horses, mules, cattle, and slaves to facilitate the operation. While the Indianans did not make contact with the enemy, they did collect some suspects. The Federals resorted to the common tactic of forcing the local elite to pledge their wealth that no more guerrilla activity would occur. Neither the pledges nor the anti-guerrilla sweep worked well.[6]

Fear of guerrilla attack could not help but affect the Federals. A tense German-American picket, who spoke little English, mistook for guerrillas three sailors who had gone out in civilian clothes to steal a sheep. After he shot at them, other members of the 52nd Indiana arrived in time to save the sailors. Soon afterward genuine guerrillas surprised and fired on two sailors out hunting near the fort. In response, a party from the *Cairo* caught a suspect with a cache of arms and ammunition in a house near the attack site.[7]

Federals often punished civilians for guerrilla activity. After the guerrilla ambush, sailors burned nearby houses, barns, and haystacks. When two steamer captains claimed that guerrillas fired a cannon at them, a gunboat went to the site and shot a broadside into a cabin in hope of achieving a "salutary effect upon the surrounding neighborhood." Guerrillas almost certainly did not have artillery, but concern about preventing that possibility led the district commander, William T. Sherman, to order the remaining useable cannons hauled away from Forts Pillow and Randolph. Then, when guerrilla riflemen in Randolph shot at a steamer, the hard-nosed major general sent troops from Memphis to burn down the village.[8] Generally, when guerrillas had attacked and disappeared, neither the army nor the navy could do anything very effective about it. The hard war policies of numerous arrests and punitive property destruction only stiffened guerrillas' determination, for secessionists blamed the Federals for violating the rules of civilized warfare through the anti-guerrilla tactics used.[9]

Military textbooks of the time drew upon the Napoleonic and Indian wars to advocate small outposts along communication lines and frequent patrols against guerrillas. Fort Pillow became exactly that sort of station when Sherman sent the 52nd Indiana back there as a garrison on September 9. Soon afterward the navy stopped stationing a gunboat at the fort but kept several ships, such as the *Silver Cloud,* cruising a long stretch of the river to the north and south. While sailors hunted for guerrillas and smugglers, both those groups did their best to avoid the warships.[10] Most of the work of policing the area fell to the new army garrison (see Tables 5 and 6).

Expeditions from the fort followed the hard war policies of seizing most weapons and many foodstuffs from civilians. Provost Marshal Ross Guffin shipped so much food upriver that the district commander soon ordered the garrison to forage for just enough to feed itself. A patrol of Indianans sent to Fulton in September again found and confiscated goods, this time salt and shoes possibly headed for the Confederates. One company stayed at the village for a month to quell smuggling.[11]

When the post commander at Bolivar asked for a foray in his direction, Captain Guffin took seventy-five men, partly on foot and partly mounted on seized horses. A large force of inexperienced partisan rangers under Captains Faulkner and Haywood surrounded and attacked the encamped Federals at dawn on September 17 near Durhamville. The Federal veterans took advantage of available cover to put up a stiff resistance into the afternoon, when the attack ended. The Confederates left twelve dead men behind but killed only one Federal and wounded eleven others. Guffin deemed it prudent to retreat to the fort. Partisan rangers would never attack the fort's patrols again. Lacking experience and enough weapons, they emphasized recruiting and conscripting instead.[12]

After Guffin's return, some army official mistakenly ordered the 52nd to Columbus, Kentucky, from which it soon returned to the fort. The district commander at Columbus sent out a small force of cavalry, infantry, and artillery to join the garrison in striking back at Faulkner and Haywood, now active around Covington. As most of the column plodded along, elements of the 2nd Illinois Cavalry under Captain Franklin Moore charged ahead. After finding burnt cotton along the road and in the town square, Moore trailed some of the well-mounted rangers to Durhamville without catching them. The operation's commander complained that some of Moore's men "behaved more like brigands than soldiers," abusing and despoiling civilians. From an opposite perspective, an infantryman later wrote: "When we could not gain respect by easy words we applied the rod with a vengeance, which never failed to produce a good effect." Further illustrating the hard war viewpoint, he added that "the policy of protecting and fighting an enemy at the same time will never win." Federals would continue to debate how far the hard war policy should go.[13]

Due to increasing guerrilla activity, unionists found themselves more vulnerable. Seeking to gain revenge and to avoid Confederate conscription, more sought Federal enlistment. Haywood's rangers captured one group of unionist recruits before they could reach a Federal post. Around thirty Tennesseans joined the 52nd Indiana at Fort Pillow, while volunteers from Arkansas received transportation to Helena, where their state's regiments were forming.[14]

Some unionists found other ways to serve. The young Samuel B. Lanier had stayed behind on his family's Craighead Point plantation when his mother and brother fled southward. This wealthy and well-educated gentleman now openly revealed his Union allegiance. Preferring that Federals rather than partisan rangers take the plantation's livestock, Lanier convinced the post provost marshal to start giving out receipts to unionists for seized livestock. Because he collected information for the Federals, his elegant family mansion was no longer safe as a regular abode, and he often stayed at the fort instead. Lanier volunteered to serve as a scout for patrols and as a member of the provost court, which judged prisoners brought in by patrols. He and Guffin became close friends.[15]

Not only unionists, but also some slaves wanted to aid the Federal cause. Slaves sought as well to gain their freedom by fleeing masters or following patrols to the fort. One group brought several bales of their owner's cotton and cleverly managed to get a white to sell it for them, since the army seized an owner's property brought by runaways. The post sent the earliest arrivals to a large contraband camp, which the army had established at Columbus; later ones went to a newer camp at Island No. 10. At some uncertain point in the fort's occupation soldiers started hiring some contrabands as cooks and servants.[16]

Lincoln's Preliminary Emancipation Proclamation surprised the nation on September 22, 1862. It threatened to free slaves in all areas remaining attached to the Confederacy on January 1, 1863. Responding to the proclamation's terms for exempting areas that demonstrated loyalty, unionists met at Ripley, resolved to return to the Union, and petitioned for permission to elect U.S. congressmen. Military governor Andrew Johnson ordered balloting to occur in West Tennessee in December, and Provost Marshal Guffin administered the loyalty oath required for voting. The army vainly hoped that oath-taking would eliminate support for guerrillas in occupied areas.[17]

General Grant had still another use for the oath—he required that both cotton buyers and sellers take it. They could then obtain permits from a post provost marshal, who would enforce trading rules, such as the one banning liquor shipments into Grant's department. The rules came from both army commanders and the Treasury Department in an effort to reduce the chances that trade would benefit either secessionists or the Confederate army. Except for brief breaks caused by the more lenient Treasury Department's objections, the army's rules existed through early 1864. The revival of the cotton trade met important needs and created significant profits for both sellers and buyers. Because the district commander restricted the landing of goods to military posts, merchants began to set up stores at the fort. In turn, a large quantity of cotton started to flow through the fort.[18]

Trade restriction, like other hard war policies, moved most hostility to the Federals from open to covert forms. Driven by real need, many secessionists took the oath of allegiance in hope of marketing cotton, purchasing supplies, and halting theft by soldiers. Fear also motivated civilians, according to a newspaper correspondent, who commented that "not the one hundredth part of those professing loyalty to our forces are honest." Behind seeming acquiescence to Federal authority, many continued their support for guerrillas and partisan rangers.[19]

In November, Colonel Robert V. Richardson came into the area with Confederate commissions to raise a brigade of partisan rangers and to systematize conscription. Richardson brought a larger force than Faulkner and Haywood, both of whom had left the area. The colonel organized an extensive network of agents for recruiting and conscripting.[20] To meet this challenge, the garrison seized numerous horses, mules, saddles, and bridles from civilians in order to transform two companies into mounted infantry, a common anti-guerrilla tactic. It also requested cavalry reinforcements, and in December Captain Franklin Moore's Company D of the 2nd Illinois Cavalry relocated to the fort. During the early years of the war Federal commanders commonly parceled cavalry regiments out as individual companies or battalions, not from a shortage of horsemen but as a tactical preference. Not only had Moore's company fought West Tennessee guerrillas and rangers for months, but, as previously mentioned, it had participated in one operation near Fort Pillow.[21]

After just one skirmish with Richardson, the garrison had to turn to a more serious threat. In December rumors abounded about major Confederate cavalry raids being undertaken by Brigadier General Meriwether "Jeff" Thompson in Southeast Missouri and by Brigadier General Nathan Bedford Forrest in West Tennessee. Only Forrest's operation actually occurred. Forrest, a tall and striking forty-one-year-old with a dark beard, had risen by sheer talent from poverty to wealth in antebellum times. He showed similar intuitive brilliance as an untrained soldier. Forrest's raid contributed to the ending of Grant's first advance on Vicksburg.[22]

Brigadier General Thomas A. Davies, commander of the District of Columbus, responded to the perceived danger by ordering the New Madrid garrison, six companies of the 32nd Iowa Infantry, to go by steamboat to Fort Pillow. He judged Fort Pillow the more defendable post of the two, if reinforced. Although New Madrid lay outside Davies's district, he incorrectly thought he had received authority to do this in the current crisis. John Scott, the Iowans' colonel, obeyed very reluctantly. The 32nd brought with it fifty German-American members of the 2nd Missouri Artillery, who had been arrested after a dispute over their term of service led to a refusal to perform military duties. After abandoning well-built winter quarters, the newcomers had to pitch tents at the fort in snowy, windy weather.[23]

Although Colonel Edward Wolfe, the fort's commander, had the garrison on the alert for an attack, Scott quickly realized that the fort needed artillery and more troops to have a chance at a successful defense. Scott traveled upriver by steamer to Cape Girardeau, where he could telegraph his old department commander that "As far as I can see, we are of no use here." To Scott's surprise, his previous superior had him arrested for abandoning his post at New Madrid. After winning exoneration in a court martial two months later, Scott returned to Fort Pillow. By that time Forrest had left West Tennessee without coming close to the fort. The fear the raid generated had led not only to expansion of the fort's garrison but also to cancellation of the congressional election.[24]

Subsequently, a threat by Richardson to attack the fort kept the Federals on alert. One member of the 32nd Iowa later remembered a night-long vigil during a lightning storm in fearful expectation of an assault that did not come. On another wet, cold night most of the guards at the Fulton

Road gate withdrew a short distance to build a bonfire. Around midnight they heard cries and shots from the two pickets remaining at the gate. They rushed back to learn that enemy cavalry had supposedly approached the gate and then wheeled back into the dark. After waiting silently a while in a wet snowfall, several men scouted down the road and discovered tracks from cattle rather than horses in the mud.[25]

Early in 1863, much construction put a new face on the site. In front of the Fulton Road gate lay a trench bridged by heavy planks (taken up at night). Just inside the gate the 2nd Illinois Cavalry built its huts. As one followed the road down a ravine and farther into the fort, a smaller ravine appeared on the east side. There the 52nd Indiana had its cabins, a hospital, and a drill field. At the mouth of the central ravine by the river Provost Marshal Guffin erected an office. Immediately to the south, on a promontory called Wolfe's Hill, Colonel Wolfe had his post headquarters. On the hill to the north of the central ravine lay the 32nd Iowa's quarters, hospital, chapel, and parade ground. Just to the north on higher ground at a breastwork behind the bluff, the arrested Missourians camped.[26]

The New Year also brought noteworthy legal developments for blacks living near the fort. Lincoln's final Emancipation Proclamation liberated all slaves in Arkansas but for political reasons exempted those in Tennessee, where the Second Confiscation Act still promised freedom to secessionists' slaves who entered Federal lines. As a response to African American interest and the army's manpower needs, the Proclamation also allowed blacks to enlist.[27]

In actual practice, some slaves preferred to stay at home, especially if they liked their masters, distrusted Federals, or considered it prudent to wait longer to see how matters would develop. Aleck, a runaway from Haywood County, to the east of the fort's Lauderdale County, advised other slaves that "if they have good homes that they had better stay where they are . . . if they run off they have no homes, and perhaps can't get any work." An owner might also keep a slave by making concessions. Allowed to haul goods from the fort purely at his own profit after every trip delivering his master's cotton, the slave Shaddrack earned enough to buy a horse. Despite some local masters' fears that slave rebellions would accompany the Proclamation, nothing happened. Individual slaves ready to seek freedom simply fled to the fort as before.[28]

The escaped slaves did not always get a positive reception. A drunk Federal forcibly took a coat from the runaway Addison. The contraband called upon Captain Joseph Cadwallader of the 32nd Iowa Infantry to rectify matters, but the guilty soldier slugged Addison, while a crowd of racist soldiers threatened the captain and denounced him as a "damned abolitionist." In February a rumor circulated among antislavery members of the 32nd Iowa that Colonel Wolfe had allowed a master to retrieve a slave who was then whipped to death. Whether true or false, it predisposed those soldiers for outrage when Wolfe permitted another owner (probably a unionist) to remove two contrabands who worked for the 32nd's wagonmaster. An infuriated Colonel Scott secured their release.[29] Afterward, Wolfe and Scott differed over several other issues relating to their powers, and Scott soon applied to have his regiment transferred. Years later, Scott and his wartime adjutant would claim that they belonged to an "Abolition Regiment," while the 52nd was proslavery. Some fights did break out between members of the two units over emancipation, but neither regiment had unanimity on the issue. Although the clash of the colonels' egos added to tensions, the conflict growing within the garrison reflected a larger one building within the nation.[30]

Emancipation, as a major change in race relations, caused political disputes within the Republican Party and especially between the Republicans and the more vociferously racist Democrats. One member of the 52nd Indiana wrote the Democratic paper back home that Lincoln's Proclamation had moved Republicans in the regiment to renounce their party. Another correspondent of the same paper exclaimed that he did not want to undergo the suffering of military life to free slaves, whom he considered ignorant and promiscuous, to move north and take whites' jobs for lower pay. He felt betrayed by the president's change of policy. Albert L. Towne of the 32nd Iowa wrote home that emancipation would lengthen the war by making the enemy more determined. He viewed the contrabands in camp as lazy, dishonest, and unhappy. In January a member of the 52nd Indiana claimed that his company had started discouraging runaways from entering the fort.[31]

On the other side, some soldiers in both infantry regiments encouraged fugitive slaves. An Iowan told a complaining master that "you will only have to work with your own hands as we have to do in the North." A man from the 52nd Indiana told his hometown Republican paper that Federals "can shoot just as well to free the slave as to save the Union if it will bring the hostilities to a close any sooner." Another wrote to deny that anyone had left the Republican Party because of emancipation.[32]

Both Wolfe and Scott were Republicans leading politically divided units. While a pro-war, anti-emancipation faction of the Democrats had its supporters, few if any Federals favored the party's pro-peace wing, which one Iowan considered "responsible for the death of every [killed] soldier."[33] The 32nd Iowa seems to have had a strong Republican majority; at an assembly the regiment gave a nearly unanimous voice vote for resolutions endorsing the Lincoln Administration and the Emancipation Proclamation.[34] The 52nd Indiana, though, probably had a closer split, which made Wolfe reluctant to speak out on emancipation, while Scott felt no inhibition.

Besides the intensification of the racial issue, another significant development in early 1863 was the placement of the mounted Indiana troops under Captain Moore's command. Colonel Wolfe did not attempt to mount Iowa companies for combat duty, probably because of their inexperience and equipment problems. That unit could not always get ammunition for the three different types of weapons it had.[35]

Moore, a tall, auburn-haired farmer from Illinois in his thirties, seemed instinctively to devise effective anti-guerrilla tactics. He carefully gathered intelligence from unionists and possibly from slaves. Unionist recruits and refugees who knew the area guided his skillfully managed expeditions, which often had specific targets. The mounted force maintained pressure on the enemy by spending about half of its time on the road. Operations stressed speed and surprise. The horsemen often traveled at night with minimal equipment and breaks. On some short trips they would find meals and shelter along the way. Their attacks frequently occurred at dawn or in the late evening, in the hope of catching the enemy resting. To do the most damage, Moore preferred to assault the partisan rangers' camps; extensive ranger recruitment had reduced the number of civilian guerrillas, anyway. Attacking upon contact (not getting into a formation first), Moore's patrols suffered almost no casualties that year. He consistently succeeded in killing a few Confederates in skirmishes and capturing more. The territory covered by Fort Pillow's patrols ranged over a portion of West Tennessee from the Mississippi River eastward to Jackson, and from the Obion River in the north to Moscow in the south.[36]

Moore's first major operation came after two unionists fled Confederate conscription agents. These men led Moore's force in single file along a faint path through woods to a ranger camp at Durhamville. At sunrise on January 7, 1863, the patrol attacked about two hundred Confederates there. Cavalryman John Ryan remembered: "We charged into there [*sic*] camp like a freight train going through a village. The enemy was completely surprised. I never saw so much confusion." He added that after another charge against a few Confederates firing from the top of a hill, the enemy "melted away like snow." The expedition killed sixteen and captured forty-four, while only one Federal suffered wounds. Most of the Confederates who escaped did so on horseback, since the exhausted Federal mounts could not pursue them. The skirmish had initiated a handful of Iowans, replacing ill Indianans, into combat. One admitted that "I then gazed for the first time upon the bodies of men killed in battle, and badly as I hate the rebels, I turned in sorrow from the view." The victors ate a fine breakfast civilians had cooked for the rangers. Moore impressed a wagon and team to haul away the wounded man and enemy supplies. For fear of a counterattack, his men marched back to the fort in rain for twelve hours without a stop. The entire garrison turned out to celebrate.[37]

The fort's guardhouse could not hold all the prisoners, so the Federals locked some in ammunition magazines. The post always forwarded prisoners to district headquarters (then Columbus, Kentucky, and later Memphis, Tennessee) for evaluation. Military courts convicted some suspected guerrillas of crimes connected to irregular warfare and sentenced them to imprisonment, hard labor, or even execution. Others just went to prisoner-of-war camps. Occasionally authorities released a captive for lack of sufficient evidence.[38]

In early February 1863, Moore went out after Captain Albert Cushman, a recruiter for Richardson, and "the dread of all cotton buyers," according to a secessionist's diary. Because Confederates captured numerous buyers, confiscated their cash, and burnt the cotton, farmers increasingly had to abandon sales or risk delivering the staple to the fort. Cushman had recently murdered a civilian, probably for resisting conscription. Those wanting to stay out of the Confederate army had to flee to the fort. When Moore missed his prey in Ripley, he ordered the ranger's family out of the house of Cushman's father-in-law and destroyed it with fire. Cavalryman Ryan later commented that "I am willing to give Capt. Moore much praise as an industerious [*sic*] officer. But I Condemned [*sic*] the act then and I Condem [*sic*] it now as I think of that poor woman with her children standing in the street in the snow Crying and Shivering with the Cold. . . . It was cruilty [*sic*] only that and nothing more." One account also has Moore announcing that he would do the same to anyone who aided guerrillas. That night the Federals caught Cushman and several associates sleeping in a nearby plantation mansion. House-burning, not surprisingly, seemed barbaric to Confederates, and Richardson seems to have sent Wolfe a threatening note about it. Significantly, Moore burned no more houses. This restraint may explain why guerrilla and counterinsurgency warfare around Fort Pillow never entered the escalating cycle of destructiveness that occurred in other places, such as Missouri.[39]

On February 27, Moore led his mounted force and a company of the 32nd Iowa on foot toward one of Richardson's bases at a Methodist camp meeting ground near Bloomington. After traveling by steamer to Randolph, they marched eastward all night and surrounded the camp by dawn. Following an opening volley, which riddled the chapel, the Federals charged and captured a mere eight rangers inside. Lying asleep on the floor, all of them had survived the volley. They had stayed behind to round up some unreporting conscripts when Richardson left.[40]

Following this incident, two pincer operations sought to trap Richardson's force against the flooded Hatchie River. Both times other Federal cavalry pressed upward from the south, while Moore had the task of closing off the Hatchie River ferry crossing. In the first effort Moore received his orders late. As soon as possible he got his men spread out along ten miles of the river, only to learn that Richardson had already escaped. In the second operation Moore found the ferryboat burnt. His troops left their horses behind, took dugout canoes across the river, and marched to Covington, where they skirmished with a few rangers. Search parties failed to find any more of the enemy in that area. The rangers had dissolved into small groups for flight.[41]

In March, Wolfe decided to mount two cannons, which the fort had received after the scare over Forrest's raid. One turned out to be unusable, but the Federals replaced it by successfully removing the spike from one of the fort's remaining Confederate cannons. Early in the training of an artillery crew from the 52nd, Wolfe ordered it to fire a blank salute for a returning patrol. After the loading of one charge, the commanding sergeant decided on his own to add a second. As Private John Adams started to ram down the extra charge, an unobservant soldier lit the fuse. The explosion blew Adams fifteen feet into the air, over the rampart, and to the ground thirty feet beyond with all his clothes torn off him. A mangled arm that required amputation led to Adams's discharge from the army.[42]

Later spring patrols continued the focus on partisan ranger recruiters. Federals attacked one, a Captain Porter, at home near Key Corner. They caught five of his men and sacked his house, but he escaped across the

Forked Deer River. The patrol then proceeded toward Eaton in search of Captain William D. Cotter, another of Richardson's recruiters. To ensure surprise, their unionist guide led them through a muddy river bottom "that looks like the foot of man nor beast had never trod since Noah's flood; our horses would often sink to their bellies," according to an Indianan. The route worked, for the troops caught Cotter and twenty-four men. During the return trip, other Federal cavalrymen mistook Moore's force for Confederates and briefly opened fire, but without doing any damage. When the patrol arrived at Fort Pillow, the gunners this time safely fired a cannon salute in celebration. Continual Federal pressure kept Richardson's force fragmented until he and much of his command escaped eastward.[43]

The mounted portion of the garrison came to know the countryside and its inhabitants. While secessionists avoided serious confrontations, some did tauntingly call the Federals "nigger-lovers." Tired of this, Private Bill Butler responded one day in Brownsville by grabbing a slave baby and mockingly proclaiming his love for the child.[44]

A more significant sore point was some civilians' violation of trading regulations. These grew tighter after the district commander banned the shipment of goods into interior areas without special permission. As part of the hard war policy, the restrictions would make it more difficult for rangers, guerrillas, and their supporters to take advantage of restored trade. Wolfe stationed a company of the 32nd Iowa at Fulton to prevent smuggling. The occasional forays of these troops did not go out very far, unlike those from the fort.[45]

When one patrol from Fort Pillow went to Key Corner to search for smuggled goods, several soldiers had to swim their horses across the South Forked Deer River to surprise and hold the hamlet while the rest came the long way by a ford. The advance party decided to undress, cross the river, and then send someone back in a skiff for their dry clothes. Finding the skiff sabotaged, they had to run naked through the community to a lumber-yard to get raft materials. Any smugglers present wound up amused rather than caught. Some of the other patrols had more success, but at least one Federal thought the ongoing effort was hopeless. Rumors arose that some officers made money through improper trading, although no investigation ever occurred.[46]

Union forces did have some positive interactions with civilians. A planter friendly to both sides occasionally invited officers to his home near the fort for dinner. Once guerrillas attempted to capture the visitors, but he talked them out of it lest this violate his hospitality and honor. While on one patrol, Corporal Sleeth stayed overnight at a farmhouse near Ripley. Not only did he get to sleep in a bed for the first time in two years, but the family also entertained him with fiddle music that evening. Passing a schoolhouse on another patrol, Sleeth saw the children line the road and hand the troops holly branches as a friendly token. He commented that "This little thing so simple in itself had an effect. . . . Most of us had been little more than school children when we went in the army and . . . this touched us in one of the tender places left in our hearts." Involving deeper emotions, courtship and marriage took place between several of the men and local women.[47]

Civilians disdained but could do nothing about the Federals' increasing interference with slavery. In late May 1863, the army inaugurated the enlistment of contrabands at the fort (the navy had probably already enlisted a few blacks there). Wolfe decreed that military personnel must not object should a black employee wish to join. Recruiting aroused little comment at the post. Private Albert Towne did not think that blacks had the necessary courage. Two of the Iowa officers, but none from Indiana, applied for positions in black regiments.[48] All members of the new black units faced great hostility from the Confederacy. Concerned about both property rights and the specter of slave rebellion, the Confederate Congress refused to recognize blacks as soldiers and left it to state authorities either to return captured ones to owners or to execute them as insurrectionaries. It also advocated the trial of white officers for inciting slave rebellion. Reports that the Confederates had implemented these policies after their first clashes with black troops moved Lincoln in the summer of 1863 to threaten retaliation if the enemy did not treat all captured Federals as prisoners of war. In actual practice, few if any official Confederate executions of black Federal soldiers or their white officers occurred.[49]

The Federal army commonly provided for the black recruits' families in refugee camps established for contrabands. Wolfe chose Captain Joseph Cadwallader of the 32nd Iowa as superintendent of contrabands at the fort. Cadwallader set up a camp, probably composed of tents and huts, by the road a little southeast of the central ravine. There he provided for runaway slaves while encouraging them to enlist or to find jobs with the army or businessmen. Wolfe declared the camp off-limits to soldiers after dark, probably because of either harassment or illegal activity. To create space for newcomers, the superintendent periodically sent the unemployed contrabands to the larger and better developed camp at Island No. 10. The fort became a magnet, drawing more fugitives from greater distances. Some came after learning of the Emancipation Proclamation; others simply sought to take advantage of wartime conditions. A journalist noted two groupings in particular: those with scars "frightful to behold" which proved their suffering in slavery and those with savings which demonstrated ambition for a much better life than bondage allowed.[50]

In June, major changes occurred in Fort Pillow's garrison. After several major patrols resulted in few captives, Captain Moore's force received orders to move to Memphis. Before parting, "many of those Infantry boys Came to our Camp to bid us good bye and wish us good fortune," wrote cavalryman John Ryan. Colonel Wolfe paid the horsemen tribute for "zeal and energy . . . in capturing and scattering the lawless bands of guerrillas [; efforts] . . . seldom equaled never excelled." During rides averaging some fifty miles per week, they had captured about three hundred Confederate recruits.[51] Later that month, when the 32nd Iowa Infantry left for Kentucky, Wolfe kept silent, not surprising given past tensions. One Indianan gleefully wrote home about the departure since "I never seen as many nigger love[r]s in my life." On the other side, an Iowan expressed pleasure to his hometown newspaper at no longer having the "Hoosier colonel to abuse and vilify us." The 32nd took with it the remaining three arrested German-Americans from the 2nd Missouri Artillery. The other forty-seven had trickled away in desertion, since the army had not yet tried the obstinate group. The 32nd's departure required Wolfe to appoint a new contraband superintendent, Lieutenant Baxter K. Logan from the 52nd Indiana.[52] Only that regiment remained.

Also in June 1863, the post received its first Treasury agent, who would inspect trade goods landed at the fort in order to uphold civil regulations. The number of merchants and the volume of trading at the fort increased during the second half of the year. Between June and September, goods worth over $50,000 would pass through the place. Controversies over the application of rules arose repeatedly. The first Treasury agent left the post after Wolfe filed a complaint about his competency; the second one quit to open a store at the fort.[53]

The army supported the Treasury agents by continuing the search for smugglers, who now moved most goods by skiff to isolated river landings at night. Some black marketers, especially those dealing in liquor, still tried to operate under the Federals' noses. Soldiers once found whiskey kegs concealed inside barrels of potatoes in a warehouse at the fort. Another time

Colonel Wolfe tried to revoke Harris and Company's trade permit partly because one of its agents had sold liquor. Confiscated liquor went to the post hospital, although the confiscators usually treated themselves first.[54]

Benefitting from trade protection in 1863, Lauderdale County unionists invited the mounted infantry to a Fourth of July barbecue near Ripley. Corporal Sleeth later remembered: "We . . . had a fine day's enjoyment and a splendid dinner. The strange thing about it was Union and Rebel citizens and Federal soldiers all met on this day under the old flag with the kindliest feelings and celebrated." Several officers gave speeches at the event, but Colonel Wolfe stayed at the fort for the ceremonies there. Starting with an artillery salute, those proceedings included songs, speeches, and a sword presentation to the commander. Several days later the gun crew fired another salute in honor of major Federal victories at Gettysburg and Vicksburg.[55] Although the Union side seemed to be gaining the upper hand in the war, the local resistance persisted.

The remaining mounted infantry, when on a patrol to Brownsville, found a roving band of rangers too large to attack. After resorting at least once during the summer to sending out a large patrol of foot soldiers, Wolfe rounded up enough horses in Tipton County (south of the fort's Lauderdale County) to create a third mounted company.[56] Fortunately for the garrison, Captain Moore, now leading the 1st Battalion of his regiment, returned to the fort in late July. All the horsemen then went to Jackson to participate in another pincer operation against Richardson. In a skirmish at Denmark, they captured six rangers, killed two, and dispersed the rest. The combined Federal attacks forced most of Richardson's men to flee precipitously into Mississippi, where they came under Forrest's control. Richardson soon lost his command because he had released some West Tennesseans from conscription in return for $1,000 payments.[57]

Moore tightened discipline in late summer because of "many complaints rendered against this Battalion." He sternly warned the mounted troops against the depredations he had permitted in the past and banned falling out of ranks on the march. Men could get water or relieve themselves only with an officer's written pass. The captain repeated these orders before subsequent trips, along with commendations for the good behavior that mostly resulted. The fort's mounted forces stayed active, probably due to the district commander's use of cavalry patrols crisscrossing interior areas to search for Confederate recruiting parties. By September his scouts could find but a few suspicious persons in the area, and the army transferred Moore with all but one of his companies.[58]

Also during the fall, the racial issue surfaced again due to a letter that Private John D. Purcell of the 52nd Indiana signed and sent to a Democratic newspaper back home. It charged that several unnamed Democrats among the regiment's officers were "Judases" who expected rewards for becoming Republicans and that abolitionists were cowardly "nigger-lovers." After the highly partisan missive caused a big stir in camp, Wolfe confronted the issue. He had it read at a dress parade and demanded that those who agreed with it step forward. None dared do so, but the document's critics freely groaned in disapproval. Purcell recanted his part in the matter, after assigning the authorship to a civilian visitor and claiming to have signed it thoughtlessly. Wolfe unsuccessfully tried to arrest the author, and the Democratic newspaper involved carried no more news from the 52nd.[59]

The next month insubordination by Lieutenant Logan led Wolfe to remove him as contraband camp superintendent and to give the job to Lieutenant James C. Alden. In October, 311 African Americans lived in Fort Pillow's contraband camp. By that time forty-three had enlisted, mostly in the 4th United States Colored Heavy Artillery (U.S.C.H.A.). The post had hired ten to cut wood or drive teams, and civilians employed fifty-three. Developments at the fort may have inspired an elderly slave living near Fulton on an absent owner's farm to start acting as if he owned the place. He sold property, spent proceeds, and even hired two white laborers.[60]

As blacks found expanding opportunities during Federal occupation, white civilians faced increasing difficulties. Immediately after Moore left, Confederate guerrillas and rangers reappeared to burn cotton and hunt for conscripts. Meanwhile, the Federal army continued to search homes for guerrillas and encourage slaves to run away. Both sides seized horses, mules, and foodstuffs from farmers. Consequently, many rural people fell into mere subsistence farming or serious hardship. Not surprisingly, bands of vicious bandits appeared in interior areas. When the sheriff of Tipton County hanged two whites and a black who had robbed and killed a neighbor, tensions in the community ran so high that he requested troops from the fort as guards. That duty seemed to Corporal Sleeth "one of the most trying scenes on the nerves we had to witness in four years service."[61]

Unionists faced special dangers. Because of Confederate guerrillas, William P. Posey "had to be prudent about his talk." M. Virginia Johnson noted later that "it was periling your life to go in the [Federal] lines on any pretence . . . You were branded at once as a[n informer] and dealt with by the guerrillas accordingly." On at least one occasion guerrillas murdered a unionist near the fort, stripped him, and threw the body into a stream. In response to worsening guerrilla activity, Military governor Andrew Johnson authorized the creation of several West Tennessee unionist regiments for home defense. Some recruiting for these regiments took place at Fort Pillow in late 1863.[62]

Fear of guerrilla attacks upon steamboats during 1863 led Wolfe on one occasion to send troops as a guard aboard a commercial steamer. Several other times expeditions sped to accidentally sunk steamers, lest guerrillas get the cargo first. In one case the troops recovered a shipment of whiskey, and Corporal Sleeth observed that "it was not long till two hundred and ninety of the three hundred boys were tight and singing yelling and capering about making things lively." Luckily, that time no guerrillas were present to snipe at them.[63]

That fall, Faulkner and nearly a hundred of his men returned to the area for recruiting. A number of other Confederate officers received leaves to go to their homes for the same purpose. By November, the gradual loss of horses had reduced the fort's mounted infantry to 125 men. This forced the group to patrol very cautiously. On the other hand, the recruiters operated too far from Confederate lines to obtain help or arms from their army. Faulkner later complained, "I was compelled to keep on the move almost constantly."[64]

In November a more serious threat, Forrest's cavalry, marched into West Tennessee to absorb as many partisan rangers and guerrillas as possible while conscripting men, laying in supplies, and collecting horses. Forrest, who had little tolerance for inept superiors and worked best with a degree of independence, had received a new command on the condition that he build up its numbers. As many guerrillas earlier had joined the partisan rangers, many rangers, including Faulkner's, now became cavalry raiders. Raiding was meant to boost Confederate morale and to slow Federal advances by hitting weak spots behind the lines. Capturing many Federal soldiers and supplies while keeping casualties down required rapid movement, the use of surprise, and avoidance of major battles. Shaken by Forrest's bold and ominous presence, Major General Stephen A. Hurlbut, the commander of a Federal corps in western Tennessee and Kentucky, ordered the enrollment of all able-bodied, male civilians into a militia. Wolfe signed up most businessmen living at the fort.[65]

Unaware that Faulkner had joined Forrest, Captain John McCowick led the fort's mounted force on a night march to attack a ranger camp at Ripley, only to learn that it had moved up a road. He proceeded and located a Confederate picket outside Woodville just before dawn. After presenting his force as partisan rangers in order to relax the sentry, the captain opened fire and led a charge. A civilian in the village warned McCowick that not only had the Federals passed by a large camp of enemy cavalry but that other encampments lay beside the two remaining roads out of town. The captain, not able to escape through the countryside due to rough terrain, ordered his men to return immediately the way they came. The noise had prompted a large group of conscripts to attempt an escape, which drew the Confederates' attention long enough for the Federals to get out with five captured pickets. However, when the exhausted patrol stopped at Ripley to rest, eat, and feed the horses, Confederates soon appeared in battle order. According to Corporal Sleeth, "we had ridden forty five miles since ten o'clock the night before and were in better humor to fight than run." The pursuers apparently withdrew for lack of enough men to attack, and so McCowick's force returned to the fort without trouble.[66]

Wolfe immediately requested cavalry reinforcements. Instead, he received the 178th New York Infantry and a warning against further patrolling. The very new and inexperienced 178th suffered from ethnic tensions and poor discipline. Fortunately for the fort this time, Forrest turned back to Mississippi to escape Hurlbut's cavalry at the end of the year. Except for one group accidentally left behind in Tipton County, Forrest had absorbed all the guerrillas and rangers near the fort.[67]

On December 31, what Corporal Sleeth called "one of the saddest [incidents] . . . in all our Regimental history" took place. That day Provost Marshal Guffin sent Lieutenant Edwin Alexander and eight men in a yawl on a fruitless search for a smuggler five miles upriver from Osceola. Near dark during their return a windy snowstorm started. Rough water beached them on a sandbar below Osceola. The soldiers and a civilian guide they had picked up unsuccessfully tried to start a fire. Then they dragged the yawl to the bar's Arkansas side, where a powerful gust shot it away with just the guide and one infantryman aboard without oars. Those two eventually got to shore and reached the fort about noon the next day. The rest tried walking during the subzero night to keep warm. By morning only three privates who eventually had taken shelter in a clump of trees still lived. An Arkansas unionist rescued them, but two subsequently died.[68]

In January 1864, General Sherman, now commanding the Department of the Tennessee, ordered Hurlbut to "abandon . . . Fort Pillow absolutely, removing all public property." Wanting to initiate a major strike into the Deep South, Sherman saw small outposts behind his lines as no longer useful and would write that "I am not going to bother myself about guerrillas . . . if they can't do our main arteries harm."[69] After Hurlbut relayed the order, black artillerymen from Memphis removed the fort's two mounted cannons, and Lieutenant Alden took all unemployed contrabands to the Island No. 10 camp. The post's closing caused stores to shut down at short notice. Harris and Company, which had somehow avoided the revocation of its license, could not secure transportation for some of its wares and had to sell them at a loss to Samuel Lanier, who stayed long enough to retail them locally. Most of the troops at the fort went downriver to serve in Mississippi. Once again a gunboat, *New Era,* became the only Federal presence at the site.[70]

When the fort had enough mounted men and skillful leadership from Captain Moore, its garrison had hindered but never ended Confederate recruiting, conscripting, guerrilla activity, and collecting of supplies. Without enough horsemen, the occupiers were ineffective, except for some inhibiting of smugglers. While the Federal army could afford to leave garrisons behind the main lines, it would never gain full pacification and dominance. While guerrillas preserved an environment into which Confederate forces could return, raiding cavalry would only pass through occasionally. The guerrillas did relatively little damage to the Union war effort, and Confederate conscription decreased their numbers. Veterans, such as the 52nd Indiana Infantry, the 2nd Illinois Cavalry, and Forrest's cavalry had great effectiveness in their operations, while beginners, such as the 32nd Iowa Infantry, the 178th New York Infantry, and recruiting partisan ranger units had little impact.

The Federal hard war policy intensified some secessionists' commitment through hardship, though it deprived them of foodstuffs, horses, and slaves' labor that would have benefitted the Confederacy. Unionists supported their own cause at great risk and received a little protection and some trading privileges in return. Runaway slaves gained much more in contraband camps, enlistment, employment, and tentative freedom. But, some of the Federals, who encouraged blacks and unionists to help the war effort, disparaged and distrusted both groups. In all Federally occupied areas, the war acquired greater ugliness as both sides broke past conventions of warfare and condemned only their opponent. The bloodiness, length, and frustrations of the Civil War had moved it away from traditional rules. Social conflict and individual suffering resulted. In the Fort Pillow area only the limited scale of operations and the rangers' desire to avoid combat kept the level of bloodshed and destruction low.

Chapter Five

The Last Garrison and the Massacre

MAJOR William F. Bradford led a unionist battalion, the mis-named 13th Tennessee Cavalry, to Fort Pillow on February 8, 1864. This intrepid thirty-six-year-old from a politically promi-nent family may have led a home guard force in Obion County, the state's northwest corner, before beginning to organize the cavalry unit in late 1863. While most of Bradford's men settled into the barracks emptied by the 32nd Iowa, Company B camped separately, probably in the huts of the 52nd Indiana, near the outer fort's two gates, where they performed picket duty.[1] As the Federal army often used black troops for garrison service, Lieutenant Alexander Hunter and a detachment from the 2nd U.S. Colored Light Artillery (U.S.C.L.A.) took up duties at the fort on February 21. The new unit, composed mostly of contrabands, brought two fieldpieces with it. Bradford's superiors ordered the post to follow the hard war policy: "You will subsist your command upon the country as far as possible, and take the stock necessary to keep it well mounted, giving vouchers to loyal men only." Although the new garrison functioned much like Colonel Wolfe's force, local secessionists probably found it much more objectionable, since they condemned the pro-Union residents of their region as renegades.[2]

In reopening Fort Pillow, General Hurlbut violated General Sherman's orders. No known contemporary document specifically says why he did this. Later Hurlbut stated that he reopened the fort because its location held strategic control over the river and would facilitate enlistment. Brad-ford's orders to continue recruiting, to improve the fort's defenses, and to suppress guerrillas fit with these explanations. General Ralph P. Buckland, whose West Tennessee District now included the fort, had also advised Hurlbut that "the people in that region are very anxious to have a small force." Perhaps most importantly, Hurlbut responded to pressure from the area's chief Treasury agent by promising to reopen trade at Fort Pillow, once he could garrison it. Sherman unintentionally had intensified interest in trading by ending his predecessors' restrictions.[3]

The new garrison made the fort a safe haven once again for entrepreneurs, contrabands, and unionists. The small town near the landing soon boasted stores, warehouses, residences, and a hotel. Charley Robinson of Minnesota opened a photograph shop aimed mostly at the market for soldiers' portraits. Edward B. Benton, another Northern businessman, bought 215 acres beside the fort and contracted contraband laborers from the Freedmen's Department, an army agency in Memphis. That office's rules for contracted contrabands required fixed wages ($10 per month for men and $7 for women), food, shelter, clothes, and medical care for them. The officials intended the program to serve as a transition from slavery to wage labor. Benton, no doubt hoping for great profits, had his workers plant cotton. As runaway slaves and unionist refugees arrived at the fort, Bradford opened a new contraband camp under a superintendent from his unit. It grew to contain about fifty women and children. Unionist refugees probably lived there, too.[4]

The major primarily focused his energy on recruiting West Tennesseans. Some unionists enlisted to help protect or support their families, as the war had disrupted the safety and economy of interior areas. Confederate deserters, especially drafted unionists, often felt safer in the Federal army. Still, enlistees trickled in so slowly that Sergeant Wiley G. Poston wrote his wife to encourage more unionists to come from his neighborhood in Haywood County, the source of most new recruits. He assured her that the army provided well for him and "we all have a lively time," but that soldiers stayed too busy to become "wild." When Bradford finally filled one new company, he could not persuade officials to come promptly from Memphis to complete the mustering process.[5]

During Bradford's brief command at the fort several issues arose. Harris and Company once again faced charges for violating trade rules but escaped punishment due to extenuating circumstances. When General Buckland learned that recruiters for a black regiment had conscripted a unionist master's slaves, he ordered Bradford to see that this stopped. The major, himself, created controversy when, seeking to benefit from veterans' experience, he gave two lieutenancies to Northerners instead of to Tennesseans. Other outsiders would come to the fort to serve as post surgeon, hospital steward, provost marshal, and clerk. Friction within the unit, late pay, worries about families, and the attractions of other recruiting regiments caused a number of desertions.[6]

Bradford used *New Era* to send out at least three foot patrols searching for guerrillas. Except the one time when the gunboat ran aground and required hours of toil to get afloat, all went very smoothly. Each effort resulted in the capture of between one and four suspects. So, Sergeant Poston could brag that "I feel perfectly safe hear [sic]," but he spoke too soon.[7]

In mid-March, Forrest, now a major general, led his cavalry north from Mississippi in an effort to finish manning and equipping his command as well as to harass the enemy. General Sherman magnified the raider's modest goals into an effort to undermine the impending Atlanta campaign by diverting troops from it. He demanded that his district commanders handle the raid without reinforcements.[8]

Forrest skillfully assigned one of his two divisions to keep watch on Memphis, General Hurlbut's base, and led the other toward western Kentucky. A regiment detached to take the garrison at Union City, Tennessee, gained the post's surrender through bluffing Colonel Isaac R. Hawkins into thinking that he faced Forrest's whole force. By this point in the war, captured Federal weapons and provisions, like those obtained at Union City, played a significant role in supplying Confederates. Having surrendered twice to Forrest's troops, Hawkins had become a major contributor. Forrest's main force proceeded to Paducah, where Colonel Samuel G. Hicks commanded a fort garrisoned by both white and black troops.[9]

Forrest had never previously encountered the controversial black Federals. Before the war he had gained wealth as a slave trader, but beyond that fact he did not record his racial views. Like many Confederates, the general probably felt galled by the arming of runaways. Ignoring the Confederacy's policy of treating black Federals as rebellious or runaway slaves, he took the unusual but practical step of offering to accept the entire Paducah garrison as prisoners of war. He did threaten that, if he had to assault the fort, he would grant no quarter, a threat he had used twice before in 1862 to garner quick surrenders. Because Forrest liked to use clever psychological tactics, the seriousness of the threat is uncertain. When Hicks relied on his fort's strength and refused to capitulate, Forrest chose to back down. After capturing some supplies in town, Forrest headed south for Jackson, Tennessee.[10]

Meanwhile, Hurlbut, a general of very limited capabilities, took his time in responding to Forrest's raid. He eventually sent some forces searching for Forrest, who drove them back. On March 28, Hurlbut strengthened Fort Pillow with two additional cannons and the 1st Battalion from the 6th United States Colored Heavy Artillery (U.S.C.H.A.) under Major Lionel F.

Booth, whom one superior had praised as "steady, intelligent, and worthy." Having enlisted in the regular army in 1858 and then in a Missouri regiment early in the war, the dark-haired and bearded major had accumulated some military experience by 1864. While most successful applicants for officer's positions in new African American regiments gained a higher rank, Booth went from sergeant to major in less than one year.[11]

Despite being only in his mid-twenties, Booth had a slightly older commission than Bradford and so took command of the fort. Hurlbut thought Forrest more likely to attack elsewhere but still directed Booth to strengthen the fortification and to limit civilian access. The general thought the fort had more than enough men to hold off attackers until help could arrive. Insisting that "the post must be held," Hurlbut shipped two more field cannons there, for a total of six.[12]

The 6th U.S.C.H.A. camped beside the 2nd U.S.C.L.A. inside the small earthwork where the arrested Missouri artillerymen had lived in 1863; there they pitched tents over board floors. The black troops had been recruited in Memphis and LaGrange, Tennessee, plus Corinth, Mississippi. Some had enlisted under pressure from Federal patrols. Private Joseph Key's son later remembered that "All of us children stood around and hollered and cried. I don't know whether they were compelled to go or not, but . . . all the able-bodied Negroes on the place did go." Other recruits felt a strong desire to use arms against the pro-slavery Confederacy. A popular journal represented Daniel Tyler as saying, "I had dreamed for two long years of escape from my bondage . . . in one second of time I leaped out of slavery into freedom" through enlistment.[13]

Blacks joining the Federal army found themselves treated as second-class soldiers. The government gave them lower pay than whites, no enlistment bounty, no officer commissions, and in West Tennessee units, such as the two at Fort Pillow, only some of the sergeant positions. While whites had a double log cabin in the central ravine for a hospital, sick blacks received separate medical care in tents behind the cabin. African American regiments, like at the fort, often received assignments away from the main fronts.[14]

Ultimately, the garrison contained about six hundred men due to late arrivals and new recruits. Because all three units remained in the formative stage, only a few officers had experienced combat. Bradford's Battalion probably obtained training before arriving. The 6th U.S.C.H.A. had received training in drilling as well as the use of both artillery and rifles, but the 2nd U.S.C.L.A.'s men lacked prior instruction. The black troops practiced both infantry and artillery drill at the fort.[15]

Booth energetically prepared for the possibility of an assault during the two weeks of his command. All available able-bodied soldiers worked under his direction to rebuild the small fortification around the black troops' camp from a crescent into a larger inverted "w" shape. While the revised earthwork held the entire garrison, he made a major error in letting the barracks cabins remain very close on the south side. Deep ravines outside the work and high ground beyond that further weakened the position. In final form, the new inner fort had a high earthen wall planked on the inside and cut with six narrow openings for the artillery. A ditch about six feet deep and twelve feet wide lay in front of the fort. The troops also dug rifle pits southeast of the fort and close to a ravine.[16] Major Booth kept sailors busy hauling lumber for the inner fort and collecting information along the river. He worked out plans for cooperation with Acting Master James Marshall of the *New Era* in case of a battle. The small wooden sternwheel steamer could serve as a mobile battery, since it carried three cannons on each side.[17] Booth also may have reinstated an enrolled militia unit for civilians.

A Federal captain who was captured at Union City and then escaped to Fort Pillow advised the major that he had heard Confederates discuss an attack on the fort but that he had seen no signs of preparation. Subsequently, the *New Era*'s sailors captured a few of Forrest's men near Randolph, and Bradford's cavalrymen caught several more in a skirmish during a reconnaissance to Brownsville. Still, because "everything seems to be very quiet within a radius of from thirty to forty miles around," the major drew the wrong conclusion: "I do not think any apprehensions need be felt, or fears entertained in reference to this place being attacked or even threatened, I think it is perfectly safe." Satisfied that nothing unusual would happen at the fort, Bradford requested permission for several of his men to go on a recruiting trip to Columbus, Kentucky.[18]

On April 4, Forrest reported to his superior, Lieutenant General Leonidas Polk, now commander of the Department of Alabama, Mississippi, and East Louisiana, an intention to attack the forces at Fort Pillow because "they have horses and supplies which we need." Booth saw little Confederate activity because Forrest briefly delayed the attack so that he could build several bridges on his route and allow some of his West Tennessee troops to visit nearby homes. Shortly after the assault, Forrest would note an additional motivation: a desire to punish West Tennessee unionist regiments in general for "oppression, murder, and plunder." Yet, he had made just one specific complaint about Bradford's command, back in March, and that only involved a civilian's confinement without a charge. Like Federal troops there earlier, the battalion arrested suspected guerrillas and did at least a little looting. It unquestionably appropriated horses and food from civilians, as both armies commonly did by this time. These typical elements of Federal occupation caused real suffering, yet in less than three months Bradford's Battalion had little time to build much of a distinct reputation. However, it may have received blame by association for the misdeeds of Colonel Fielding Hurst's infamous unionist regiment, the only unit that Forrest criticized in detail at the time.[19]

Before the operation against Fort Pillow, Brigadier General James R. Chalmers regained a division command lost in a petty squabble initiated by Forrest over possession of a large tent. Although a careful planner, Forrest also had a very fiery temper, probably originating in his impoverished and overburdened youth.[20] Perhaps as a conciliatory gesture, Forrest assigned Chalmers to lead Walton's Battery and the two brigades closest to Jackson in opening an attack on the fort. Colonel "Black" Bob McCulloch's Brigade (Chalmers's Division) contained the 2nd Missouri Cavalry, Willis's Texas Cavalry Battalion, the 5th Mississippi Cavalry, Duff's 8th Mississippi Cavalry, McDonald's Tennessee Cavalry Battalion, and the 18th Mississippi Cavalry Battalion. Colonel Tyree H. Bell's Brigade (Brigadier General Abraham Buford's Division) consisted of Barteau's 2nd Tennessee Cavalry, Wilson's 16th Tennessee Cavalry, and Russell's 15th Tennessee Cavalry. To divert Hurlbut's attention, Forrest sent out his other two brigades, one toward Paducah and the other above Memphis.[21]

Late on April 10, Bell's Brigade started riding from Eaton toward the fort. At dawn the men stopped for one hour on the banks of the South Forked Deer River, and then crossed one of the newly built bridges. They took another one-hour break at 10:00 A.M. and a three-hour rest at 3:00 P.M. Early on April 11 Chalmers and McCulloch's Brigade departed from Poplar Corner, near Jackson. Forrest and his escort, Wisdom's Alabama Cavalry Battalion, left Jackson later that morning. With McCulloch a little ahead of Bell, the column of about fifteen hundred troops, mostly veterans, kept riding all that dark, rainy night. Captain Elisha T. Hollis of Bell's Brigade called it an "awful march," since besides the bad weather it was his unit's second night without much sleep. Forrest's escort, traveling behind the others, rested for part of the night so it would be fresh in the morning.[22] The Confederates' rapid movement would deny any warning to the Federals.

At a cool and cloudy dawn on Tuesday, April 12, 1864, the Federals started the usual procedures of reveille, dressing, and roll call. Outside the fort, McCulloch's Brigade halted and dismounted. Following standard cavalry practice, every fourth man held horses while the rest prepared for battle. A civilian showed the Confederates a spot at which a party could cross the outer embankment between picket posts without detection. A small group did so and surprised the guards at the Fulton Road gate. After a brief skirmish, one or two of those Federals escaped. The gunfire caused pickets at other posts and the rest of Bradford's Company B to flee toward the river.[23]

Upon sending out skirmishers, McCulloch directed his troops both northwest along the road toward the river and north over the middle hill. The first column discovered the contraband camp and set it afire. At least some of the residents fled toward the landing. At the nearby post hospital, the mobile ones among the sick black soldiers moved to tents in Booth's inner fortification for safety. Outside Fort Pillow, a contraband laborer awakened Edward Benton at his farm to warn him of the attack. Benton feared for his life, since he had hired runaway slaves, and fled to the inner fortification. A few of his hired contrabands followed.[24]

Alerted by the pickets, Major Booth sent out a skirmish line, which anchored itself at the old Confederate breastwork on the fort's middle hill, to meet McCulloch's second column. He also had Captain Theodorick Bradford, the unionist major's brother, signal the *New Era* to shell the Confederates in the central ravine. At the inner fortification, Booth ordered two unfinished artillery stations prepared for action. The men quickly threw together a wooden platform for one and rolled the guns into place. About an hour into the battle, Bradford's adjutant noticed that no one had raised the fort's flags, and he did so to the cheers of the troops. Meanwhile, to the right of McCulloch's force part of Bell's brigade entered the Ripley Road gate, another part came up from Cold Creek, and Colonel Clark Barteau's regiment trudged through the creek bottoms toward the north side of the inner fort.[25]

By 8:00 A.M. the Federal skirmishers had retreated to the rifle pits and to the inner fort, located, as Forrest later noted, "on the bluff . . . of the Mississippi River at the mouth of Coal [Cold] Creek." Black crews opened artillery fire, but numerous defective shell fuses somewhat reduced their effectiveness. Private Samuel Green's group was "'working for all our worth,' as it was life or death." The rest of the garrison stood on a low bench behind the fort's wall to fire single-shot carbines while exposing only their heads and shoulders. The Confederate combatants outnumbered the Federals roughly two to one.[26]

Booth had armed at least eight civilians, including photographer Charley Robinson and planter Edward Benton. If the major had reinstated the enrolled militia, some civilians either had exemptions or withheld their cooperation, as several stayed just to watch the battle or their stores. A large group of noncombatants at the landing boarded a coal barge, which *New Era* towed up alongside Flour Island. Barteau's sharpshooters, now at the mouth of Cold Creek, started firing at these vessels. The civilians took shelter in an abandoned log cabin, while some sailors engaged in small arms fire with the snipers. Directed by signals from Captain Bradford, *New Era* focused its shelling on the Cold Creek area north of the fort.[27]

A little before 9:00 A.M., Dr. Charles Fitch, the post surgeon, became the first wounded Federal, but a minor flesh wound on the leg did not stop him from setting up a field hospital marked off with red flags on the riverbank. More wounded Federals soon came in from an unsuccessful sortie to burn the barracks just south of the inner fort. Around that time, Confederates killed Major Booth as he walked along the lines encouraging his men. Major Bradford then resumed command of the fort. Meanwhile, the southbound steamer *Liberty* picked up from Flour Island all civilians who wished to leave and headed for Memphis to report the attack.[28]

Chalmers's forces had coalesced into a long crescent investing the inner fort by the time Forrest arrived at 10:00. While Forrest conducted a reconnaissance over the area, Federals shot two horses out from under him, and the falls caused him some bad bruises. The general judged the military situation as relatively simple. It only required that he keep the enemy surrounded and pressured by his superior numbers while using available cover. Forrest stationed sharpshooters on high ground and then ordered a forward movement. Moving from the central ravine and Cold Creek bottoms, some troops proceeded out of sight up the ravines near the fort. The Federal cannons could not be lowered enough to hit these Confederates, had they been noticed.[29]

Around noon, McCulloch's men made major gains by occupying the barracks and thereby forcing black troops in the rifle pits to withdraw into the fort. Soon the Confederates sheltered in the barracks close to the fort picked off most of the artillery crews at the two southernmost gun ports.

Forrest sent Major Charles Anderson of his staff with one or two pieces of field artillery to the first hill south of the central ravine to drive *New Era* upriver. By this time the Confederates had probably ensured themselves a victory. They had gained an excellent position for rendering the vulnerable defenses less effective and for launching an assault.[30]

In the early afternoon Confederate fire slackened as ammunition ran low. A long delay ensued before new supplies came forward from wagons parked at the fort's outer earthworks. Forrest may have completed the Federals' entrapment by positioning detachments near the riverbank above and below the fort during this delay. However, the smoke of three steamboats coming upriver elated the Federals. Bradford gloated that reinforcements would soon land.[31]

At about 2:00 P.M. Forrest sent a flag of truce toward the fort's south side with a demand for surrender. Acknowledging that "the conduct of the officers and men garrisoning Fort Pillow has been such as to entitle them to being treated as prisoners of war," he included by implication the black troops, as he had done at Paducah. In a noticeable shift from the explicit threat of no quarter used at Paducah, he added: "Should my demand be refused, I cannot be responsible for the fate of your command." This represented either just another attempt to intimidate a post commander into surrender or a new concern about controlling his men. Bradford responded in a note signed with Booth's name to cover up the commander's death and to hide his own presence as a unionist leader. He asked for an hour to consult with his officers and *New Era*'s commander. In response, Forrest granted only twenty minutes, since he suspected that his enemy wanted the time to get reinforcements from the approaching steamboats.[32]

Prior to the truce, Surgeon Fitch counted fewer than thirty dead and wounded Federals. Feeling secure in the fort, the garrison entered energetically into the bantering which often occurred between the two sides during a Civil War truce. A Confederate newspaper correspondent considered the Federals "defiant and insolent . . . [as] they ridiculed the idea of taking the fort, and intimated that the last man would die before surrendering." Sergeant Achilles V. Clark reported them as "threatening that if we charged their breast works to show no quarter." Taunting by blacks and Southern white unionists particularly antagonized the Confederates, who had time to ruminate about it during the truce.[33]

The approaching steamboats caused Forrest, if he had not already done so, to send a detachment commanded by Major Anderson to the riverbank below the fort. When the ships, merely commercial steamers, neared the fort, those Confederates fired a warning volley to prevent a landing. Two steamboats continued upriver; the third turned back. Brigadier General George F. Shepley, a passenger on *Olive Branch,* the largest one, had ordered its captain to run past the fort and to make contact with *New Era,* which had gone upstream near Flour Island to clean its artillery during the truce. *Olive Branch* carried some artillerists and their cannons. Since the cannons could not be elevated enough from the level of the island to hit the Confederates in front of the fort and since the men lacked small arms, Shepley believed that they could provide little help. Actually, if not rendered ineffective by the terrain or enemy snipers, they might have had a significant impact against the Confederates on the riverbank. In any case, the *New Era*'s commander urged that they proceed immediately to Cairo with his request for more ammunition, as he had little left. Their departure caused great disappointment in the fort.[34]

One last important development took place during the truce. As several Federals later alleged, some enemy soldiers and officers slipped into the fort's trench, for Captain John W. Carroll of the 16th Tennessee Cavalry would reveal in his autobiography that "while the flag of truce was up Captain James Stinnett and I with some picked men crawled up close under the guns to be ready in case they refused to surrender, to prevent them from discharging their cannon into our ranks." Whether or not additional Confederates moved into ravines close to the fort during the truce, as some Federals later claimed, is impossible to resolve.[35]

Within the fort boldness and inexperience prevailed, despite the deteriorated situation at the southern gun ports. Unanimously supported by his commissioned officers, Bradford decided not to surrender. He knew of the successful defense of Paducah by Colonel Hicks, as well as of the disgraceful capitulation at Union City by Colonel Hawkins, a recruiting rival. Bradford suspected that the Confederates were trying a ruse similar to the one at Union City. After the battle he told Dr. Fitch that he refused to surrender because "his name was not Hawkins." At the truce parlay, because the Federals expressed doubt about Forrest's presence, the general rode over and identified himself. The Federals nevertheless delivered a note refusing to surrender. By dragging out discussions, Bradford probably made the truce last longer than Forrest wished.[36]

Forrest, though, had the fortification completely surrounded on land. Posting himself at the breastwork on the middle hill, which had a good view of the field, he sent staff officers to the two brigade commanders to urge that each state's troops seek the honor of entering the fort first. At about 3:15 P.M. a bugler sounded the charge. Firing reopened between the defenders and the sharpshooters outside, as the attackers, surprisingly closer than many Federals expected, rushed out of the ravines toward the fort. Captain Carroll's group in the trench quickly dispatched one gun's crew. The Federals, meanwhile, could not shoot rifles at the enemy pouring into the ditch without mounting the fort's high wall and completely exposing themselves to the sharpshooters. As Confederates helped one another climb atop the embankment, Federals backed away and, according to Northerner Charley Robinson, "stood their ground until the top of the breastworks was just crowded by the rebels."[37]

The Federal line broke under the firepower of the enemy's superior numbers. A rout ensued, and Robinson observed that "our men ran or rather tumbled down . . . [the steep bluff] & tried to get behind logs, trees, stumps, etc. to shield them from the rebel bullets." Lieutenant Daniel Van Horn suffered an inguinal hernia from a long downhill jump. Since Confederates held the riverbank to the north and south, the Federals soon found themselves trapped. Robinson added that "Our boys when they saw that they were overpowered threw down their arms and held up their handkerchiefs and some their hands in token of surrender."[38] At this point discipline broke down in portions of the Confederate force.

During the preceding months some of Forrest's newer men had shown a lack of discipline. Just before the West Tennessee campaign began, a group of nineteen recruits started home without permission. Forrest caught them, condemned them to execution before his assembled forces, but granted reprieves at the very last minute. Officers also could be contrary, like the colonel who led and died in an unauthorized charge at Paducah because he wanted to put up more of a fight in his hometown than Forrest did. Even if the circumstances seem to make these incidents unusual, the Confederates' encounter with black troops at Fort Pillow was a more extraordinary event. Although Bell's men may have seen and sniped at uniformed blacks at Paducah, none of the Confederates at Fort Pillow had ever fought them before this in close combat.[39]

A Confederate newspaper correspondent wrote afterward that "the sight of negro soldiers stirred the bosoms of our soldiers with courageous madness." Such anger probably involved a common Southern belief that the Federals' enlistment of slaves to fight against whites constituted an atrocity.

Most of the Confederate comments, reported later by Federals, expressed racial hostility. One angry Confederate told a black soldier, "God damn you, you are fighting against your master," and another shouted, "You'll fight with the niggers again will you?" as he fired at Charley Robinson. For blacks to join the Federal side with whites, especially with Southern unionists and deserters from the Confederate army, was inflammatory. Additionally, many of Forrest's men came from West Tennessee or North Mississippi, the same homelands as many garrison members, and their families may have suffered from the Federal emancipation and hard war policies, in some cases enforced from Fort Pillow during the previous one and a half years.[40]

With weakened self-control after going without rest or food for at least twenty hours and "exasperated by the Yankees' threats," as Sergeant Clark put it, many Confederate officers and enlisted men refused to accept prisoners. Clark vividly described the scene: "The slaughter was awful. Words cannot describe the scene. The poor deluded negroes would run up to our men[,] fall upon their knees and with uplifted hands scream for mercy but they were ordered to their feet and then shot down. The whitte [sic] men fared but little better. Their fort turned out to be a great slaughter pen. Blood, human blood stood about in pools and brains could have been gathered up in any quantity."[41]

Since Forrest's veterans commonly carried two six-shot revolvers besides their rifles, they could quickly dispose of many enemies at close range. The officers' sabers also facilitated rapid killing. One Confederate and several Federals later mentioned the use of bayonets, which if present probably belonged to a few of Forrest's newest men, since veteran cavalry preferred lightweight carbines, which usually did not hold bayonets. When out of ammunition, assailants obtained more from prisoners or used rifle butts as clubs.[42]

Several Confederate officers, including Clark, tried to stop the massacre. Clark believed that his effort failed because "Gen. Forrest ordered them shot down like dogs," but, as a young man who had enlisted just a few months earlier, he may have believed certain Confederates who, according to several Federal survivors, ran about shouting that Forrest had ordered a massacre. Wrathful men may have used the general's name without authorization. One early account and many later documents by Confederates hint that they used the lack of a formal post surrender to rationalize the massacre, as if individual attempts to surrender did not count.[43]

A cruel spirit animated many of the Confederates. Charley Robinson recounted afterward that one of Forrest's men shot a surrendering Federal at point blank range "right in the head scattering the blood & brains in my face." Some Confederates robbed victims before executing them. Several ordered surrendering Federals to fall into a line and then shot a volley, which killed many in it. Other prisoners had to walk up the bluff through a gauntlet of firing riflemen. Some officers encouraged the slaughter or even ordered reluctant men to participate. Dr. Fitch saw most of the wounded in the field hospital "chopped to pieces with Sabres" by some particularly vicious individuals. Others killed sick soldiers in the post hospital and in tents at the inner fort. One ill black soldier received three severe saber cuts on his head, plus one on his hand as he tried to protect himself.[44]

Federals generally persisted in trying to surrender, but some, seeing a massacre underway, resumed fighting or flight, and thus added to the confusion. A few managed to run through Confederate lines or to find a hiding place, not always secure. Some Federals tried to save themselves by pushing a coal barge off the bank, but their enemy killed all who tried to get in it. According to a Confederate newspaper correspondent, a number "so great, that they resembled a drove of hogs" tried to swim the Mississippi only to be picked off by veteran marksmen. After observing these developments, some Federals just lay down and acted dead.[45]

Major Bradford, "crying at the top of his voice that he surrendered," held up both hands while backing across the riverbank amid whizzing bullets until he found himself in the water. After swimming a distance out, he gave it up and returned. When some soldiers again shot at the major, he ran up the bluff into the fort before locating an officer who accepted his surrender.[46]

Surgeon Fitch survived by walking closely beside a Confederate lieutenant who was leading a horse up the bluff. Upon Fitch's request, that officer pointed out General Forrest, who had ridden into the fort to direct the movement of a Federal cannon to the bluff's edge to fire at the *New Era.* When Fitch demanded the protection due a prisoner, Forrest angrily accused him of being either a black regiment's doctor or a Southern unionist. After Fitch denied both, Forrest still replied, "I have a great mind to have you killed for being down here." Forrest's comments may have indicated support for a massacre or may have only amounted to irate talk, for he then ordered a soldier to guard Fitch. As the trooper took the doctor outside the southern end of the fort for safekeeping, other Federals rushed over for protection. Nearby Confederates shot down most of the blacks within the group. Even though more guards came on duty, several Confederates, who had consumed liquor from the town's stores, robbed and fired at prisoners. When General Chalmers saw this, he arrested one miscreant and ordered a still stronger guard to form a two-row square around the captives.[47]

Forrest meanwhile used the Federal cannon to drive off *New Era*. Then he ordered subordinates to stop the fighting, and a soldier cut down the fort's flag to signal the battle's end. Clearly by that point no Federal still fought back. Forrest helped to enforce his order, for a captured captain saw the general shoot a Confederate who continued to kill. The firing, according to Forrest's first battle report, lasted thirty minutes after the charge began. Years later Fitch noted that "What was done was done very quickly" and, in his opinion, without Forrest's knowledge.[48]

No evidence provides unquestionable proof of Forrest's guilt or innocence regarding the massacre. Sergeant Clark's account indicates that the general had not ordered a massacre when he initiated the final charge yet could have done so after the Federals' rout, although no one ever claimed to have heard him issue a massacre order. He definitely had not taken special precautions to prevent a massacre, but he had never been in this situation previously. Forrest may not have known about the spontaneous killing of twenty-five to fifty wounded black Federals after a Confederate victory at Olustee, Florida, though an Atlanta newspaper ran a candid report of the incident in early March. Certainly, one pattern in Forrest's life was the impulsive act of anger followed later by a humane resolution of the problem. How promptly he stopped the fighting we do not know. Benjamin Robinson, a black sergeant, later claimed to have seen someone Confederates called Forrest observing but not halting the killing. However, another Federal reported an enemy officer as shouting that the general wanted Federals taken as prisoners, and several black soldiers contended, like Samuel Green, that "if it had not been for General Forrest coming up and ordering the Confederates to stop killing the prisoners, there would not one of us been alive today."[49] The general's offer to accept African Americans as military prisoners and his provision of protection to one group of captives support the possibility of his innocence.

When the shooting stopped, Forrest asked Major Anderson and Captain John T. Young, a prisoner, to go to *New Era* to arrange for it to receive the wounded Federals, but Young could neither find a skiff nor get a response from waving a white flag. Probably not trusting the victors, the *New Era*'s commander picked up the civilians remaining on Flour Island and headed upstream. Forrest detailed several Confederates to organize some prisoners for gathering up the wounded Federals and burying the killed. The latter process forced a few Federals to quit acting dead. A Confederate surgeon commented that the field of dead and wounded represented "decidedly the most horrible sight that I have ever witnessed. . . . They sure heaped upon each other." By nightfall the prisoners had managed to bury officers in individual graves and some enlisted men in the ditch on the fort's south side.[50]

Crews placed those with major wounds in four or five barracks cabins, but white unionists in one cabin drove blacks outside. Rather than letting Fitch minister to the wounded, Forrest ordered him held as a prisoner because Federals had confined a Confederate surgeon left with wounded Confederates at Paducah. Some Union soldiers later claimed that sporadic killing of the wounded continued through the evening and night by men beyond their officers' control. The riotous atmosphere of the massacre makes this seem possible. One writer has suggested that guerrillas might have done such killing, but no other source mentions guerrillas in the area before, during, or after the battle.[51]

By 4:00 P.M. the fort echoed with the sounds of celebration and looting. One Confederate, observed by Dr. Fitch, "had taken off his [Booth's] uniform, and was parading around with it on." Others filled empty bellies, as well as indulged in liquor, found replacements for worn-out clothes, and looted merchandise from the warehouses. Confederates then burned the town buildings and nearby stables. At 10:00 P.M. Forrest moved his troops and all but severely wounded prisoners to several campsites a little east of the fort. Officers released most white civilians with passes but kept about forty black women and children for return to masters. Exhausted and bruised, Forrest turned matters over to Chalmers and rode off to spend the night in a farmhouse. Major Bradford, alarmed by hearing numerous West Tennessee Confederates call for his death, obtained permission to stay at Colonel "Black" Bob McCulloch's headquarters. Many a tired Confederate had a need for sound sleep that evening. Bradford took advantage of the situation to escape from McCulloch's camp during the night. After obtaining civilian clothing, he struck out for Memphis. Late in the night Corporal Jacob Wilson of the 6th U.S.C.H.A. crawled out of a hiding place in the river, helped three wounded blacks aboard a coal barge, and cut it loose only to get beached on an island several miles downstream.[52]

The victors had suffered casualties of only thirteen to twenty deaths and eighty-three to eighty-six wounded; no count exists of how many died from wounds. As their diary entries and letters written shortly afterward contained estimates of Federal deaths running from 65 to 86 percent, the Confederates clearly understood that a great bloodletting had occurred. In actuality, deaths from the battle and from the massacre, which cannot be tallied separately, ran between 47 and 48 percent (277–295) of the garrison (see Table 7). Sixty-one Federals survived their wounds. To have more than twice as many men killed than wounded was rare in Civil War battles and indicated the likelihood of something unusual. Despite the roughly equal numbers of black and white Federals, the death rates by race alone were 65 percent for blacks and 29–33 percent for whites (including thirteen officers of black troops). These figures demonstrate that a Confederate newspaper correspondent only slightly exaggerated when he stated that "the whites received quarter, but the negroes were shown no mercy."[53]

The battle of Fort Pillow lacked great significance in a purely military sense, though it did weaken Federal occupation in West Tennessee. Forrest easily took the fort, since he understood its weak strategic position and effectively used his superior numbers. Although he had done some recruiting and conscripting during the raid, his army largely consisted of veterans very efficient at fighting, while the garrison mostly contained men without combat experience. The Federals' flight and attempt to surrender by throwing down arms created the opportunity for a massacre. Equipped with revolvers, the victors had the means to conduct efficient mass killing, as some of the cavalry raiders reverted to the terrorism of the guerrillas. Anger about Federal military occupation and the long forced march without much food or rest—one of the hardships of soldier life—probably contributed to the breakdown of Confederate discipline. Racial hostility against blacks rejecting slavery, political enmity toward Southerners joining the Federal army, and a concomitant antagonism toward white Northerners officering those units are not surprising. Easily identified by race and uniform, the condemned did not seem to deserve the protection due enemies under the military practices of the time. That social message carried more impact than a military victory over a small outpost away from the major war zones in 1864.

Chapter Six

The Massacre's Aftermath

I N the morning twilight of April 13, the *Silver Cloud*, a "tinclad" gun-boat similar to the *New Era* but larger and plated with thin iron armor, traveled toward Fort Pillow. The ship and its interracial crew had left Memphis the previous evening in response to the first report of the attack. A transport loaded with reinforcements would have gone, too, except that news of the fort's fall arrived first. The slow warship benefitted from a gracious towing by the speedy passenger steamboat *Platte Valley*. As the ships approached Island No. 34, a blue-clad soldier signaled from a coal barge aground there. A small boat went from the *Platte Valley* to pick up Corporal Jacob Wilson of the 6th U.S.C.H.A. and three wounded comrades. The four soldiers gave the first account of the nightmarish massacre to an outside audience.[1] A major controversy, focusing on racial conflict and the rules of warfare, would soon develop over the incident.

That morning most of Forrest's men began preparations for a march. General James Chalmers sent a detachment back to the fort to collect small arms, to dispose of remaining Union supplies, and to burn buildings. A number of Federal survivors later alleged that some of these soldiers killed more of the wounded that morning.[2] The attitudes of the massacre may have reawakened, though no other evidence confirms this.

While the detachment worked at the fort, the *Silver Cloud* drew close and disconnected from the *Platte Valley* to steam ahead. With dawn's illumination slipping over the bluff, sailors and passengers observed, according to a St. Louis newspaper correspondent, "numerous dead bodies strewed along the river and on the sides of the bluff." Seeing enemies scurrying around the fort, the gunboat's captain started shelling. The Confederates then hastily set buildings and tents on fire as they tried to finish their assignment. The flames burned some Federals who may or may not have already been dead. Other Federals concealed in the terrain silently signaled the gunboat to land and then rushed out as it approached the shore. Confederates opened fire but killed only one. *Silver Cloud* continued shelling as the men clambered aboard and it returned to midstream.[3]

The sound of the cannon fire traveled miles away to General Nathan B. Forrest, who, preparing to depart, dispatched Major Charles W. Anderson, a few troopers, and the prisoner Captain John T. Young to try again to arrange a truce for the delivery of disabled Federals. Around 8:00 A.M. Anderson succeeded in instituting a truce to run until 5:00 P.M., not only for the sailors to gather up the sick and wounded but also to bury the dead. He ordered the other Confederates out of the fort. His small group efficiently helped to bring survivors to the landing and to write paroles. The *Platte Valley* drew up to the landing, and its captain volunteered to transport the wounded. Soon the gunboat *New Era* and passenger steamer *Lady Pike* came downstream. The civilian refugees on the *New Era* had already transferred to the *Lady Pike,* which stayed only forty-five minutes before heading south. A work crew from *New Era* participated in burying the dead. General Chalmers and his staff appeared with a group of wounded captives, who had received some care from doctors in the Confederate camps. About fifty-five soldiers, two contraband laborers, and a civilian clerk boarded *Platte Valley.* The group included Dr. Charles Fitch, whom Chalmers had paroled at the request of Confederate surgeons. Fitch, another surgeon from *Silver Cloud,* and several passengers on *Platte Valley* busied themselves in providing medical care.[4]

Reporters, Federals, and others who went ashore saw many bodies repeatedly wounded at close range and a few charred ones in the burnt structures. This, plus the survivors' accounts, prompted them to question the Confederates. Federal accounts recorded two responses: most asserted that so many Federals died because they refused to surrender, but some, including General Chalmers, supposedly admitted the occurrence of a massacre because Federal enlistment of blacks had infuriated the enlisted men. Chalmers stressed that, while Confederate law would allow the execution of rebelling slaves, he and Forrest had neither approved nor ordered a massacre.[5] While those who reported these discussions obviously could have distorted their enemies' statements, significantly, subsequent Confederate documents would contain the same two conflicting versions of the battle's aftermath.

Several indiscreet Federal officers traveling on *Platte Valley* disgusted some passengers by treating Major Anderson to a drink and inviting General Chalmers to lunch. When the steamboat's departure bell interrupted the meal, an unperturbed Chalmers hastily debarked while joking that "he had learned to run as well as to fight." *Platte Valley* then headed for the army hospital at Mound City, Illinois.[6]

Activity continued during the rest of the afternoon. The large hospital ship *Red Rover,* en route to Memphis, landed and took on thirteen wounded men, who arrived late from another Confederate camp, as well as some civilian refugees. Fearing trouble from Confederates downstream, the *Red Rover*'s crew loaded the ship's single cannon but did not need to use it. One soldier on *Red Rover* and eight on *Platte Valley* would die from wounds while traveling. Back at the fort, sailors surreptitiously violated the truce by moving a little ammunition from the *Silver Cloud* to the depleted *New Era.* The sailors' task of burying the dead near where they fell was left unfinished at the truce's end. While the *Silver Cloud* returned to Memphis, the *New Era* anchored at Island No. 34 after picking up more refugees and wounded soldiers from hiding places along the way. Anderson's party finished burning buildings and tents before it left.[7]

Chalmers and most of his troops had already marched away with captured horses, supplies, artillery, Federals, and contrabands. Believing "it was not healthy for Niggers to complain," Samuel Green and some other wounded black soldiers kept silent about their injuries and marched. On the road that day Chalmers received an order to redirect his force to Mississippi.[8]

Also on April 13, the 7th Tennessee Cavalry, which Forrest had conscripting men south of the fort, caught and identified Major William Bradford. Colonel W. L. Duckworth forwarded him with a group of conscripts to Forrest, but on the road between Brownsville and Jackson, guards took Bradford into a woods and shot him. They reported that he died during an escape attempt. One of the conscripts later fled into Federal lines and recounted the murder. When Forrest subsequently received an official complaint, he agreed to investigate, but nothing happened, either because the evidentiary trail had grown too cold or because Federals had not pursued murder charges that Forrest filed against Union colonel Fielding Hurst's troops. After the war, Duckworth would admit to learning that several of his men had murdered the major.[9]

At Fort Pillow on April 14, the supply ship *Volunteer* delivered the ammunition that *New Era* had requested two days earlier, and the gunboats *Hastings* and *Moose* arrived as reinforcements. Besides picking up more contrabands, white refugees, and wounded soldiers, the warships shelled some Confederates, probably from the 7th Tennessee Cavalry, who had set an empty coal barge and several woodpiles afire. The next day the sailors hastily buried the remaining dead. *Moose* then headed to Mound City with additional wounded (nine soldiers and one contraband woman), while *Volunteer,* accompanied by *Hastings,* left for Columbus with the civilian refugees. River traffic, which commanders at Cairo and Memphis had halted since the night of April 12, soon resumed.[10]

On April 23, 1864, a detachment of survivors from the 6th U.S.C.H.A. returned to the fort to rebury the dead in coffins. Amid this effort, Lizzie Booth arrived to have her husband's supposed remains–there was some uncertainty about the location of his grave–exhumed for interment in the North. The Federal army abandoned Fort Pillow after the massacre. *New Era* remained stationed near the fort until late June; thereafter, it and other gunboats cruised by the site periodically as they patrolled long stretches of the Mississippi.[11]

The *Memphis Bulletin* broke the Fort Pillow story on April 14, but most Northerners first learned about it the next day, when all newspapers belonging to the Associated Press ran a brief telegraphic dispatch that reported a massacre after the fort's surrender as well as allegations about a truce violation, the burning of wounded soldiers, and the killing of civilians. On April 16 a second Associated Press dispatch added the charge that Confederates buried some wounded men alive. Since the dispatches came from Cairo, the information probably originated with sources aboard the *Platte Valley.* For a few days some papers ran wildly incorrect stories about the garrison surrendering, all blacks being killed, and other matters, but those tales then disappeared from subsequent reports.[12]

During the following weeks, six newspapers ran letters from individuals who had visited the fort on the day after the incident and talked to paroled Federals. The correspondents mentioned four sources by name: Private Daniel W. Harrison (Bradford's 13th Tennessee Cavalry Battalion), Corporal Jacob Wilson (6th U.S.C.H.A.), Captain John T. Young (post provost marshal on detached duty from the 24th Missouri Infantry), and Dr. Charles Fitch (post surgeon), all of whom would make similar statements later. Significantly, survivors could not have created a common story, since some had stayed hidden by themselves after the incident and others were dispersed in several groups as prisoners. Only limited collusion could have occurred among the authors of the letters because they traveled on three different ships and at least three were not professional journalists. All collected similar details, except for the one writer on the *Lady Pike;* his major misunderstandings probably resulted from the brevity of the steamer's stop at the fort.[13]

The fullest account, printed in the *St. Louis Missouri Democrat*, concluded that the enemy particularly sought to kill black troops and that General Hurlbut showed total "imbecility" in dealing with Forrest. The reporter demanded revenge in the form of no quarter for Forrest's cavalry and added: "Especially let every colored soldier when going into battle remember that with him it is victory or death, and when called upon to surrender, let him 'Remember Fort Pillow.'"[14]

Many Republican editors, especially radical ones, quickly reacted to early accounts of the incident with shock and outrage. A *Cincinnati Gazette* editorial called it "one of the most horrible that has disgraced the history of modern warfare." Like many other radical papers, the *Springfield Illinois State Journal* drew upon antislavery thought when it professed that "Such are the atrocities which men have been educated by slavery to commit." The *New York Tribune* added that "the Rebel leaders meant to impress upon this struggle every possible feature of cruelty." Several radical Republican papers charged that both the Federal army's unequal treatment of black troops and Lincoln's lenient reconstruction policy encouraged the massacre by demonstrating a lack of respect for blacks. Besides policy changes, they demanded retaliation through punishment or execution of captured Confederates.[15]

Other Republican papers criticized the massacre and the proposal of violent revenge. The moderate *Cincinnati Commercial* suggested placing some enemy prisoners on hard labor instead and warned against uncivilized retribution. The conservative *Washington National Intelligencer* urged great caution, especially so that no retaliation take place against the innocent. The *Boston Journal* advised that "Strict vengeance is out of place, but an increased determination to suppress these monsters of cruelty and to annihilate the cause which breeds them, ought to fire the heart of . . . every man amongst us."[16]

On the other side of the partisan divide, the *Portland [Maine] Advertiser* proclaimed that "Dressing a monkey in the uniform of the government . . . cannot convert the monkey into a real soldier and attach to him the rights and immunities of a prisoner of war." While that paper viewed blacks as too savage and uncivilized for the military, the *Chicago Times*, a major mouthpiece of Peace Democrats, emphasized the claim of several surviving members of Bradford's Battalion that cowardly black troops caused the defeat by breaking and running during the last Confederate assault. The newspaper charged the Republican administration with recruiting a race that could neither fight well nor receive respect from the enemy. The *New York World* simply urged fellow editors to withhold comment until more fully informed, since "The country has so often been deceived by reports touching the conduct of rebels to black soldiers, that it has lost implicit faith in all such stories." Some editors from both parties agreed in blaming Federal military leaders for a blundering response to Forrest's raid.[17]

Abolitionist and African American newspapers understandably blamed the massacre on the racism fostered by Southern slavery. Gerrit Smith, a longtime abolitionist leader, took very high ground in stating that "The guilt of this crime is upon all her [the United States'] people who have contributed to that public sentiment which releases a white man from respecting the rights of a black man." The incident convinced a black clergyman, writing to the *Philadelphia Christian Recorder,* that "Although we may have to pour out rivers of blood, liberty is not attainable without it." He advocated a no-quarter policy toward Confederates, as did a black regiment's white officer whose "blood chills within my veins" in response to the massacre. Individuals writing the *Boston Liberator,* edited by pacifist William Lloyd Garrison, though, considered violent retaliation unchristian and uncivilized. A female reader noted that executions of Confederate war prisoners would only lower the Federals to their enemy's level. One abolitionist advocated making Confederate officers do manual labor; others demanded legal equality for blacks as the only appropriate response.[18]

The incident also inspired artistic efforts by several Northerners. Printmakers, none of whom had witnessed the event, focused on unarmed black victims and brutal Confederate killers. The unanimously sympathetic portrayal of blacks was unique, since denigrating racial images predominated in wartime prints. A few white officers appeared in the prints to imply that blacks were under white control. Following an established pattern, the artists emphasized the viciousness of the Confederates.[19]

Poets shared in condemning the enemy but downplayed the African Americans' role. A melodious and sentimental song by Charles and James E. Haynes, "The Massacre at Fort Pillow," completely ignored the issue of race while stressing the tragedy and need for renewed patriotism with lines like:

> O'erpowered by the rebels they threw down their arms,
>> With hands raised for mercy they cry,
> In vain they appealed for protection from harm,
>> The traitors had doomed them to die.

Like the song, the poem "Fort Pillow" by "Lizzie P." implicitly blamed Southern culture for the massacre, avoided mention of race, and demanded the defeat of an evil enemy. The poem contended:

> Ah! just as long as history owns a record,
>   This foulest shame upon the South shall rest.

Neither of these works advocated revenge. However, Private James T. Ayers, a recruiter of black troops, did so in an angry unpublished poem:

> And altho they for mercy Cry
> Mercy must not be given
> The murderers' death they all must dy,
> Grant it God of Heaven.[20]

Within the Federal army, the Fort Pillow incident quickly generated a number of official documents. The first report from a survivor, Lieutenant Daniel Van Horn of the 6th U.S.C.H.A., on April 14, stressed, "There never was a surrender of the fort." Both his report and an unfiled one by his regimental commander clearly wanted to make Booth's Battalion look good. On April 15, Acting Master James Marshall described seeing a massacre from the *New Era*. Additional reports soon followed from 6th U.S.C.H.A., 2nd U.S.C.L.A., and Bradford's Battalion officers who, though not present at the incident, interviewed their units' survivors. The commander of the *Silver Cloud* and an army officer traveling on the *Platte Valley* filed accounts of the carnage seen and the stories heard on April 13.[21]

It seems highly unlikely that early accounts of a massacre resulted from military pressure, given their rapid production, the number of survivors and interviewers, and corroboration from civilian combatants. The strongest single piece of Federal evidence is a private letter to relatives from Charley Robinson, a photographer who probably belonged either to a revived enrolled militia or to Bradford's Battalion as an unmustered recruit. After securing release as a civilian from the Confederates and hiding in the woods until April 17, he caught a steamer to Columbus, Kentucky. When writing home the next morning, he in all likelihood had not seen any journalist's account of the attack, because the Confederates had cut Columbus's telegraph wire and the Federals had halted steamer traffic. He never reported to military authorities again and did not appear in the battalion's records.

Robinson's letter significantly affirmed that some Confederates entered the fort's trench during the truce and that a gory massacre ensued when the troops threw down guns and tried to surrender. Civilians Edward Benton and Hardy Revelle made similar points in newspaper interviews.[22]

The responsibility for reacting to the massacre fell to General William T. Sherman, who disliked black enlistment. Having ordered Fort Pillow shut down and not having noticed it listed on his departmental returns (where it actually appeared at least once), he was furious with Hurlbut's disobedience and seeming deception, for if the fort had not reopened, a massacre could not have occurred. Sherman suspected this was "the first fruits of the system of trading posts designed to assist the loyal people of the interior." Grant, now a lieutenant general and general-in-chief, ordered Hurlbut removed. Sherman approved because of Hurlbut's "marked timidity" in responding to Forrest's raid.[23]

Hurlbut, offended by the loss of his command, blatantly denied ever receiving an order to close the fort and demanded a court of inquiry in hope of clearing his name. He also ordered an investigation into the rumor that the 6th U.S.C.H.A.'s commander, Lieutenant Colonel Thomas J. Jackson, had stated that Major Lionel Booth fruitlessly begged Hurlbut for reinforcements before the battle. Although five officers claimed to have heard Jackson make such allegations, the lieutenant colonel denied it and suggested the rumor originated with Booth's wife. Lizzie Booth had arrived in Memphis after visiting the wounded black soldiers at Mound City Hospital. They had told her in general terms that Booth had unsuccessfully sent for reinforcements. This had angered her, but she later calmed down when both Jackson and the Memphis post commander assured her that the request only came after the assault. The investigation of Jackson halted when Grant denied Hurlbut's appeal of his removal.[24]

Without any knowledge of the developing uproar, Chalmers and the two brigades at Fort Pillow marched back to Mississippi. On the way, Sergeant Achilles Clark wrote his sisters a letter that graphically and sadly described a massacre. One historian has questioned Clark's reliability because of supposed errors regarding the number of defenders, the time of the final charge, the location of the most killing, and Forrest's role. Clark did incorrectly give the Federal garrison's size as 790, but no Confederate at the time had an accurate knowledge of the garrison's size. Forrest himself and other members of his force overestimated their opponents' numbers as between 650 and 800, apparently because of something misleading in the captured post records. Clark's correct statement that "At 2 P.M. Gen. Forrest demanded a surrender and gave twenty minutes to consider" presumably led to the accusation of wrongly placing the final assault at 2:20, but the Sergeant actually mentioned no specific time for the Confederate charge. Similarly, while Clark focused on the scene at the riverbank, he did not claim that most of the killing took place there. While the early evidence is not clear on the location of most deaths, the quick rout of the Federals actually makes the riverbank a strong possibility. Clark blamed Forrest for ordering a massacre but did not specifically claim to have witnessed the general doing so. He probably heard and believed other Confederates attributing such an order to Forrest.[25]

Clark's letter does convey the sincerity of a conscientious man troubled by what he had observed: "In as much as I am a member of Forrest's Cavalry modesty would direct that I say nothing in our praise nor will I but will tell you in as few words as possible what was done and leave you to judge whether or not we acted well or ill."[26] Finally, it seems most unbelievable that a committed Confederate could have any reason for falsely accusing his comrades of perpetrating a massacre.

Several other Confederates wrote about the event. Chalmers, after reaching Mississippi, issued a congratulatory order which scornfully but ambiguously asserted that his men had "taught the mongrel garrison of blacks and renegades a lesson long to be remembered." Surgeon Samuel H. Caldwell, who could not actually watch the battle on account of his work, relayed to his wife the story that "They refused to surrender—which incensed our men & if General Forrest had not run between our men & the Yanks with his pistol and sabre drawn not a man would have been spared."[27] If true (several Federals said similar things), Forrest had to be stopping Confederate fire, as no sensible commander would have done this while the enemy persisted in fighting or fleeing.

After the incident, Forrest had returned to Jackson for recuperation from his bruises. On April 15 the commander commented in a report that "The river was dyed with the blood of the slaughtered for 200 yards. . . . It is hoped that these facts will demonstrate to the Northern people that negro soldiers cannot cope with Southerners." He wrote his president, Jefferson Davis, that the Federals caused themselves a high death toll by continuing to fight or to seek escape rather than surrendering. His report portrayed the Federals as retreating, rather than fleeing, to the riverbank, a claim unusual among the early sources. Either guilty subordinates had misinformed him or he had begun to rationalize about the incident in an effort to cover it up. Only if the general and other Confederates somehow did not hear or see the events that took place mostly on the riverbank, as Dr. Fitch came to believe, could they have sincerely believed in the troops' innocence. Since Captain Young told several reporters that Forrest shot a Confederate who refused to stop firing, it seems hard to believe that the general did not observe the massacre.[28]

Forrest, not knowing that his men had robbed Federals of their currency, actually bragged that no one in West Tennessee wanted Federal greenbacks. Chalmers, though, had learned about the thefts and tried to confiscate the money. He also required men who had turned captured black soldiers into personal servants to surrender them. Except for a handful of escapees, captives would generally reach a prisoner-of-war camp, in many cases the infamous one at Andersonville, Georgia. Treating the African Americans as captured slaves, the Confederates diverted some of them to labor on for-tifications at Mobile, Alabama. Among the captives, 71 percent from white units would die as prisoners, while only 13 percent from the black units did.[29] Perhaps the white unionists had lower morale or particularly suffered at the hands of their guards. While blacks on work details probably benefit-ted from better food and the activity, the former slaves among them may have had more determination and better survival skills.

Shortly after the Fort Pillow massacre, two similar incidents occurred. On April 18 a Confederate army beat a much smaller force of black and white Federals at Poison Spring, Arkansas. Confederate diaries and letters noted that the victors generally refused to grant quarter to African Ameri-cans, although most of the Federals eventually escaped. As at Fort Pillow, these Federals had protected and enlisted contrabands as well as taken foodstuffs from secessionist civilians. Unlike other Confederate massacres, this one involved Indian allies who participated in the killing. The victors, who had very few casualties, killed 117 men (27 percent) from the African American regiment during and after the Battle of Poison Spring.[30]

On April 20, another Confederate army enveloped a biracial garrison at Plymouth, North Carolina, and issued it a surrender demand worded like Forrest's at Fort Pillow. The Federal commander refused at first; then, after Confederates broke through the defenses, he tried to surren-der for fear of a massacre like Fort Pillow only to see one start anyway. Some black Federals resisted briefly before fleeing into a swamp. Almost forty (31 percent) of them died in the skirmish and afterward. Both forces

knew of the Fort Pillow incident, and the Confederates may have con-
sciously copied it. The incidents at Poison Spring and Plymouth received
little attention at the time, due to limited information, their small scale, and
their location in peripheral war theaters. But they demonstrated that Fort
Pillow fit into a larger pattern that accompanied early Confederate defeats
of black troops.[31]

Within the Confederacy, the *Mobile Advertiser and Register* on April 17
broke the Fort Pillow story with a widely reprinted telegraphic dispatch
from a correspondent who reported an "indiscriminate slaughter followed
[the battle.] . . . The fort ran with blood; many jumped into the river and
drowned or [were] shot." Subsequently, several other brief pieces of newspaper correspondence emphasized the high number of casualties. On
April 26, the same paper published a fuller report from a correspondent
in Barteau's Regiment, "Marion," who specifically stated that Confederate
soldiers gave no quarter to black troops. This document and Clark's letter
provide the strongest evidence for a massacre. The early public reports
convinced the *Memphis Appeal*'s editor that an "unprecedented slaughter
of five-sevenths of the garrison" had occurred. Basil Gildersleeve, an edi-
torialist for the *Richmond Examiner,* more explicitly assumed that a massacre occurred. Alleging without specifics that Federals had been killing
captured Confederates, he contended that only revenge in kind would stop
it: "We must mete out to them strict justice. . . . Repeat Fort Pillow. Repeat
Plymouth a few times and we shall bring the Yankees to their senses."[32]

Reacting to the first reports of the Fort Pillow incident, the U.S. Army
and Congress quickly initiated investigations. Acting first, Secretary of War
Edwin Stanton on April 16 sent an order to General Sherman, who assigned the investigation to Brigadier General Manson M. Brayman, commander of the District of Cairo. Between April 17 and 30, Brayman had
several officers collect sworn affidavits from twenty-four soldiers and three
civilians who survived the violence. The general obtained Lieutenant Van
Horn's report as well as statements, some sworn and some not, by six witnesses of the scene on the day afterward. The testimony read as if the
interviewers did not indulge in biased questioning but asked witnesses to
tell only what happened and to whom. Two Federals said that they watched
the enemy kill civilians. Three women reported finding on April 13 the
burning body of a Federal who seemed nailed to wood planks. Six soldiers
claimed that Confederates broke the truce by crawling closer to the fort,
although a sergeant whose cannon port overlooked the barracks disproved
a story that Confederates took those buildings during the truce. Mostly

short and factual, the wounded soldiers' accounts of a massacre had much consistency with one another.[33]

Brayman's April 28 report concluded that "violations of the laws and usages of civilized war and of those obligations of common humanity which even barbarians and heathen tribes, in some sort observe, have been perpetrated." Specifically, he believed premeditation was proven by Forrest's threat to give no quarter at Paducah, and by a Confederate subordinate's similar surrender demand at Columbus.[34]

The initial report, that Confederates massacred the garrison after it surrendered, moved Congress to consider holding its own investigation. This caused the Joint Committee on the Conduct of the War to undertake its own study. The committee delegated Senator Benjamin Wade, its chairman and a leading radical Republican, as well as Congressman Daniel Gooch, a more moderate member of the same party, to travel west with a stenographer to collect evidence. On April 18, Congress passed a resolution directing the Committee on the Conduct of the War to focus on "the truth of the rumored slaughter of Union troops, after their surrender" and whether or not the army could have successfully reinforced or evacuated the fort. That same day, Lincoln gave a speech in Baltimore. Along the lines of his 1863 threat regarding Confederate mistreatment of black troops, he announced, "If there has been the massacre . . . and being so proven, the retribution shall as surely come." A few days later he signed the congressional resolution.[35]

The subcommittee started to take sworn testimony at Cairo on April 22. The members probably discussed the army investigation with General Brayman, their first witness, and apparently decided to seek more information than he had. Between April 22 and 26, a shorter span than the army inquest, the two congressmen would interview fifty-one soldiers, sailors, and civilians who witnessed the incident. Of the returned soldiers, 38 percent gave testimony to at least one of the investigations, but both sets of affidavits over-represented the 6th U.S.C.H.A. a little. The congressional report would include some other interviews and correspondence, plus selections from Brayman's reports. Besides taking more sworn affidavits than the army investigators did, the subcommittee generally obtained longer and more specific answers. The questions appeared in the record, another difference from most army affidavits.[36]

The subcommittee's questions, after identifying a witness, tended to turn to an open-ended query, such as "What did you see done there?" Next, they usually asked specific questions, most often "Did you see any-

body buried alive?" and "Did you see any one burned?" Forrest later denounced the interrogatories as "leading questions," a legal term for word-
ing unacceptable in a courtroom. Significantly, he ignored the fact that the
subcommittee did not conduct a trial but a legislative investigation, which
commonly used such questions. The two congressmen sought information about specific allegations that had received little attention in the army
affidavits. Furthermore, nearly all of the subcommittee's questions had a
straightforward and unemotional nature, rather than one prejudicing the
response or pointing to a single answer. Instead of being led, the majority of testifiers who were asked about the burning or burying of wounded
Federals reported that they did not see it. The few questions about observing Confederates violating the truce or killing civilians also drew a couple
of negative responses. The congressmen, to their credit, repeatedly distin-
guished between a witness's personal experience and hearsay. Perhaps by
seeking more information they also evoked a few more sensational statements than the army investigators did.[37]

On April 30, Dr. Charles Fitch, who had received permission to recuperate at home in Iowa and thereby missed both investigations, submitted
a particularly lengthy and vivid description of the massacre to the army's
Medical Department. He portrayed the massacre as arising from a spontaneous breakdown of Confederate discipline. Although he described Forrest
as speaking menacingly to him, he did not blame either Forrest or Chalmers and noted that they provided protection for prisoners. After a superior
grossly misjudged the document and Fitch by claiming that "the horrors of
the massacre are but faintly depicted in this paper. The mind of Dr. Fitch is
impaired, and I fear permanently injured by the scenes witnessed," it was
filed away without notice to either investigation.[38]

One historian has challenged the usefulness of Fitch's report by accusing him of incorrect statements about the removal of all black women and
children from the fort, the occupation of the barracks in violation of the
truce, and the number of captured Federals. Like Fitch, the log-keeper of
the *New Era* recorded that the gunboat towed a coal barge loaded with
civilians upriver. The doctor and the log-keeper simply did not know that
others remained in the area. The forty black women and children captured
by Forrest most likely were caught at the contraband camp and the quarters of Edward Benton's contract laborers.[39] In regard to a truce violation
by occupation of the barracks, Fitch could not have seen it from his field
hospital on the riverbank and must have thoughtlessly repeated an inac-

curate story heard from other survivors. As for the captured Federals, Fitch only counted the 101 in his group but had no access to the others. Fitch's errors are understandable; he does not show a general pattern of careless-ness or falsification. As his report expanded upon his April 13 interview with the *St. Louis Missouri Democrat* reporter, it could not have resulted from peer pressure.[40]

On May 2, the congressional investigators returned to Washington and notified Lincoln that they had confirmed all the charges about Fort Pillow. The next day the president informed his cabinet members of the verdict and asked each to write an opinion advising him on a course of action. Secretary of the Navy Gideon Welles felt very uncomfortable doing this without having seen the evidence: "There must be something in these ter-rible reports, but I distrust Congressional Committees. They exaggerate." At a May 6 cabinet meeting the president received what Attorney General Edward Bates called a "very diverse" set of responses. All seven agreed that the president should demand an explanation of Confederate policy regarding the incident. Most advocated that at least Forrest and Chalmers should be indicted for war crimes. Four cabinet members, including Stan-ton, favored retaliation in some form against captured Confederates, if the enemy did not respond satisfactorily. This proposal gravely troubled the other three. Welles later noted in his diary that "The idea of retaliation—killing man for man which is the popular noisy demand is barbarous and I cannot assent. . . . The whole subject is beset with difficulties." Secretary of the Interior John P. Usher advised that for the sake of appearances Lin-coln should retaliate only if Grant won the upcoming Virginia campaign. Lincoln closed the meeting and decided to give the matter more thought before acting.[41]

The Joint Committee on the Conduct of the War approved a quickly written statement from the subcommittee and decided to bind it and the testimony together with a report on the suffering of Federals in the Confed-erates' prisoner-of-war camps. Congress chose to print and distribute sixty thousand copies, an unusually large number. While the report exonerated the Federal army for not succeeding in reinforcing or evacuating the fort, it focused primarily on condemning the Confederates. Obviously intending the report to stiffen the war effort, Wade and Gooch used a very emotional style in their brief introduction to the evidence. The committee viewed the massacre not as a spontaneous breakdown of discipline but as the result of Confederate policy: "It is the intention of the rebel authorities not to recognize the officers and men of our colored regiments as entitled to the treatment accorded by all civilized nations to prisoners of war." Recognizing that the fort did not surrender, the report held that individual Federals trying to surrender "fell victims to the malignity and barbarity of Forrest and his followers." Claiming that "no cruelty which the most fiendish malignity could devise was omitted by these murderers," the report also charged that the Confederates broke the truce in order to move closer to the fort, killed some civilians, buried some of the wounded, and burned some of the wounded.[42] The subcommittee obtained more evidence on these subsidiary charges than the army did, although this still involved relatively few witnesses.

The charge of truce violation was true on at least a small scale, as Confederate captain John Carroll later admitted his participation in a group of Confederates who on their own initiative hid in the fort's ditch during the truce. Early Confederate sources discredit claims that troops sneaked into the ravines during the truce. Although not mentioned in Confederate accounts, reinforcements sent up during the truce could have prompted the Federal allegations. A later Confederate defensive argument that the Federal charge arose from a misunderstanding of Major Anderson's move of several companies to the riverbank to stop the steamboats from landing is irrelevant, because no Federal mentioned that particular movement.[43]

A few civilians definitely died as well. The Mound City hospital register listed a black soldier's wife who died from wounds, and the *New Era*'s log recorded that sailors found and buried one woman with the other dead at the fort on April 13. The sailors did not record finding wounded or dead children at the site, despite several allegations of such made by survivors. The bodies that Confederates reportedly threw in the Mississippi might have included some women and children. In 1866, the army would find two children's graves at the fort, but without any indication of the time of death. The scarcity of noncombatants' corpses and the presence of forty contrabands among Confederate captives would indicate that few civilians suffered.[44]

Likewise, the burial alive of wounded men probably involved few individuals. A civilian combatant saw a black die while buried up to his head. Sailors from *New Era* dug out one soldier who died soon afterward. Another soldier, Private Daniel Tyler of the 2nd U.S.C.L.A., testified that, while acting dead for fear of being killed, others tossed him into a burial trench. A Confederate rescued Tyler upon noticing that he remained alive. Workers could have buried still other Federals unconscious from severe wounds. In a manner intended to be amusing, one Confederate wrote a newspaper shortly after the incident that he deliberately buried some of those acting dead: "Vitality was not restored until breathing was obstructed, and then the resurrection began."[45]

A handful of witnesses, including a burial crew, reported seeing at least two bodies nailed to wood and presumably burnt alive, though no one claimed to see this happen. Two Federals did report observing the enemy burn down buildings containing wounded men on April 13. Lieutenant Mack Leaming of Bradford's Battalion stated that the hut where he had rested was torched just as Confederates received a warning that men remained inside; these Federals seem to have helped one another out. Leaming's original testimony did not specifically attribute fault to the enemy, as he would in a report nine months later, possibly after some angry brooding. Three wounded Federals said that Confederates removed them from buildings or tents before starting fires. Moved by the mood of the massacre, some Confederates could have intentionally burned a few Federals alive on the morning of April 13. However, *Silver Cloud*'s shelling rushed the setting of fires and thereby promoted carelessness. Some of those burnt may have already been dead.[46] The evidence for this charge remains particularly inconclusive.

Most of the allegations subsidiary to the massacre contain some truth in regard to at least a few individuals. That the subcommittee believed all charges without qualification indicates the suspiciousness and hostility of Wade and Gooch toward Confederates. A few of their witnesses definitely conveyed incorrect information. However, when pruned of some obviously biased and sensational statements, the testimony fits well with the earlier evidence and therefore seems mostly reliable.[47]

In response to the army and congressional investigations, Lincoln on May 17 drafted a plan for action. It demanded that by July 1 the Confederacy agree to not allow similar massacres in the future and to treat captured members of African American regiments "according to the laws of war," including access to prisoner exchange. Otherwise the United States would carry out unspecified retaliations against captured officers for the Fort Pillow massacre and against enlisted prisoners for any other mistreatment of black Federals. The president never finished the document nor implemented it, probably because of his consistent tendency to avoid actions that could make the war more vengeful. The document itself stated that "blood can not restore blood, and government should not act for revenge." Soon the subject largely disappeared from the newspapers. According to Lincoln's secretaries, Grant's very bloody campaign in Northern Virginia "crowded out of view and consideration a topic so difficult and hazardous as whole-sale retaliation." That, together with widespread racial prejudice, probably limited the depth of the incident's impact on Northern public opinion.[48]

During the time of the Federal investigations, the Confederates started to defend themselves. "Memphis," someone at Forrest's headquarters, penned a letter on April 18 in response to critical Federal comments made the day after the incident. Writing to the *Memphis Appeal,* then published in Atlanta, Georgia, the author seemed unaware of the full list of charges made in Northern press reports on the incident. After overrating the fort's cap-ture as "one of the most brilliant achievements of the war," the letter por-trayed all Federals as continuing resistance or seeking flight rather than sur-rendering. The author twice repeated his main defense for Forrest's force: "Still the enemy would not or knew not how to surrender [after fleeing to the riverbank]. The Federal flag, that hated emblem of tyranny, was still proudly waving over the scene. . . . General Forrest begged them to surren-der, but he was told with an air of insulting defiance that he could not take the place, and that they asked for no quarter. Not the first sign of surrender was ever given."[49] The letter hinted that the failure of the garrison to sur-render as a whole justified unchecked killing by Confederates. This ratio-nalization implied that few or no Federals attempted individual surrenders and ignored that the Federals' rout made a flag lowering unlikely.

By April 25, Forrest had learned of the Northern newspapers' allega-tions and had decided to write a rebuttal endorsing the emphasis on a Fed-eral failure to surrender. Honor meant a great deal in the South and prob-ably influenced this very defensive document. His second, fuller report of April 26 reiterated that the Federals "retreated toward the river, arms in hand and firing back, and their colors flying," in a "short but desperate struggle" and added that they expected covering fire from *New Era.* He reduced the time of fighting after the final charge from thirty minutes, as stated in his April 15 report, to twenty minutes. After numerous newspa-pers printed the report, all but one other Confederate account gave the time period as twenty minutes or less.[50]

Similar accounts followed Forrest's. Major Anderson, whose presence below the bluff should have entailed knowledge of what happened there, filed a report that covered up his men's guilt by implying that a foolish and hopeless resistance by the Federals accounted for their casualties. Chalmers's May 7 report similarly attributed high Federal casualties to persistent resistance and escape efforts. Also in early May, Isham G. Harris, Tennessee's Confederate governor who had accompanied Forrest to Fort Pillow, gave a newspaper interview in which he held, like Forrest, that most Federals kept firing until the bitter end. Yet, unlike Forrest, he described a rout of the enemy down the bluff and admitted that "a few, black and white, threw down their arms and made signs of surrender." The governor excused their deaths because "in the heat, din, and confusion of a fire of such close quarters there was no chance of discrimination."[51]

The *Memphis Appeal* printed an April 27 letter from Forrest's headquarters, this one by "G.W.A.," who, if the "G." had accidentally replaced a "C.," likely was Charles W. Anderson. It introduced a new, highly questionable accusation that black troops drunkenly sang a rallying song during the truce.[52] It denigrated the African American troops as a way of countering Federal claims.

Confederate newspapers quickly adopted a consensus denying the occurrence of a massacre. Ironically, the *Charleston Mercury* on the day after printing the "Marion" letter, the last acknowledgment in 1864 by a Confederate of the massacre, ran an editorial expressing concern about Federal retaliation for something that did not happen. The *Mobile Advertiser and Register,* which had originally run "Marion's" statement, ignored it to assert that "accounts of 'massacre,' 'butchery,' etc. are the fruits of Yankee invention and told with the hope of inciting Lincoln to retaliation." According to the *Atlanta Intelligencer,* Northerners fabricated the tale of a massacre for anti-Confederate propaganda purposes.[53]

Both the Confederate Congress and President Jefferson Davis upheld the innocence of Forrest's troops in the face of Federal allegations. The Confederate failure to change official policies toward captured black Federals served as one of the U.S. government's grounds for halting most prisoner exchanges in the summer of 1864. However, some of these blacks did actually go to prisoner-of-war camps, a practice indicating that the outrage expressed by the Federal side over the massacre had an impact.[54]

Still, some Confederates would not treat African Americans as legitimate soldiers. On July 30, 1864, at the Battle of the Crater outside Petersburg, Virginia, 439 black soldiers died during and after an assault into a giant hole blown in Confederate fortifications. According to Confederate letters, a number of blacks tried unsuccessfully to surrender after being trapped in the crater. Whether the death toll, higher than that at Fort Pillow, arose from casualties in the larger-scale battle or from a more extensive massacre cannot be determined. Confederate sources also reveal that on September 16 their forces wiped out twenty-seven black soldiers, most of a small company, after its ammunition ran out at Flat Rock, Indian Territory (today's Oklahoma). Following a Federal defeat at Saltville, Virginia, on October 3, 1864, some Confederates killed twelve to forty-six wounded black Federals on the field or in hospitals. General Robert E. Lee ordered a trial, but the flight of the accused parties and the war's end prevented it.[55] No massacre of black troops other than that at Fort Pillow attracted much attention. All, except the one at the Crater, involved small numbers killed in minor war theaters. Federal authorities seem to have had extensive evidence only from Fort Pillow.

Partly spurred by the black troops' sacrifices at Fort Pillow and elsewhere, the U.S. government moved toward policy revisions. One congressman mentioned the incident when favoring the abolition of slavery through the proposed 13th Amendment to the U.S. Constitution, and Congress approved equal pay and bounties for black soldiers in 1864. Before the end of the war the army would also commission a small number of black officers.[56]

Lizzie Booth personally lobbied for a change in pension laws to benefit African American applicants. Having learned that most families of Fort Pillow's black dead could not get pensions because slave marriages had no legal standing under Southern state laws, she traveled to Washington to discuss the problem with Lincoln. He viewed her concerns as worth attention and sent her to a leading senator. Less than two months later Congress amended the pension law to grant payments to a legally unmarried widow of a black soldier provided that she had affidavits from "credible witnesses" that she had lived as the man's spouse for at least two years before enlistment, the couple had not lived in a state that would have registered their marriage after they escaped slavery, and the applicant did not remain in slavery. While the new rules could pose difficulties, many benefitted.[57]

The Fort Pillow massacre also affected the battlefield. General Sherman somewhat presciently advised Secretary of War Stanton: "I know well the animus of the Southern soldiery, and the truth is they cannot be restrained. The effect will be of course to make the negroes desperate, and when in turn they commit horrid acts of retaliation we will be relieved of the responsibility. . . . Let soldiers affected make their rules as we progress. . . . [Confederates] will heed the slaughter that will follow as the natural consequence of their own inhuman acts."[58] As if in response, Lieutenant Colonel

Jackson of the 6th U.S.C.H.A. held a military ceremony in which Lizzie Booth returned a blood-stained flag that Corporal Eli Cothel had given her when she visited Booth's men in the Mound City Hospital. After Confederates had cut the fort's flags down, he wrapped one around a wound on his right leg both to save the flag and to staunch his blood flow. Mrs. Booth made an impassioned speech during the ritual: "I have given to my country all I had to give—my husband—such a gift! Yet I have freely given him for freedom and my country. Next to my husband's cold remains the dearest object left to me in the world is this flag . . . I give to you, knowing that you will ever remember the last words of my noble husband, '*Never surrender the flag to traitors.*'" Colonel Jackson accepted the flag, called the troops to kneel down, and led them in swearing to avenge the victims of the Fort Pillow massacre.[59]

Sherman himself instigated a series of major expeditions against Forrest. In the face of the first one, Forrest's remaining forces departed from West Tennessee in early May 1864. The second operation ended in a severe Federal defeat at Brice's Crossroads, Mississippi, on June 10. After the battle a black brigade conducted a tough rear guard defense for the retreating column. According to a Confederate source, the black troops came with and then discarded hatbands and guidons bearing the slogan "Remember Fort Pillow," imitating a similar slogan used by Texans in 1835 after the massacre at the Alamo. Some antagonized Confederates granted the black troops no quarter. However, a concerned Forrest supposedly visited those taken prisoner to promise them security from harm. Fort Pillow had created a problem that would long shadow his reputation.[60]

Shortly after the battle, Forrest wrote Hurlbut's successor, Major General Cadwallader C. Washburn, to object to the rumored no-quarter policy of black troops toward his men, because "in all my operations since the war began I have conducted the war on civilized principles." Washburn replied that the "attempt to intimidate the colored troops by indiscriminate slaughter has signally failed," and asked what policy Forrest would follow toward them in the future. If Confederates intended to execute all black captives, Washburn would allow his troops to respond as they so chose. In reply Forrest explicitly denied the occurrence of a massacre at Fort Pillow and claimed that he held black troops as captured property, which he never mistreated. If Federals started to execute captured Confederates, he threatened to retaliate in the same manner. Major General Stephen D. Lee, commander of all cavalry in the department to which Forrest belonged, also wrote Washburn to endorse all that Forrest had said and to defend his subordinates. Lee, though, stressed that Federals had committed inflammatory transgressions: "You had a servile race, armed against their masters and in a country which had been desolated by almost unprecedented outrages." Needless to say, the Federals continued to follow a hard war policy, and black regiments persisted in fighting Forrest's cavalry fiercely.[61]

African American troops shouted "Remember Fort Pillow" during combat at least at Brice's Crossroads (Mississippi), James Island (South Carolina), Mariana (Florida), Petersburg, Aquia Creek, and Richmond (Virginia). The slogan only antagonized Confederates at the battles of Brice's Crossroads and the Crater.[62] In the name of vengeance for Fort Pillow or Poison Spring, black troops killed small numbers of prisoners at Mariana, Petersburg, and Jenkins Ferry (Arkansas). When they could avoid attracting attention, some black and white Federals in several war theaters refused to accept prisoners. Robert Strong, a white Illinoisan, after his first battle at Resaca, Georgia, wrote home that his comrades immediately killed a surrendering Confederate with a "Fort Pillow" tattoo, and observed, "I shall never forget his look of fear."[63]

Some troops had no interest in violent revenge, and some officers urged the men in black regiments to abide by the rules of war for prisoners. Surgeon Humphrey Hood of the 3rd U.S.C.H.A. wrote, "I regret very much that the ridiculous farce [the 6th U.S.C.H.A.'s revenge oath] enacted here got into the news." Whatever their purpose, black soldiers fought with great determination, as they expected little mercy if captured. In early 1865 the Confederate army agreed to trade captured black Federals, and this reopened major prisoner exchanges during the war's last months.[64]

Before the Civil War, the U.S. Army in practice had fought war differently depending upon whether the enemy was considered white or not. All the sizeable massacres of the American Civil War involved racial conflict. Besides the ones conducted by Confederates, Federal forces massacred around 250 Shoshoni Indians at Bear River, Idaho, and 130 Cheyenne at Sand Creek, Colorado. The Committee on the Conduct of the War investigated and condemned the Sand Creek incident.[65] In this investigation and the one on Fort Pillow the committee questioned different warfare rules for racially different opponents.

The Civil War's massacres reveal several things about American society then. First, in one sense the sectional hostility did not run as deep as the racial one. The massacres focused on particular minority groups, rather than on Northerners and Southerners. In at least this category the whites of both sides could generally respect each other's rights on the battlefield. Second, while atrocities resulted from conflicts present in American society, they did not become a common part of the war. The great majority of soldiers on both sides did not participate in massacres, even when opportunities appeared. In fact, the number of Civil War massacre victims pales beside the world's more recent ethnic massacres. Third, while perpetrators of massacres denied wrongdoing by dehumanizing the enemy and thus placing them beyond coverage by the rules of war, other witnesses objected at least privately. Fourth, the public retained a divided memory of the major incidents. Some condemned injustice to the victims on moral and political grounds. Others defended the alleged victimizers from supposed slander by stressing their innocence and cultural superiority, while condemning the alleged atrocities of the victims, views which had contributed to the massacre in the first place.[66]

The debate over Fort Pillow contributed to ongoing contention over change in race relations. However, the controversy had one positive outcome: the implicit public admission by leaders on both sides that a massacre motivated by racial antagonism was wrong or at least should not occur. Confederate Secretary of War James Seddon realized that the law allowing execution of slave soldiers became inoperative because of "the embarrassments attending this question and the serious consequences which might ensue from the rigid enforcement of the act."[67] That ultimately required a tacit Confederate acceptance of black Federal enlistments, which limited the number of subsequent massacres. Without this turn, the war would have taken a very different and even uglier route.

Chapter Seven

Public Memory and Fort Pillow

B Y the end of the war the fort resembled a ghost town. The only indi- cation of life at the otherwise empty site was the small group of en- trepreneurs once again operating stores at the steamboat landing. Weeds abounded on the fort's parade ground, and the flagpole stood un- used. Graves, mostly without headboards, lay scattered about the site. Ero- sion had exposed some human bones, and the Mississippi had washed away those buried beside it.[1] Signs and memories of past violence persisted.

In 1866 the army created a formal, fenced cemetery south of the massacre site where barracks had stood. Work crews exhumed around 250 bodies, including those from the Federals' pre-massacre cemeteries (the records say nothing about the Confederate graveyards). Identification existed for only forty-one persons, most of whom had died before the massacre. After placing all remains in new coffins, laborers buried them in a cemetery with separate sections for each race. Every new grave received a plain oak marker. The next year the army moved all the bodies to a Fort Pillow sec- tion of the new Memphis National Cemetery. National cemeteries repre- sented an innovative approach to commemorating the country's wars and inevitably played an important role in early memorializing of the Civil War, the United States' bloodiest struggle.[2]

Just as the dead at Fort Pillow had repeated reburials, the story of what happened and the site where it occurred would undergo periodic modifi- cations, for the changing concerns of the present reshape remembrance of the past. While much took place at Fort Pillow, only the incident of April 12, 1864, made a strong impression on public memory. Some people would seek tangible commemorations, like a cemetery, while others would pre- serve the event by writing about it. Sectional politics especially affected pub- lic memory of the war.[3] Postwar interpretations of the Fort Pillow incident started with two basic versions, each connected to one side of the war.

Northern accounts relied exclusively upon the congressional investi- gation.[4] Few exhibited a neutral tone. Influenced by Northern sectionalism, most used the incident as proof that barbarism characterized Southern society. Willard Glazier, for example, called the massacre an "outgrowth of . . . slavery," perpetrated by a "fiendish" Forrest. Henry H. Lloyd falsely claimed that Forrest refused an offer to surrender by Booth. Coming at the subject from a different direction, *Black Cudjo, or, the Contraband Spy: A Thrilling Story of the Fort Pillow Massacre,* a thin novelette, utilized the Northern stereotype of slaves as clumsy and cowardly until liberation and enlistment by the Federal army made them manly.[5] All these works reaffirmed Northern whites' heroic self-image and sense of mission. This version also preserved the memory of the incident in order to condemn the perpetrators and honor the victims.

After the war, Federal survivors published at least three brief accounts. Without referring to postwar Southern writings, Dr. Charles Fitch commented on their major assertions in an 1879 letter to James R. Chalmers. He described only Confederates as violently drunk (after consuming liquor from the warehouses) during the incident. While remembering that Forrest's men charged Bradford's Battalion "with doing many things that were mean" toward secessionists, he did not rate such feelings as a main cause of the incident. The doctor blamed the massacre on the attackers' prejudices and drunkenness, rather than a Federal refusal to surrender. At the same time he exonerated both Forrest and Chalmers from blame for the slaughter on the ground that they were unaware of it. In contrast, Lieutenant Thomas W. McClure, a captured officer from the 6th U.S.H.C.A., declared in an 1884 memoir that he heard the two Confederate leaders speak approvingly of the massacre afterward. While they may have expressed such thoughts, this would not prove they initiated or permitted the killing, as McClure assumed. Thomas C. George, the hospital steward, in 1888 made the unique claim that Forrest stopped only the killing of whites. While his memory in all probability was wrong about that, he correctly recalled the intense hostility of many Confederates toward the garrison.[6]

General Sherman, whose involvement with the incident was indirect, thoughtfully suggested in his *Memoirs* that Forrest's men committed the massacre in anger over black enlistment. Sherman thought that Forrest did not know about the massacre and respected prisoners.[7] None of these short commentaries attracted much attention at the time.

Writers on the Confederate side found Northern allegations of a massacre and of Southern savagery offensive. They rejected the congressional report as biased, yet often cited portions of it useful to their case. Testimony in the report by the *New Era*'s commander convinced Virginia journalist Edward Pollard of the correctness of Forrest's assertion that the Federals retreated to the riverbank under a plan to receive cover from the gunboat's cannons. This scheme, he asserted, failed and forced the Federals to fight too long and to suffer excessive casualties. Pollard made the limited concession that "for some moments, the Confederate officers lost control of their men, who were maddened by the sight of negro troops opposing them."[8] His theory about a planned retreat quickly became a common part of the Confederate interpretation, while the admission of a small amount of unnecessary killing reappeared occasionally.

After the war, General Forrest rarely offered public comments on the controversy. In an interview after his surrender he brought racial prejudices into the Confederate defense by claiming that blacks never made truthful witnesses. Holding that open beer and whiskey barrels sat in the inner fort, he alleged that widespread drunkenness (expanding this charge to white troops as well as blacks) made the garrison fight recklessly hard. The former general did not specifically claim to have seen the liquor and probably had acquired this new information from Colonel Clark Barteau. The massacre issue clearly upset Forrest and provoked defensiveness as a matter of honor: "The charges made against me, are as false and black as the hearts of the men who made them. . . . [I condemn any] liar who says I ever overstepped the bounds of civilized warfare."[9]

Public discussion of the incident left Forrest angry and distraught. In 1866 he protested to President Andrew Johnson that "I am at this moment regarded in large communities, at the North, with abhorrence, as a detestable monster, ruthless and swift to take life, and guilty of unpardonable crimes in connection with the capture of Fort Pillow. . . . This mis-judgement of my conduct and character . . . pains and mortifies me greatly." Forrest held that the congressional investigation had "*exparte* proceedings . . . leading questions, and willing witnesses whose prompted evidence should, therefore mislead no one." The general offered to submit to a trial in order to defend himself, but the president had no interest in prosecuting war crimes. Shortly after writing Johnson, Forrest attended a reception in Memphis for Senator Ben Wade. A report later circulated that, when conversing about Fort Pillow, Forrest admitted the occurrence of a massacre while Wade conceded the former general's innocence. If true, either the men's pride or Congress's move toward more radical reconstruction measures sabotaged the rapprochement, for neither leader ever corroborated the tale. To Forrest's detractors, his subsequent involvement in the Ku Klux Klan confirmed his guilt.[10]

Forrest ultimately responded to critics through an authorized biography by Thomas Jordan and John P. Pryor, two former Confederate officers who were not at the battle. In 1868, when their side lay economically undermined and politically subordinated, they sought to boost its self-esteem. The book fit within the new "Lost Cause" movement, which defended and venerated the Confederacy.[11] A highly influential chapter packaged three main emphases in the pro-Confederate interpretation of Fort Pillow: the garrison's depredations, drunkenness, and desperate resistance. Jordan and Pryor essentially blamed the victims for their own suffering.

The coauthors maintained that numerous depredations and rapes committed in a region between the fort and Jackson by the Bradford Battalion aroused Confederates to fight hard in the battle. Jordan and Pryor exaggerated depredations into the sole reason Forrest wanted to take the fort. Forrest's awareness of his men's vengefulness motivated his comment that he could not be responsible for the Federals' fate if they refused surrender. However, no records show Bradford's cavalry traveling farther east than Brownsville. The detailed diary of a secessionist from the Jackson area never mentions misbehavior by Bradford's Battalion, for Hurst's cavalry committed the depredations there. Before the Jordan and Pryor biography, no one had charged Bradford's men with rape, a subject from which Confederates did not shy away (one had published such an assertion about black troops in the Brice's Crossroads campaign). The rape story probably arose from the tendency of "Lost Cause" writings to emphasize the chivalric protection of women's sexual honor. Furthermore, the contemporary evidence indicates that whatever depredations Bradford's Battalion committed had limited significance to Forrest in 1864. His surrender demand spoke of the garrison's conduct as entitling it to prisoner status, and that day he did not mention allegations of criminality.[12]

The real issue was probably not the behavior of the final garrison during its brief service at the fort but the Federals' hard war policy in occupied areas since late 1862. The common Federal practices of arresting suspected guerrillas, restricting trade, emancipating slaves, and appropriating goods from civilians understandably offended Confederates. These policies did harm to secessionists in the area around Fort Pillow, although not to the degree experienced in Missouri or Virginia's Shenandoah Valley.[13]

Jordan and Pryor portrayed most Federals as madly drunk after freely dipping into open whiskey and beer barrels in the fort. Both sides during the Civil War made repeated use of this common propagandist device for discrediting opponents who put up a particularly desperate fight. As humanity has long known the dulling impact of liquor on a soldier's judgment and effectiveness, it would require extreme foolishness for a commander to distribute liquor during a battle. If this had occurred, some Federals would surely have criticized it, since survivors did not refrain from accusing one another of contributing to the defeat. The coauthors identified Colonel Clark Barteau, rather than Forrest, as the source of information about the intoxicating beverages.[14] "G.W.A." had claimed black Federals were drunk, but neither the newspaper correspondent "Marion," who wrote from Barteau's camp shortly after the incident, nor any other writer in 1864 had mentioned beer and whiskey barrels.[15] After all, Colonel Barteau commanded some of the Confederate troops fighting on the riverbank, where most of the massacre probably took place, and had reason to want to defend his troops.

Even if present, liquor's availability does not prove drunkenness on the part of the Federals. A private letter by Charley Robinson, a Northern civilian, did refer to beer somewhere around the inner fort. It was definitely in the landing's warehouses, and may have been in a camp sutler's stores. Just as victorious Confederates broke into alcohol in the warehouses, they could have opened any barrels at the inner fort.[16]

Only the third allegation, the one blaming the Federals' reckless resistance for the high death toll, appeared immediately after the incident and in a number of accounts, including Forrest's. Jordan and Pryor estimated that 45 percent of the garrison died. While close to accurate, their calculation incorrectly counted everyone on their prisoner list as captured at Fort Pillow, when the 1864 version of the list designated some individuals as captured elsewhere in West Tennessee. Using a European philosophical work on international law from the 1700s, they claimed that civilized warfare allowed for killing all enemies when their commander failed to surrender an untenable position.[17] Significantly, this argument attempted to legitimize rather than deny unnecessary killing. No subsequent writer would repeat this argument, but many Confederates would hint at agreement by emphasizing the post's failure to surrender, as if that justified indiscriminate killing until Forrest symbolically had the Federal flag cut down.

Jordan and Pryor considered the garrison's losses to be normal for a fort taken by storm, but also contended that Federals chose to resist too long and thereby forced the attackers to kill many. They held that Confederates killed only a few Federals trying to surrender and attributed that to "insania belli," the craziness or momentum of combat. Soldiers failed to surrender, according to the coauthors, because they were left directionless by the death of most officers—but most officers actually survived the battle. According to an interview with wounded survivors in the Mound City Hospital, some Federals frantically sought escape or continued to fight, but they did so because of the Confederates' refusal to grant quarter.[18] The charge of unyielding resistance, the strongest part of the Confederate argument, would hold great weight, except that several Confederates admitted the occurrence of a massacre.

Jordan and Pryor staunchly denied all of the congressional committee's charges. Concurring in Forrest's belief that the investigators conducted a completely biased inquiry, they showed their own bias in presenting Confederates as completely honorable and Federals as deserving of the punishment received. By combining and expanding upon previous Confederate defenses, the two biographers, with Forrest's blessing, set the pattern for most subsequent Southern writings on Fort Pillow. After losing the war, former Confederates gradually gained cultural as well as political dominance in the South on a platform of unified white supremacy. The "Lost Cause" version of the war became a central part of Southern identity. Forrest, who died in 1877, became a popular folk hero as a skillful trickster on behalf of the Confederate underdogs.[19]

Confederate memoirs often followed the lead of Jordan and Pryor but sometimes modified the story in ways that tried to strengthen the defense's case. At least nine participants in the attack published personal accounts between 1879 and 1925. Five brought up the issue of the Bradford Battalion's depredations and insults, although one (James R. Chalmers) admitted that he did not know the truth about the alleged abuses of civilians. James Dinkins, at the late date of 1897, made the first allegation that black troops participated in Federal depredations and even in raping white women. The latter claim, which reappeared in later works, most likely arose from the rape scare that accompanied the South's transition to segregation and black disfranchisement. Nothing in the black units' records indicates notable disciplinary problems. Four participants describe much drunkenness among Federals, but only Richard Hancock specifically stated that he saw liquor in the fort. Starting with his memoir, beer disappeared from the pro-Confederate narrative in favor of a more potent intoxicant, whiskey. Six accounts emphasized desperate resistance by Federals. Charles W. Anderson mentioned no individual efforts to surrender, but stressed Bradford's rejection of the surrender request and Forrest's final order to "fight everything '*blue*' between wind and water until yonder flag comes down."[20]

Chalmers, a lawyer and congressman after the war, denied any personal wrongdoing. Unlike what Northern newspapers reported him as saying on April 13, 1864, he declared in 1879 that the incident "for political purposes, has been, by false testimony, and I believe willful perjury, represented as a bloody massacre." Yet, he undermined his credibility by calling Fitch's letter to him "a complete vindication of the Confederates."[21]

Gustave A. Hanson in 1887 created a spurious story, repeated by Thomas F. Berry in 1914, that the garrison officially surrendered in order to fool the Confederates and then resumed firing when the Confederates stopped. Dinkins inaccurately held that many Federals died from falling down the bluff as they fled attackers who had fought all the way into the fort's trench before the truce. A few other obvious factual errors or memory lapses appeared in the several accounts written years after the event.[22]

A few memoirists openly made admissions. John W. Carroll described violating the truce by leading some men into the fort's ditch to gain an advantage during the subsequent charge. Hancock admitted that some Federals tried to surrender. Berry allowed that a massacre occurred, but he presented most details incorrectly. Thomas D. Duncan asserted that some unnecessary killing took place but tried to excuse it: "Aside from the outcropping of natural race prejudice, which is dangerous enough under normal peaceful conditions of life and which had been blown to its fiercest form by the breath of war, there was nothing brutal or savage." Still, most of the Confederate recollections displayed a strong defensive tone. Commenting on Fort Pillow, a veteran of Forrest's forces not there wrote that "our own (Southern [men]) make to[o] many apologies. It needs none."[23]

Late in the century and early in the segregation era, John Allen Wyeth, another Confederate veteran not at Fort Pillow, published a Forrest biography so popular that it would go through multiple reprintings. For the most part Wyeth's book repeated the arguments of Jordan and Pryor. He estimated Federal deaths at 40 percent, lower than Jordan and Pryor had allowed, and introduced the contention that a lack of Federal retaliation after the incident proved Confederate innocence. Probably because the new argument overlooked Lincoln's compassionate personality, only one subsequent biography of Forrest reused it. Wyeth's main contribution to the debate was his collection in 1898 of sworn affidavits from a group of Confederate participants. He intended them to counter the "irreparable damage to the cause of the South" done by the sworn testimony of the congressional report.[24]

Wyeth quoted thirteen witnesses' testimony, briefly summarized portions of five, and listed thirty-eight others whom he contended gave similar evidence. Recurrent topics in responses suggest that he sent out a questionnaire asking for comments on particular points: first, that no massacre or atrocities occurred; second, that the garrison members never surrendered but either kept fighting or sought escape; third, that the respondent saw whiskey in the fort; and fourth, that the Federals acted drunk. Wyeth reported that all his deponents swore agreement on the first two points and the great majority concurred on the last two.[25]

The fate of the original affidavits is unknown, and Wyeth's reading of them raises questions. For example, he asserted that "All but two of these witnesses [J. K. Dodd and Joseph Smith] swear that they saw the whiskey which had been freely distributed to the troops within the works," but Charles Anderson's affidavit, the only one given in full, does not specifically say so. Five of the quoted veterans do make that statement, and four claim the Federals were drunk. Two men, according to Wyeth's summaries, remembered filling their canteens with Federal whiskey in the fort, but a semantic issue about the "fort" clouds the matter. The traders' warehouses, where Confederates unquestionably found a large amount of liquor, sat in the town downhill from the inner fort but within the larger fort.[26] Bitter debates can create temptations to mislead with true, but incomplete, statements.

Wyeth reported that the affidavits unanimously denied the occurrence of a massacre. Yet, Wyeth's quoted sources mostly said that Confederates shot no one after the Union flag's lowering (Chalmers's testimony granted that he arrested one Confederate who continued shooting afterward). "Black" Bob McCulloch's assertion that "Not a gun was fired . . . after the surrender was made" means little if it refers to a point at which all Federal survivors had *successfully* surrendered. Except for W. C. Wert's and William J. Shaw's mentions of individuals' attempts to surrender prior to the Union flag's lowering, all the quoted testimony could fit with a rationalization that the lack of a formal surrender by the garrison justified Confederates in continuing to kill until ordered to stop. Shaw's affidavit specifically reported a Confederate who refused to accept a Federal's surrender during the period of shooting. Such actions offer an alternative explanation for Barteau's assertion that "Some even, who had thrown down their arms, took them up again and continued firing." A very strong indication that rationalization affected the affidavits appeared in the case of Tyree H. Bell, who swore to Wyeth that no massacre took place. A few years later, just before his death, he wrote in an unpublished autobiography that "There was promiscuous shooting for some time at different places, whenever they saw a negro or white man running. This was contrary to the commands of the commanding officer." [27] Taken long after the event in a context of defensiveness, unavailable today except for the quoted material in the book, and questionably interpreted, Wyeth's affidavits are of very limited usefulness.

· Wyeth, like Jordan and Pryor, felt called upon to justify the "Lost Cause," honor Confederates, and criticize their opponents. Wyeth assumed that the Federal side acted immorally more often during the war. Believing in white supremacy, he stated that "White men, [were] more intelligent than their colored comrades." Wyeth speculated that when a foolish Bradford distributed liquor during the truce, black troops did most of the indulging because masters had tried to prohibit drinking in slavery. Conversely, the author portrayed Forrest as a leader with a nearly perfect character. He also implied that Confederate troops, exemplified by the mostly churchgoing deponents, were on the whole too religious to do wrong. The book urged Northerners to give respectful consideration to Southern thinking about the war.[28]

In 1903, following Wyeth's assertive defensiveness, the United Confederate Veterans Historical Committee, chaired by Stephen D. Lee, Forrest's former superior, publicly condemned a Northern author for describing Forrest and his men as barbarous during the incident. Like Wyeth, the members wanted Northerners to pay more attention to the Southern version of the war. The movement for sectional reconciliation at that time tried to reduce partisan Northern writing on the war. The popular "Great Commanders Series," published by D. Appleton and Company in New York City, included a 1902 biography of Forrest written by a Confederate veteran, James H. Mathes, who endorsed his predecessors' interpretations of the 1864 incident.[29]

James Ford Rhodes started a trend among Northern writers to agree with Southerners on racial inequality but to uphold the moral justice of emancipation. He gave attention to Wyeth's arguments but did not accept them. Estimating a distinct disparity between the death tolls of the blacks and the whites in the garrison, he judged that racial prejudice among Forrest's men caused a spontaneous massacre for which Forrest was innocent.[30]

During Rhodes's life, graduate training in history emerged. Simultaneously, the sectional reconciliation movement and western civilization increasingly emphasized racial hierarchy and minimized African Americans' role in public memory of the Civil War. Early professional historians from Confederate backgrounds generally ignored controversial topics, such as Fort Pillow. Those with Northern or unionist parentage presented the massacre briefly and in neutral language. The subject no longer garnered one or two pages in books on the Civil War.[31]

Southern society experienced the high point of the "Lost Cause" movement after the turn of the century. One commander-in-chief of the United Confederate Veterans received a gavel carved from an oak at Fort Pillow and inscribed with "General Forrest chased the niggers and Yankees on a day of glorious vengeance." The presenter explained that the oak symbolized the emotional strength of Confederates as well as the authoritative establishment of white supremacy in the South after the war.[32]

The first decade of the twentieth century was the most active time for Southern communities to commemorate the Confederacy with monuments, generally in prominent municipal locations. Memphis erected an equestrian statue of Forrest in a city park. A group of Ripley men undertook the strenuous task of moving a large siege gun from Fort Pillow's bluff defenses to a monument near the Lauderdale County courthouse to honor the military strength of the fort and the Confederacy. They acted with opportune timing, for in 1908 thirty acres of the bluff around the southern end of the fort caved into the Mississippi when a current shift and low water weakened the bank. Several old cannons disappeared as a result. If the river landing and its stores still existed, the landslide shut them down by moving the channel southward.[33]

By 1931, farmers owned the fort's site and cultivated small plots on the more level ground. A cotton patch filled the inner fort. Theodore A. Mills, a visitor, found the earthworks "in a splendid state of preservation." Since gravel roads now facilitated tourist trips to the fort by car, several local leaders advocated the establishment of a state park there. R. M. Pritchard, a major booster of the site and a banker who lived nearby, scoured the fort for artifacts, especially after heavy rains. He also obtained a few relevant documents and firsthand accounts. Still, hampered by the Great Depression, the effort to create a park did not succeed.[34]

In the 1930s the Fort Pillow debate seemed an irrelevant reminder of past sectional squabbles to many. The passage of time and the passing away of most veterans led to more dispassionate writing. James G. Randall, the leading Civil War specialist among a new generation of professional historians, concluded that contradictory evidence prevented a determination of what actually happened at Fort Pillow. For forty years this became a common refrain among scholars. African American historians such as W. E. B. Du Bois, John Hope Franklin, and Benjamin Quarles dissented and insisted that the congressional report contained a core of truth.[35] In a study of the Committee on the Conduct of the War, T. Harry Williams, a Northern white, also concluded that a massacre occurred but criticized the committee's report for exaggerations. On the opposite side, E. Merton Coulter firmly rejected the occurrence of a massacre when he wrote on the Civil War for a multivolume history of the South by white historians from the region.[36]

Nonprofessional historians who wrote Forrest biographies continued to use the Jordan and Pryor arguments against the massacre interpretation, but with some qualifications. Eric W. Sheppard suggested that, despite Forrest's efforts to control his men, they engaged in some unnecessary killing. But Sheppard partially excused him on the ground of the battlefield's many demands upon a commander. Andrew N. Lytle did not criticize Forrest at all but granted that some private vengeance took place even after Forrest ordered the shooting to stop. As a member of the Southern Agrarian Movement of writers, Lytle praised Forrest as a rough-hewn and bold common man, a product of rural Mississippi. This increasingly popular image of the general emphasized his rise from poverty, untrained genius for warfare, and aptitude for leadership. Sometimes it also included his racial prejudices, which Lytle left out. Both Lytle and Sheppard estimated that over 50 percent of the Federals died, a notable increase over previous writers' calculations and probably a little high. Robert S. Henry's biography returned to Wyeth's lower death toll estimate of 40 percent. As the first writer to quote the letter written by Confederate sergeant Achilles V. Clark on the occurrence of a massacre, Henry also conceded that some Federals died trying to surrender.[37]

However, John L. Jordan, a retired army colonel, sought to revive a purer pro-Confederate interpretation in 1947. Stirred by a controversy over the army's consideration of naming a training camp for Forrest during World War II, he published an article arguing for a 31 percent death rate, the lowest estimate ever made. Convinced that too few Federals died for a massacre to have occurred, he judged the massacre interpretation a "grave injustice . . . done General Forrest and the Southern Confederacy." He asserted that any Southerner who criticized the Confederates' role in the incident "denounced his ancestors." No writing since Wyeth's had supported the "Lost Cause" so fervently. Like all previous casualty estimates, Jordan's built on sketchy and misleading bits of information in published records.[38]

After World War II, the civil rights movement slowly instituted a profound change in American race relations. By emphasizing widely shared Judeo-Christian morals and American political ideals, the movement not only fostered more assertiveness by African Americans but also slowly induced more self-examination and tolerance among whites. Government, the mass media, and academia gradually came to take prominent roles in endorsing reform of race relations. In scholarly discussion of Fort Pillow, blanket generalizations about blacks' low intelligence, disposition to lie, and attraction to liquor disappeared. Within this new context, Dudley T. Cornish's 1955 work on black regiments reiterated the view of Fort Pillow as a racist massacre. Since pro-Confederate writers had long rejected the congressional report as propaganda, Cornish tried to strengthen his case by treating the more moderate army report as the key evidence.[39]

In 1958 a young historian, who once had accepted the pro-Confederate interpretation, reexamined the available evidence. Albert Castel observed much consistency among Federal witnesses on the occurrence of a massacre but found fatal contradictions in Confederate reports and memoirs regarding the length of time that shooting occurred after the final charge, whether Federals conducted an orderly retreat or fled in drunken disorder, and whether the shooting stopped because of Confederate officers' actions or the Federals' ceasing of resistance. He concluded that Confederates had sought to evade admitting the massacre. The likelihood of a higher death toll for blacks convinced him, like Rhodes, that racial antagonism primarily motivated the unrestrained killing. Castel held that both sides had distorted the truth, for the congressional committee had included additional charges without proving them. Although Castel's seminal article built a strong case, most historians at that time ignored it and continued to uphold Randall's position of uncertainty.[40]

A few years after Castel's article came the Civil War centennial, which greatly increased public interest in the war and inspired a wave of new studies. Probably because of its minor military significance and controversial nature, which the commemoration avoided, Fort Pillow did not attract special attention then. Around the time of the centennial, though, the Southerner Perry Lentz worked on *The Falling Hills,* a long and vivid novel about the Fort Pillow incident. It followed the pro-Confederate interpretation, except for portraying Forrest's men as violating the truce and killing some surrendering soldiers. Lentz depicted both black troops and white unionists very negatively. In fact, the dark work, printed in the shadows of the Cold War and the Vietnam War, had but few admirable characters, all minor ones.[41]

A somewhat different story appeared in James Sherburne's 1972 novel, *The Way to Fort Pillow,* which climaxed with the massacre. Showing the power the pro-Confederate interpretation had gained through a century of repetition, this Northern writer kept liquor present in the inner fort and had the Federals engaging in desperate resistance. Still, he avoided stereotypes and presented black troops sympathetically in the book, which had as a theme the difficulty of living by moral principles. The main character, a white abolitionist, seemed much like a civil rights activist, and an intriguing minor character resembled the black militants prominent at the time Sherburne wrote.[42]

In the wake of the Civil War centennial, a movement reappeared for a state park at Fort Pillow. By then most of the site had returned to a wilderness condition, although that had not stopped relic-seekers from visiting and damaging it. A fishing camp operated on Cold Creek Chute Lake, a water body created by the 1908 landslide. Farmers did a little cultivating and logging on the fort grounds; one landowner had covered the Fulton Road gate with a dam and pond. No one now knew where most of the earthworks lay within the thick forest. In 1971 the state acquired 1,628 acres, and the first park superintendent explored the area on horseback. Development of the site as both a historic and a recreational area followed.[43]

As the state began to develop the park, most general studies of the Civil War finally adopted Castel's interpretation of Fort Pillow. This viewpoint received support from the publication between 1973 and 1985 of key documents written by Charley Robinson, Achilles V. Clark, "Marion," and Dr. Charles Fitch. At the same time the rapid growth of the prosperous

Sun Belt economy made the South more cosmopolitan and, along with the influence of the civil rights movement, further reduced but did not eliminate "Lost Cause" thinking. Still, a U.S. government official, influenced either by Northern sectionalism or controversies over the recent Vietnam War, offended some of those living near the fort by asserting, "Fort Pillow must stand always as a shameful reminder of how close we are to . . . barbarism," when he formally designated Fort Pillow a National Historic Landmark. The fact that local popular belief ran at odds with the professional consensus created a challenge for park officials.[44]

In the late 1970s, the state decided to rebuild the inner fort with slight modifications for durability. Dr. Robert C. Mainfort Jr., from the Tennessee Division of Archaeology, did extensive research to clarify the design of the inner fort. The contractor, though, incorrectly placed one section of the restoration. Mainfort's digs at the site produced some military and civilian artifacts for a small museum.[45] The museum's colorful, attractive displays covered the fort's story from construction through its capture by Forrest. The exhibit on the massacre controversy followed Randall's neutral stand, but a short slide program utilized the recently published documents to support the massacre interpretation.

The slide show quickly offended believers in the pro-Confederate interpretation. Feelings may have run higher then, due to a statewide African American protest against memorialization of Forrest and the movement's call for the removal of Forrest's statue from a Memphis city park. Not surprisingly, some participants in the controversy blamed him for the Fort Pillow massacre. That campaign encountered a countervailing trend toward increased popularity for the general among some whites. After sharply worded complaints from his devotees and alleged mechanical problems, the Fort Pillow museum suspended the slide show.[46]

The reviving controversy over Fort Pillow motivated Lonnie E. Maness, a local college professor, to write in 1982 the first defense of the pro-Confederate interpretation since John L. Jordan's 1947 article. Besides agreeing with Jordan's claim that too few Federals died to rate the incident as a massacre, Maness accepted without question the arguments of Jordan, Pryor, and Wyeth. He judged accounts by Sergeant Clark, Dr. Fitch, and "Marion," as untrustworthy. However, few Ph.D. historians have questioned in print the professional consensus on Fort Pillow.[47]

In the same year, Joyce Hansen, an African American writer, published a vivid children's novel about a runaway slave who ended up at the fort. She drew her readers into empathy with the black troops and fit the massacre into the larger context of racist abuses by whites. While the story included humane whites, Hansen emphasized the need of blacks not to depend on them but to work together assertively for the race's welfare.[48]

A few years later, Gregory J. Macaluso, a civil engineer and Civil War buff, published a book implying that a justifiable massacre occurred. Macaluso discovered that General Hurlbut had deliberately disobeyed orders in reopening the fort in 1864. The study asserted without citing concrete proof that the fort protected illegal activities, mostly unlicensed dealings in cotton and trade goods. Confederates, the author believed, had many substantial grudges against these Federals, especially over property confiscation, emancipation, and harboring of deserters.[49] Despite its limitations, the work raised a new and noteworthy point about Hurlbut.

In the mid-1980s, the state produced a videotape for the Fort Pillow museum on the 1864 incident. Essentially based on the earlier slide show, it added more qualified phrasing while still demonstrating why professional historians accept the massacre interpretation. It has proven to provoke less controversy than the slide show. Around this time two exhibits dominated the museum lobby outside of the display room. Possibly in an effort to reach two conflicting constituencies with special interest in the park, each highlighted a heroic aspect of one side of the April 12 battle. One praised Forrest's military talents, while the other lauded the contributions of African American troops to the Federal war effort.[50]

Several films near the end of the twentieth century fostered public empathy with black Civil War soldiers. The commercially successful movie *Glory* delved deeply into the trials and accomplishments of the 54th Massachusetts Infantry, an African American regiment. Ken Burns's extremely popular *The Civil War* documentary series on public television emphasized the war's tragic nature, as well as its limited contributions to racial justice. However, the series mentioned the massacre only in passing, and *Glory* dealt with earlier events in a different theater of the war.[51]

Recent studies have elaborated upon the massacre interpretation. One essay utilized a variety of military records not previously consulted to present a detailed statistical analysis of Federal casualties. Brian S. Wills wrote the first biography of Forrest to accept the massacre interpretation of Fort Pillow, while recognizing the uncertainty surrounding his role.[52]

However, Richard Fuchs, the lawyer who wrote a book on the massacre, judged Forrest guilty of exaggerating the danger from the steamers as an excuse for strengthening his position during the truce, subtly encouraging a massacre by implying during negotiations that such an outcome would follow a refusal to surrender, and choosing not to control his troops for a time once the slaughter began.[53] While not implausible, this thesis runs beyond the existing evidence. Consequently, it remains a minority one on the opposite end of the spectrum from Maness's pro-Confederate view.

After over 140 years, interpretations of the Fort Pillow incident still have some recognizable connections with the two views left after the Civil War. Placed on the defensive by the congressional report, ex-Confederates advanced their version more aggressively than their Northern critics. As sectional conflict decreased in the early twentieth century, the debate stagnated until the 1950s, when the civil rights movement revitalized and reshaped it by undermining common stereotypes. The pro-Confederate interpretation's strength, despite being magnified by frequent repetition, eventually declined. Even when Maness reused Jordan and Pryor's arguments, he left out their implicit racism. At the other extreme, Fuch's negative view of Forrest's cavalry did not revive the claim of Southern barbarism. The new paradigm in social attitudes and the fuller use of available evidence has favored a massacre interpretation.

Earlier events at the site set the massacre's context and, while not having major military significance, typified major trends in the Civil War. Participants mostly entered the war as amateur soldiers. Gideon Pillow and William F. Bradford illustrate the mistakes that could result. Franklin Moore and Nathan B. Forrest, in contrast, show how experience could transform talented novices into highly effective veterans. The letters, diaries, and memoirs of Federals and Confederates serving in the area demonstrate the many hardships faced by the common soldiers. The social conflicts aroused by the war entangled these troops. African Americans and unionists asserted themselves against repression by Confederates but received limited Federal help and trust. Meanwhile, Union occupation drove secessionist resistance underground, and Confederate aid could come only sporadically.

As the war grew longer and more frustrating, the two sides bent the traditional rules of American warfare. Both armies appropriated private property. Federals attacked slavery, and some secessionists adopted guerrilla tactics. In the Fort Pillow incident, many of Forrest's men treated unionist and black Federals as so unacceptable that they could be massacred. Debate over the memory of this incident formed a part of sectional and racial conflicts for many years after the war, but the reinterpretation of the event during the last thirty years offers some hope that society can move beyond past intolerance.

Appendix A

TABLES

Table 1.
Confederate Garrison's Commanders

Colonel Patrick Cleburne *(June 6–July ?, 1861)*
Colonel Riley P. Neely *(July 18–August ?, 1861)*
Lieutenant Colonel Otho F. Strahe *(August ?–17, 1861)*
Colonel James Knox Walker *(August 17–September ?, 1861)*
Colonel James C. Tappan *(September ?–30, 1861)*
Lieutenant Colonel Mark S. Miller *(September 30–October 20, November ?–19, 1861)*
Colonel Jabez M. Smith *(October 20–November ?, 1861)*
Colonel Lucius March Walker *(November 19, 1861–February 26, 1862)*
Captain Montgomery Lynch *(February 26–March 8, 1862)*
Brigadier General Jones M. Withers *(March 8–14, 1862)*
Major Lawrence W. O'Bannon *(March 14–17, 1862)*
Colonel Alsey H. Bradford *(March 17–18, 1862)*
Brigadier General John P. McCown *(March 18–19, 1862)*
Brigadier General Alexander P. Stewart *(March 19–26, 1862)*
Brigadier General John B. Villepigue *(March 26–June 4, 1862)*

Sources: John L. T. Snead to Gideon Pillow, June 7, 1861, Gratz Collection, Historical Society of Pennsylvania, Philadelphia, Pa.; J. K. Walker to L. Polk, September 8, 1861, and J. M. Smith to Leonidas Polk, November 19, 1861, Register of LR by Gen. Leonidas Polk's Corps of the Army of Tennessee, RG 109, NA; Tennessee, *Tennesseans in the Civil War: A Military History of Confederate and Union Units,* 2 vols. (Nashville: Tennessee Civil War Centennial Commission, 1964–1965), 1:174, 183, 240, 262; James T. Poe, *The Raving Foe,* ed. J. C. Poe (Eastland, Tex.: Longhorn Press, 1967), 7–15; *Memphis Appeal,* March 9, 1862; P. G. T. Beauregard to Montgomery Lynch, March 7, 1862, Jones Withers to P. G. T. Beauregard, March 14, 1861, and Thomas Jordan to L. W. O'Bannon, March 17, 1862, P. G. T. Beauregard Papers, Library of Congress; Alfred Roman, *The Military Operations of General Beauregard,* 2 vols. (New York: Harper and Brothers, 1884), 1:559–560; J. C. Tappan to L. Polk, September 30, 1861, and John B. Villepigue to L. Polk, March 26, 1862, Gen. Leonidas Polk Papers, RG 109, NA.

Table 2.

Confederate Garrison's Size

September 1861	945 men
October 31, 1861	787 men
November 30, 1861	896 men
January 31, 1862	1,064 men
March 31, 1862	3,128 men
April 30, 1862	3,607 men
May 30, 1862	2,000 men (estimated)

Sources: OR, 3:712, 730, 7:727, 853, 10 (pt. 2):382, 476; John Villepigue to Daniel Ruggles, June 1, 1862, Daniel Ruggles Papers, Duke University Library, Durham, N.C.

Table 3.

Units in the Confederate Garrison

15th Arkansas Infantry (June 6–July 1861)

Clarkson's Arkansas Light Artillery Company (June 6–July 1861)

Flynn's Sappers and Miners Company (July–December 1861)

13th Tennessee Infantry (July 10–28, 1861)

4th Tennessee Infantry (July 18–September 5, 1861)

Stewart's Tennessee Heavy Artillery Battalion (Summer 1861)

Johnston's Tennessee Heavy Artillery Company (August 1861)

Scott's Tennessee Light Artillery Company (Summer 1861; March–April 1862)

2nd Tennessee Infantry (August 17–October 24, 1861)

39th Tennessee Infantry [also called 1st Mississippi-Alabama-Tennessee Infantry]
    (August 18–September 1861; December 1861–February 26, 1862)

13th Arkansas Infantry (?–September 30, 1861)

11th Arkansas Infantry (September 28–November 20, 1861)

1st Tennessee Heavy Artillery (December 1861; May 10–June 2, 1862)

Gallimard's Sappers and Miners Company (October 1861, March 14–April 1862)

40th Tennessee Infantry (November 19, 1861–February 26, 1862)

4th Confederate Infantry (December 17, 1861–February 26, 1862)

1st Confederate Infantry Battalion (January 29–June 3, 1862)

2nd Alabama Infantry (February 28–April 1862)

21st Alabama Infantry (March 8–14, 1862)

1st Alabama Infantry (March 9–?, 1862)

22nd Alabama Infantry (March 11–15, 1862)

31st Tennessee Infantry (March 17–April 7, 1862)

12th Louisiana Infantry (March 17–June 3, 1862)
21st Louisiana Infantry (March 17–June 3, 1862)
Stewart's Artillery Battalion (March 17–?, 1862)
Bowman Parson's Missouri Light Infantry (April–June 1862)
1st Missouri Infantry Battalion (April–June 1862)
6th Missouri Infantry Battalion (April–June 1862)
22nd Arkansas Infantry (April 13–26, 1862)

Sources: John L. T. Snead to Gideon Pillow, June 7, 1861, Gratz Collection; *Memphis Avalanche,* June 17, 1861, July 16, 1862; J. H. Atkinson, ed., "A Civil War Letter of Captain Elliot Fletcher, Jr." *Arkansas Historical Quarterly* 22 (spring 1963): 53; C. Fay CSR (Tennessee Sappers and Miners), RG 109, NA; J. C. Tappan to Leonidas Polk, September 30, 1861, L. M. Walker to Leonidas Polk, December 14, 1861, Gen. Leonidas Polk Papers, RG 109, NA; *OR,* 7:825–826, 10 (pt. 2):382, 396; James C. Edenton Diary, July 10, 28, 1861, TSLA; Tennessee, *Tennesseans in the Civil War: A Military History of Confederate and Union Units,* 2 vols. (Nashville: Tennessee Civil War Centennial Commission, 1964–1965), 1:133, 149, 174, 183, 240, 259, 262; James T. Poe, *The Raving Foe,* ed. J. C. Poe (Eastland, Tex.: Longhorn Press, 1967), 12–15; *ORS,* 1:228, 2:641, 24:252, 38:366–367, 391, 550, 66:337–338, 73:459, 476; Robert Partin, "A Confederate Sergeant's Report to His Wife during the Bombardment of Fort Pillow," *Tennessee Historical Quarterly* 15 (September 1956): 245–249; Jones Withers to P. G. T. Beauregard, March 14, 1862, Beauregard Papers; Charles Stewart to Julia Stewart, March 13, 15, 1862, Stewart Papers, Alabama Department of Archives and History, Montgomery, Ala.; Arthur W. Bergeron Jr., *Guide to Louisiana Confederate Military Units, 1861–1865* (Baton Rouge: Louisiana State Univ. Press, 1989), 101, 125; Mark Lyons to Amelia Horsler, March 14, 31, June 7, 1862, Lyons Papers, Alabama Department of Archives and History. Given the fragmentary state of the records, the Confederate garrison may have contained other units.

Table 4.

Units in the Federal Garrison

52nd Indiana Infantry (September 9, 1862–January 21, 1864)
2nd Illinois Cavalry, Co. D (December 11, 1862–June 9, 1863)
32nd Iowa Infantry, Cos. B, C, H, I, J, and K (December 29, 1862–June 19, 1863)
2nd Illinois Cavalry, Cos. C, D, L, and M (July–August 1863)
2nd Illinois Cavalry, Co. B (July 1863–January 21, 1864)
178th New York Infantry (December 21, 1863–January 21, 1864)
Bradford's 13th Tennessee Cavalry Battalion (February 8–April 12, 1864)
2nd United States Colored Light Artillery, detachment from Battery D
   (February 21–April 12, 1864)
6th United States Colored Heavy Artillery, 1st Battalion (March 29–April 12, 1864)

Sources: OR, 17 (pt. 2):205, 517; E. H. Wolfe to John Hough, December 22, 1863, and E. H. Wolfe, S.O. 19, January 21, 1864, 52nd Indiana Infantry Records, RG 94, NA; *ORS,* 7:377, 389, 424, 429, 20:765, 47:196; Post Returns for Fort Pillow, February 9, 1864, Microcopy 617, NA.

Table 5.

Federal Garrison's Commanders

Major William T. Strickland (September 9–December 9, 1862)

Colonel Edward H. Wolfe (December 9, 1862–January 21, 1864)

Major William F. Bradford (February 8–March 29, 1864)

Major Lionel F. Booth (March 29–April 12, 1864)

Major William F. Bradford (April 12, 1864)

Sources: OR, 17 (pt. 2):205; W. T. Strickland to C. W. Lyman, October 2, 1862, Fort Pillow Papers, University of Memphis Library, Memphis, Tenn.; Post Return from Fort Pillow, March 1863, Microcopy 617, NA; E. H. Wolfe, S.O. 19, January 21, 1864, 52nd Indiana Infantry Records, RG 94, NA; Tennessee, *Report of the Adjutant General of the State of Tennessee of the Military Forces of the State from 1861 to 1866* (Nashville: S. C. Mercer, 1866), 646; *New Era* Log, March 29, 1864, RG 24, NA.

Table 6.

Federal Garrison's Size

November 30, 1862	617 men
January 31, 1863	1,278 men
March 31, 1863	1,171 men
May 31, 1863	1,060 men
June 30, 1863	544 men
August 31, 1863	858 men
September 30, 1863	634 men
November 30, 1863	637 men
January 20, 1864	1,473 men
February 29, 1864	320 men
March 31, 1864	557 men

Sources: OR, 17 (pt. 2):513; Post Returns for Fort Pillow, January, March, May, June, August, September, November 1863, January, February 1864, Microcopy 617, NA; U.S. Congress, *Fort Pillow Massacre,* 38th Cong., 1st Sess., H. Doc. 65. (serial 1206), 98.

Table 7.

Impact of the Battle and Massacre on the Garrison

	Bradford Battalion	Detached Staff	6th U.S.C.H.A.	2nd U.S.C.L.A.	Total
Dead					
Killed/Presumed Dead	64–82	0	164	18	246–264
Died From Wounds	21	0	10	0	31
Subtotal	85–103	0	174	18	277–295
Survivors					
Wounded	30	1	25	5	61
Sick	8	0	0	0	8
Captured	154	3	44	12	213
Escaped	8	0	26	0	34
Subtotal	200	4	95	17	316
Total	285–303	4	269	35	593–611

COMPILING DATA FOR TABLE 7

Because the Confederates burnt all of the records at Fort Pillow, no Federal report contains a casualty count. Table 7 was derived from a number of records. Since last participating in a set of published calculations, I have learned of an easier way to track down relevant pension files and have double-checked the garrison's compiled service records. The improved results vary slightly from that previous work.[1]

Most earlier writers have relied on the fort's last monthly report, which tallied 557 men present on March 31, 1864. Other military records in the National Archives make it clear that the garrison had at least 593 present on April 12, as additional men had been recruited or had returned from other places. The head count rests primarily upon compiled service records of individuals in units assigned to the fort or on detached service there. Because the two black units retained records at their headquarters in Memphis, we know their detachments at the fort had 304 members on April 12. Personnel records and Forrest's prisoner list show that the post had four white staff members who did not belong to the three units in the garrison.[2] Bradford's Battalion, based at the fort, lost all its records. The use of its incomplete compiled service records, plus other sources, shows that it had at least 285 men in the battle. The role of eighteen additional men, presumably present before the battle, is unclear. They may be the "twenty" that the post surgeon reported as deserting during the night before the battle, or they may have been killed.[3] Eight volunteer civilian combatants and two deserters held under arrest (from other units) seemed inappropriate for inclusion.[4]

Once those present were identified, they needed to be sorted as survivors or casualties. Some individuals' compiled service records relied on a survivor's word to declare him dead, and others presumed a soldier dead for lack of further record (including Confederate prison rolls). Pension claims filed by a number of family members confirmed that some missing individuals still had not reappeared years later. The "Died From

Wounds" column includes only those listed as such in hospital records, regardless of how long life lingered. Those who died from illnesses, which may have been complications arising from wounds, were counted in "Survived Wounds." The "Escaped" category lists both those who came out of hiding after the incident and captives who got away from the Confederates soon after the battle. The former group simply reappeared in unit records after the incident without wounds or a parole.[5]

Notes

CSR	Compiled Service Record
G.O.	General Order
LR	Letters Received
LS	Letters Sent
NA	National Archives, Washington, D.C.
OR	U.S. War Department, *The War of the Rebellion: A Compilation of the Official Records of the Union and Confederate Armies,* 131 vols. (Washington, D.C.: GPO, 1880–1901). All citations are to Series 1, unless otherwise noted.
ORN	U.S. Navy Department, *Official Records of the Union and Confederate Navies in the War of the Rebellion,* 31 vols. (Washington, D.C.: GPO, 1894–1927). All citations are to Series 1.
ORS	Janet B. Hewitt et al., eds., *Supplement to the Official Records of the Union and Confederate Armies,* 100 vols. (Wilmington, N.C.: Broadfoot Press, 1994–2001). All citations are to Series 2, unless otherwise noted.
RG	National Archives Record Group
	RG 15–Records of the Veterans Administration
	RG 24–Naval Records
	RG 29–Census Bureau Records
	RG 45–Naval Records Collection of the Office of Naval Records and Library
	RG 92–Quartermaster General's Office Records
	RG 94–Adjutant General's Office Records
	RG 105–Records of the Bureau of Freedmen, Refugees, and Abandoned Lands
	RG 109–Confederate Records
	RG 123–Records of the Court of Claims
	RG 153–Records of the Office of the Judge Advocate General
	RG 217–Records of the Accounting Officers of the Department of the Treasury
	RG 233–Records of the House of Representatives
	RG 249–Records of the Office of the Commissary General of Prisoners
	RG 366–Records of Civil War Special Agencies of the Treasury Department
	RG 393–Records of the United States Army Continental Commands, 1821–1920
S.O.	Special Order
TSLA	Tennessee State Library and Archives, Nashville, Tenn.
U.S.C.H.A.	United States Colored Heavy Artillery
U.S.C.I.	United States Colored Infantry
U.S.C.L.A.	United States Colored Light Artillery

PREFACE

1. Sean Michael O'Brien, *In Bitterness and in Tears: Andrew Jackson's Destruction of the Creeks and Seminoles* (Westport, Conn.: Praeger, 2003), 149; Paul Foos, *A Short, Offhand, Killing Affair: Soldiers and Social Conflict during the Mexican-American War* (Chapel Hill: Univ. of North Carolina Press, 2002), 126; Robert M. Utley and Wilcomb E. Washburn, *Indian Wars,* 2nd ed. (New York: American Heritage, 1985), 222–225; Stephen E. Ambrose, *Citizen Soldiers* (New York: Simon and Schuster, 1997), 352–353; Gerald F. Linderman, *The World Within War: America's Combat Experience in World War II* (New York: Free Press, 1997), 121–137; James S. Olson and Randy Roberts, *My Lai: A Brief History with Documents* (Boston: Bedford Books, 1998), passim. See *New York Times,* November 13, 1999, A5, regarding an alleged massacre of Koreans at No Gun Ri in 1950.

2. On this matter, see Weymouth T. Jordan and Gerald W. Thomas, "Massacre at Plymouth: April 20, 1864," *North Carolina Historical Review* 72 (April 1995): 181.

CHAPTER ONE. THE FORT'S BEGINNINGS

1. Nathaniel C. Hughes Jr. and Roy P. Stonesifer Jr., *The Life and Wars of Gideon J. Pillow* (Chapel Hill: Univ. of North Carolina Press, 1993), 2, 39–42, 142–146, 157–160; William H. Russell, *My Diary North and South,* ed. Fletcher Pratt (New York: Harper and Row, 1965), 162; William G. Stevenson, *Thirteen Months in the Rebel Army* (New York: A. S. Barnes and Burr, 1862), 62.

2. *OR,* 52 (pt. 2):63, 69, 90; Hughes and Stonesifer, 160–172; Charles McCormick to Perceval Newman, June 2, 1861, Army of Tennessee Papers, TSLA.

3. Hughes and Stonesifer, chap. 6; Joseph T. Glatthaar, "The Common Soldier of the Civil War," in *New Perspectives on the Civil War: Myths and Realities of the National Conflict,* ed. John Y. Simon and Michael E. Stevens (Madison, Wisc.: Madison House, 1998), 120; James M. McPherson, *For Cause and Comrade: Why Men Fought in the Civil War* (New York: Oxford Univ. Press, 1997), viii.

4. Craig L. Symonds, *Stonewall of the West: Patrick Cleburne and the Civil War* (Lawrence: Univ. of Kansas Press, 1997), 21–24; *Memphis Appeal,* May 29, 1861; Gideon Pillow to ?, n.d., 1861, Goodman Papers, Memphis and Shelby County Public Library; John L. T. Snead to Gideon Pillow, June 7, 1861, Gratz Collection, Historical Society of Pennsylvania, Philadelphia, Pa.; J. G. Law, "Diary of a Confederate Soldier," *Southern Historical Society Papers,* 10 (September 1882): 381.

5. *Memphis Avalanche,* June 17, 1861; Lauderdale County Deed Register, vol. I, 72, TSLA; 1860 Census, Tennessee, Lauderdale County, 355, RG 29, NA; E. H. Wolfe to Henry Binmore, September 13, 1863, 52nd Indiana Infantry Letterbook, RG 92, NA; Richard Edwards, *St. Louis Directory* (St. Louis: Southern Pub. Co., 1860), 68; U.S. Department of the Interior, Census Office, *Eighth Census of the United States,* 4 vols. (Washington, D.C.: GPO, 1864), 1:42–43, 132–133, 3:109, 111, 451, 461, 463.

6. *OR,* 4:362, 368–369; Hughes and Stonesifer, 172–175. For Cleburne's later career, see Symonds, chapters 2–14.

7. Montgomery Lynch to Leonidas Polk, March 26, 1862, Montgomery Lynch CSR (Engineer Corps), RG 109, NA; *Memphis Appeal,* May 1, 1861, June 5, 1861.

8. Hughes and Stonesifer, 170; Stevenson, 56–58, 62; *Memphis Appeal,* June 5, July 18, 1861.

9. Leonidas Polk to James Rogers, August 24, 1861, Fort Pillow Papers, University of Memphis Library; John Cimprich, *Slavery's End in Tennessee, 1861–1865* (Tuscaloosa: Univ. of Alabama Press, 1985), 14, 16.

10. Cimprich, 13; Armstead L. Robinson, *Bitter Fruits of Bondage: The Demise of Slavery and the Collapse of the Confederacy, 1861–1865* (Charlottesville: Univ. of Virginia Press, 2005), 39, 42–47; Census Office, 1:238, 3:109–111; Lauderdale County Court Minutes, vol. D, 604–605, 615, TSLA.

11. Stevenson, 58–59; Gideon Pillow to Preston Smith, July 10, 1861, Goodman Papers; Hughes and Stonesifer, 171, 177; Mark M. Boatner III, *Encyclopedia of the American Revolution,* 2nd ed. (New York: Stackpole Books, 1994), 530.

12. Hughes and Stonesifer, 172–174, 188–195; *OR,* 4:420.

13. *OR,* 4:408, 52:69; Benjamin F. Cooling, *Forts Henry and Donelson: The Key to the Confederate Heartland* (Knoxville: Univ. of Tennessee Press, 1987), 48; Nathaniel C. Hughes Jr., *The Battle of Belmont: Grant Strikes South* (Chapel Hill: Univ. of North Carolina Press, 1991), 36–37.

14. Stevenson, 56; Joe Barbiere, *Scraps from the Prison Table at Camp Chase and Johnson's Island* (Doylestown, Pa.: W. W. H. Davis, 1868), 58; Anthony C. Rushing, *Ranks of Honor: A Regimental History of the 11th Arkansas Infantry Regiment and Poe's Cavalry Battalion C.S.A., 1861–1865* (Little Rock, Ark.: Eagle Press, 1990), 9; *OR,* 10 (pt. 2):309.

15. *Memphis Appeal,* November 13, 1861; J. M. Smith to L. Polk, November 3, 1861, J. M. Smith CSR (11th Arkansas Infantry), RG 109, NA; James Rogers to Leonidas Polk, October 23, 1861, Fort Pillow Papers; Lauderdale County Court Minutes, vol. E, 27, 69; Montgomery Lynch to Leonidas Polk, October 22, 1861, Gen. Leonidas Polk Papers, RG 109, NA; William W. Mobley to Hannah Wylie, September 8, 1861, William Wylie Papers, Duke University Library, Durham, N.C.

16. Cooling, *Forts Henry and Donelson,* 34–35; Hughes and Stonesifer, 164; Testimony, 34, Georgia M. Erwin File, Settled Cases of the Southern Claims Commission, RG 217, NA; Leonidas Polk to Jabez M. Smith, October 9, 1861, Gen. Leonidas Polk Papers, RG 109, NA; Barbiere, 58; James T. Poe, *The Raving Foe,* ed. J. C. Poe (Eastland, Tex.: Longhorn Press, 1967), 12–13.

17. Montgomery Lynch to Lewis De Russy, October 8, 1861, Montgomery Lynch CSR (Engineer Corps), RG 109, NA; Stevenson, 59–60.

18. Y. W. Goodwin to Thomas Jordan, March 16, 1862, Thomas Jordan Papers, Duke University Library, Durham, N.C.; Montgomery Lynch to Leonidas Polk, October 30, November 26, 1861, Montgomery Lynch CSR (Engineer Corps), RG 109, NA; John Scott, *Story of the Thirty-Second Iowa Infantry Volunteers* (Nevada, Iowa: Privately printed, 1896), 103; Robert C. Mainfort Jr., "A Folk Art Map of Fort Pillow," *West Tennessee Historical Society Papers* 40 (1986): 75.

19. *OR,* 7:728–729; *ORN,* 23:51; William W. Mobley to Hannah Wylie, September 8, 1861, Wylie Papers; David Winter to Leonidas Polk, November 12, 1861, David Winter CSR (Tennessee Sappers and Miners), RG 109, NA; Montgomery Lynch to Leonidas Polk, November 26, 1861, Gen. Leonidas Polk Papers, RG 109, NA; James Rogers to Leonidas Polk, October 23, 1861, Fort Pillow Papers. Several observers referred to very high numbers of slave

laborers at Fort Pillow, sometimes in direct contradiction to the hirers' records, which never mentioned more than fifteen hundred.

20. Lewis Williamson to Leonidas Polk, September 28, 1861, and James Rogers to Leonidas Polk, November 2, 1861, Fort Pillow Papers; John Houston Bills Diary, October 9, 1861, Southern Historical Collection, University of North Carolina, Chapel Hill, N.C.

21. Hughes and Stonesifer, 204–205; *OR,* 4:522, 7:728–729, 853; *Memphis Appeal,* November 10, 1861; L. M. Walker to Leonidas Polk, December 21, 23, 27, 1861, Gen. Leonidas Polk Papers, RG 109, NA.

22. William T. Avery to his wife, January 25, 1861, Gordon/Avery Families Papers, TSLA; Poe, 14–15; Mark Lyons to Amelia Horsler, March 14, 1862, Mark Lyons Papers, Alabama Division of Archives and History, Montgomery, Ala.; James I. Robertson Jr., *Soldiers Blue and Gray* (Columbia: Univ. of South Carolina Press, 1988), 48–51.

23. Larry J. Daniel, *Soldiering in the Army of the Tennessee: A Portrait of Life in a Confederate Army* (Chapel Hill: Univ. of North Carolina Press, 1991), 84; Cornelia Anderson Watkins Diary, October 30, 1861, transcript at Fort Pillow State Historic Area Museum, Henning, Tenn.

24. Daniel, 39; L. M. Walker to L. Polk, December 27, 1861, Gen. Leonidas Polk Papers, RG 109, NA; *OR,* 7:692; Royce Shingleton, ed., " 'With Loyalty and Honor as a Patriot:' Recollections of a Confederate Soldier," *Alabama Historical Quarterly* 33 (fall/winter 1971): 241.

25. Bell I. Wiley, *The Life of Johnny Reb: The Common Soldier of the Confederacy* (Baton Rouge: Louisiana State Univ. Press, 1943), 288; Poe, 10, 14; Alpheus Baker, "Island No. 10," *Southern Bivouac* 1 (October 1882): 56; Shingleton, 241; *OR,* 4:436, 512, 7:689.

26. Wiley, *Johnny Reb,* 20; Barbiere, 57–58; Rushing, 9–10; John L. Logan CSR (11th Arkansas Infantry), RG 109, NA; Junius N. Bragg, *Letters of a Confederate Surgeon, 1861–65,* ed. Helen B. Gaughan (Camden, Ark.: Privately printed, 1960), 17.

27. *OR,* 7:729, 853; L. Polk to James Rogers, December 16, 1861, and A. M. Rafter to James Rogers, December 17, 1861, February 2, 11, 1862, and Robert Turnbull to James Rogers, December ?, 1861, Fort Pillow Papers; John Q. Anderson, ed., *Brokenburn: The Journal of Kate Stone* (Baton Rouge: Louisiana State Univ. Press, 1995), 83.

28. Hughes and Stonesifer, 236–237, 246–247; Herman Hattaway and Archer Jones, *How the North Won: A Military History of the Civil War* (Urbana: Univ. of Illinois Press, 1983), 69–76, 147; Larry J. Daniel and Lynn Bock, *Island No. 10: Struggle for the Mississippi Valley* (Tuscaloosa: Univ. of Alabama Press, 1996), 21.

29. Daniel and Bock, 21–22; *ORS,* ser. 3, 2:172; *OR,* 7:920, 8:755, 757, 760, 762, 10 (pt. 2):300; Alfred Roman, *The Military Operations of General Beauregard,* 2 vols. (New York: Harper and Brothers, 1884), 1:555, 559; Thomas Jordan to W. R. Hunt, March 17, 26, 1862, P. G. T. Beauregard to J. T. Trezevant, March 26, 1862, P. G. T. Beauregard to John Adams, March 7, 15, 1862, P. G. T. Beauregard Papers. For the general's background, see T. Harry Williams, *P. G. T. Beauregard: Napoleon in Gray* (Baton Rouge: Louisiana State Univ. Press, 1955), chaps. 1–7. Later in his life Beauregard claimed to have viewed the Island No. 10 fortifications as merely a means to gain time for finalizing Fort Pillow's defenses, but the 1862 records read otherwise.

30. P. G. T. Beauregard to L. W. O'Bannon, March 15, 16, 1862, P. G. T. Beauregard to Montgomery Lynch, March 7, 8, 1862, and P. G. T. Beauregard to Jones Withers, March 11, 1862, Beauregard Papers; *OR,* 7:728–729, 10 (pt. 2):309; Charles Stewart to Julia Stewart, March 13, 15, 1862, Charles S. Stewart Papers, Alabama Division of Archives and History; Y. W. Goodwin to Thomas Jordan, March 16, 1862, Jordan Papers.

31. Daniel and Bock, 63; *OR,* 8:782; *Memphis Appeal,* March 23, 1862.

32. Jeremy Gilmer to Louisa Gilmer, March 29, 1862, Jeremy F. Gilmer Papers, Duke University Library, Durham, N.C.; Richard N. Current, ed., *Encyclopedia of the Confederacy,* 4 vols. (New York: Simon and Schuster, 1993), 2:686; George W. Cullum, *Biographical Register of the Officers and Graduates of the U.S. Military Academy,* 3rd ed., 3 vols. (Boston: Houghton Mifflin, 1891), 1:542; P. G. T. Beauregard to L. Polk, April 20, 1862, Beauregard Papers.

33. Braxton Bragg to Elissa Bragg, March 29, 1862, Braxton Bragg Papers, Library of Congress; Current, 4:1660–1661; John Villepigue to L. Polk, March 26, 1862, Gen. Leonidas Polk Papers, RG 109, NA.

34. *OR,* 10 (pt. 2):395–396; P. G. T. Beauregard to Jones Withers, March 10, 1862, P. G. T. Beauregard to A. P. Stewart, March 23, 1862, and P. G. T. Beauregard to John Villepigue, April 8, 1862, Beauregard Papers.

35. James M. McPherson, *Battle Cry of Freedom: The Civil War Era* (New York: Oxford Univ. Press, 1988), 413; P. G. T. Beauregard to John Villepigue, April 8, 1862, Beauregard Papers; Daniel and Bock, 137.

36. Roman, 1:564; Current, 2:868; Thomas J. Payne to Mary Payne, April 20, 1862, in "Thomas Joseph Payne, Captain (C.S.A.)," http://www.mindspring.com/~jogt/surnames/paynetj.htm, accessed 2003; Thomas Jordan to John Villepigue, April 10, 1862, P. G. T. Beauregard to John Adams, April 8, 1862, P. G. T. Beauregard to Thomas Hindman, April 17, 1862, Beauregard Papers; *OR,* 10 (pt. 2):396.

37. *ORN,* 22:839–841; C. W. Read, "Reminiscences of the Confederate States Navy," *Southern Historical Society Papers* 1 (May 1876): 337–339.

38. L. T. Delisdimier, "Cruise of the Steamer Price," in *The Confederate Soldier in the Civil War, 1861–1865,* ed. Benjamin LaBree (Louisville: Courier Journal Job-Printing·Co., 1895), 400–401; *OR,* 52 (pt. 1):38; Michael L. Gillespie, "The Novel Experiment: Cotton-Clads and Steamboatmen," *Civil War Times Illustrated* 22 (December 1983): 34–36; Read, 339.

39. Braxton Bragg to Elisa Bragg, March 20, 1862, Braxton Bragg Papers, Duke University Library, Durham, N.C.; James M. Williams, *From That Terrible Field: Civil War Letters,* ed. John K. Fulmer (Tuscaloosa: Univ. of Alabama Press, 1981), 45.

CHAPTER TWO. THE FEDERAL ATTACK

1. *ORN,* 22:626 (quoted), 768, 23:3–4; Spencer C. Tucker, *Andrew Foote: Civil War Admiral on Western Waters* (Annapolis, Md.: Naval Institute Press, 2000), 116–117, 155–156, 178–180.

2. Daniel and Bock, 16–18, 68; H. Allen Gosnell, *Guns on Western Waters: The Story of the River Gunboats in the Civil War* (Baton Rouge: Louisiana State Univ. Press, 1949), 16; Paul Silverstone, *Warships of the Civil War Navies* (Annapolis, Md.: Naval Institute Press, 1989), 155; Eliot Callender, "What a Boy Saw on the Mississippi," in *Military Essays and Recollections* (Chicago: Military Order of the Loyal Legion, Illinois Commandery, 1891), 1:59. See Tucker, chaps. 2–8, for Foote's background.

3. Daniel and Bock, 38; Edwin C. Bearss, *Hardluck Ironclad: The Sinking and Salvage of the Cairo,* 2nd ed. (Baton Rouge: Louisiana State Univ. Press, 1980), 50; *Logansport [Ind.] Journal,* April 26, 1862; *ORN,* 22:723 (quoted), 23:3, 675.

4. *Benton* Log, April 12, 1862, RG 24, NA; Bearss, 50; *ORN,* 23:280.

5. Delisdimier, 401; *Chicago Tribune,* April 17, 1862; *New York Herald,* April 26, 1862.

6. Augustus G. Sinks Memoir, 14, Indiana State Library, Indianapolis, Ind.; *New York Herald,* April 26, 1862; John D. Milligan, ed., *From the Fresh-Water Navy: 1861–64* (Annapolis, Md.: Naval Institute Press, 1970), 61; *Logansport [Ind.] Journal,* April 26, 1862.

7. *Benton* Log, April 13, 1862, RG 24, NA; *ORN,* 23:4–5; Milligan, ed., *Fresh-Water Navy,* 62; *OR,* 10 (pt. 2):107.

8. Ephraim A. Wilson, *Memoirs of the War* (Cleveland: W. M. Bayne Printing Company, 1893), 102; John S. Pickard Diary, April 14, 1862, Vigo County Public Library, Terre Haute, Ind.; Hugh Johnson to his wife, April 15, 1862, Hugh Johnson Papers, State Historical Society of Iowa, Iowa City, Iowa; Cloyd Bryner, *Bugle Echoes: The Story of Illinois 47th* (Springfield, Ill.: Phillips Bros., 1905), 39; *St. Louis Missouri Democrat,* April 18, 1862.

9. George R. Yost Diary, April 14–15, 1862, Illinois State Historical Library, Springfield, Ill.; Delisdimier, 401; *New York World,* April 25, 29, 1862; *ORN,* 23:675–676; *Boston Journal,* April 25, 1862; *Chicago Tribune,* April 19, 1862.

10. *ORN,* 22:316, 23:5 (quoted); *OR,* 10 (pt. 2):119–120; Daniel and Bock, 104–105, 120; Charles H. Davis, *Life of Charles Henry Davis, Rear Admiral, 1807–1877* (Boston: Houghton, Mifflin, 1899), 235.

11. Testimony, 7–8, 52, 79, Erwin File, Settled Cases of the Southern Claims Commission, RG 217, NA; Bernard Schermerhorn to Josie Schermerhorn, April 16, 29, 1862, Bernard Schermerhorn Papers, Indiana Historical Society, Indianapolis, Ind.; Bryner, 40; Wilson, *Memoirs,* 105.

12. Aden G. Cavins, *War Letters* (Evansville, Ind.: Rosenthal-Kuebbler Printing Co., 1907), 14; *Boston Journal,* April 23, 1862; Hugh Johnson to his wife, April 15, 1862, Hugh Johnson Papers; Testimony, 25–27, 49, 63, 87, Erwin File, Settled Cases of the Southern Claims Commission, RG 217, NA; John Q. Campbell, *The Union Must Stand,* ed. Mark Grimsly and Todd D. Miller (Knoxville: Univ. of Tennessee Press, 2000), 37; Mark Grimsley, *The Hard Hand of War: Union Military Policy toward Southern Civilians, 1861–1865* (New York: Cambridge Univ. Press, 1995), 8–17, 23.

13. Cavins, 14; *Boston Journal,* April 25, 1862; Hugh Johnson to his wife, April 15, 1862, Hugh Johnson Papers; Bernard Schermerhorn to Josie Schermerhorn, April 16, 1862, Schermerhorn Papers.

14. Mark Lyons to Amelia Horsler, April 15, 1862, Lyons Papers; Frank Moore, ed., *The Rebellion Record: A Diary of American Events,* 11 vols. (New York: D. Van Nostrand, 1861–1868), 5:166.

15. Roman, 1:365, 564; P. G. T. Beauregard to A. Rust, April 14, 1862, and P. G. T. Beauregard to Thomas Claiborne, April 14, 1862, Beauregard Papers; Barbiere, 209.

16. Thomas J. Payne to Mary Payne, April 20, 1862, in "Thomas Joseph Payne, Captain (C.S.A.)," http://www.mindspring.com/~jogt/surnames/paynetj.htm, accessed 2003; Delisdimier, 401; *Boston Journal,* April 25, 1862; *Benton* Log, April 16, 29, 1862; Absalom C. Grimes, "Diary," *Confederate Veteran* 22 (December 1914): 549.

17. *OR,* 10 (pt. 2):107–108, 113; *ORN,* 23:7.

18. Jay Slagle, *Ironclad Captain: Seth Ledyard Phelps and the U.S. Navy, 1841–1864* (Kent, Ohio: Kent State Univ. Press, 1996), 214; *ORN,* 23:8–12 (pp. 8 and 12 quoted), 62–63, 70, 76; James Mason Hoppin, *Life of Andrew Hull Foote* (New York: Harper and Brothers, 1874), 299.

19. *ORS,* ser. 3, 2:249; Roman, 1:565; *OR,* 10 (pt. 2):115; Watkins Diary, April 21, 1862;

P. G. T. Beauregard to W. H. Jackson, April 21, 1862, and Thomas Jordan to A. W. Water, April 23, 1862, Beauregard Papers; *Humboldt [Tenn.] Chronicle,* July 24, 1862.

20. Robert Partin, "A Confederate Sergeant's Report to His Wife during the Bombardment of Fort Pillow," *Tennessee Historical Quarterly* 15 (September 1956): 251, 248–250, 245–247; *Memphis Avalanche,* May 1, 1862.

21. Meriwether Jefferson "Jeff" Thompson, *Civil War Reminiscences of General M. Jeff Thompson,* ed. Donal J. Stanton et al. (Dayton, Ohio: Morningside Press, 1988), 159–160; Wiley, *Johnny Reb,* 79; Barbiere, 212; Delisdimier, 401; Mark Lyons to Amelia Horsler, May 10, 1862, Lyons Papers.

22. Descriptions of the final armament of the fort conflict. This study relies mostly on Captain Phelps's accounts in *ORN,* 23:51, and S. L. Phelps to A. H. Foote, June 17, 1862, Area File 5, RG 45, NA, with some consideration of reporters' versions in *New York Herald,* June 12, 1862; *Cincinnati Gazette,* June 11, 1862; *Cincinnati Commercial,* June 12, 1862.

23. J. Guthrie to C. B. Laselle, April 21, 1862, Charles B. Laselle Papers, Indiana State Library, Indianapolis, Ind.; *ORN,* 23:10, 68, 280, 397; George R. Yost Memoir, 8–9, Naval History Center, Washington, D.C.

24. *New York World,* April 25, 1862; *Cincinnati Gazette,* April 23, 1862; *New York Tribune,* June 6, 1862; *ORN,* 23:676–679, 279–280.

25. *Indianapolis Journal,* April 26, 1862; Sinks Memoir, 14; William E. McLean, *The Forty-Third Regiment of Indiana Volunteers* (Terre Haute, Ind.: C. W. Brown, 1902), 86–87; *Logansport [Ind.] Journal,* May 3, 1862; *ORN,* 23:72; *OR,* 10 (pt. 2):115; Graham Fitch to J. Pope, April 25, 1862, LR Register for Army of Mississippi, RG 393, NA.

26. *Logansport [Ind.] Journal,* May 3, 1862; Pickard Diary, April 18–27, 1862; *Logansport [Ind.] Democratic Pharos,* May 7, 21, 1862; *Benton* Log, April 21–May 7, 1862, RG 24, NA; Junius H. Browne, *Four Years in Secessia* (Chicago: George and C. W. Sherwood, 1865), 152.

27. Browne, 147–148; *St. Louis Missouri Democrat,* June 4, 1862; Yost Diary, May 15, 1862; *Cincinnati Commercial,* May 2, 1862; *Logansport [Ind.] Journal,* May 24, 1862.

28. *Logansport [Ind.] Democratic Pharos,* April 30, 1862; *Humboldt [Tenn.] Chronicle,* July 24, 1862; Watkins Diary, April 26, 1862; *Cincinnati Commercial,* April 28, 1862; McLean, 84.

29. Cimprich, 21–24, 27–29, 33–34; Barbiere, 211; *Chicago Tribune,* April 19, 1862; J. Guthrie to C. B. Lasselle, April 21, 1862, Lasselle Papers; *Cincinnati Gazette,* May 10, 1862.

30. Cimprich, 34–35; *Chicago Times,* April 30, 1862; Testimony, 4–6, Erwin File, Settled Cases of the Southern Claims Commission, RG 217, NA; *Logansport [Ind.] Journal,* May 17, 24, 1862; *Cincinnati Gazette,* April 29, 1862, May 7, 10, 1862; *St. Louis Missouri Republican,* May 1, 1862.

31. Slagle, 227.

32. *ORN,* 23:112–113; *St. Louis Missouri Republican,* June 3, 1862; *Chicago Times,* April 25, 1862; *Logansport [Ind.] Journal,* May 3, 1862; *Cincinnati Gazette,* May 7, 1862; Browne, 154.

33. *Cincinnati Gazette,* April 26, May 7, 1862; *Logansport [Ind.] Democratic Pharos,* May 21, 1862; *ORN,* 23:10–11; Hoppin, 308.

34. *Chicago Tribune,* April 19, 1862; *Cincinnati Gazette,* May 12, 1862.

35. Hoppin, 301, 303, 310–311 (quoted); *Logansport [Ind.] Journal,* May 10, 1862; G. N. Fitch to J. Pope, April 24, 1862, LR by Army of the Mississippi, RG 393, NA.

36. Thompson, *Reminiscences,* 152–153, 155; Jay Monaghan, *Swamp Fox of the Confederacy:*

The Life and Military Service of M. Jeff Thompson (Tuscaloosa, Ala.: Confederate Publishing Company, 1956), 10, 27, 38–39; Glatthaar, "Common Soldier," 127; *ORN,* 23:54.

37. Read, 340, 347–348; *OR,* 52 (pt. 1):38; P. G. T. Beauregard to Robert Pinkney, April 26, 1862, Beauregard Papers; U.S. Navy Department, Historical Division, *Civil War Naval Chronology* (Washington, D.C.: GPO, 1966), 6:269, 288.

38. *Chicago Times,* May 5, 1862; Yost Diary, April 28, 1862; Pickard Diary, April 28–29, May 3, 1862; *ORN,* 23:677; Hoppin, 310–311.

39. *Cincinnati Gazette,* May 7, 1862; *Cincinnati Times,* May 1, 6, 1862; Daniel and Bock, 91, 148; *ORN,* 23:12.

40. *Logansport [Ind.] Journal,* May 24, 1862; *Peoria Transcript,* May 15, 1862; Pickard Diary, May 2–7, 1862; *Logansport [Ind.] Democratic Pharos,* May 21, 1862; Benton Log, May 3, 1862.

41. *ORS,* ser. 3, 2:249, 269; Gillespie, 38; Barbiere, 212; Milligan, ed., *Fresh-Water Navy,* 73; *Peoria Transcript,* May 15, 1862; *Cincinnati Times,* May 14, 1862.

42. Davis, *Davis,* 222–223; *ORN,* 23:85; Gideon Welles to Andrew Foote, April 23, 1862; Area File 5, RG 45, NA; *Cincinnati Times,* May 14, 1862; Benton Log, May 9, 1862, RG 24, NA; Tucker, 199–204.

43. Thompson, *Reminiscences,* 154–155; *ORN,* 23:54.

44. Thompson, *Reminiscences,* 155–156; *ORN,* 23:14.

45. Thompson, *Reminiscences,* 157; *ORN,* 23:15, 56; ORS, ser. 3, 1:554–555; Callender, 60–61; *OR,* 52 (pt. 1):38.

46. *ORN,* 23:16, 56; Callender, 62–63; Barbiere, 212–213.

47. Thomas H. Bringhurst and Frank Swigart, *History of the Forty-Sixth Regiment Indiana Volunteer Infantry* (Logansport, Ind.: Press of Wilson, Humphreys and Company, 1888), 27; Sinks Memoir, 15; Henry Walke, *Naval Scenes and Reminiscences of the Civil War* (New York: F. R. Read and Company, 1877), 251–252; Milligan, ed., *Fresh-Water Navy,* 75–77; Barbiere, 213.

48. *ORN,* 23:15, 56; Yost Diary, May 10, 1862; Thompson, *Reminiscences,* 158.

49. Thompson, *Reminiscences,* 158; *Memphis Appeal,* May 11, 1862.

50. *ORN,* 23:14, 16–17, 20, 24, 26, 55–56; *OR,* 10 (pt. 1):889; *Memphis Avalanche,* May 12, 1862; Barbiere, 213; Davis, *Davis,* 228; U.S. Navy Department, Historical Division, *Civil War Naval Chronology* (Washington, D.C.: GPO, 1962), 2:62; Gosnell, 90. John D. Milligan, *Gunboats Down the Mississippi,* (Annapolis, Md.: Naval Institute Press, 1965), 67, and Ivan Musicant, *Divided Waters: The Naval History of the Civil War* (New York: HarperCollins, 1995), 214, judge the battle a Confederate victory because that side did more short-term damage.

51. Mark Lyons to Amelia Horsler, May 13, 1862, Lyons Papers; Thomas W. Knox, *Campfire and Cotton Field* (New York: Blelock and Company, 1865), 171.

52. *ORN,* 23:17, 24, 85; *OR,* 10 (pt. 2):202; Raimondo Luraghi, *A History of the Confederate Navy,* trans. Paolo E. Coletta (Annapolis: Naval Institute Press, 1996), 170. See Davis, *Davis,* chaps. 1–10, for his background.

53. *ORN,* 23:53, 678; Yost Memoir, 12; Benton Log, May 11–17, 1862, RG 24, NA; Milligan, ed., *Fresh-Water Navy,* 81; Walke, 269, 271.

54. Thompson, *Reminiscences,* 159; P. G. T. Beauregard to John Villepigue, May 15, 1862, and P. G. T. Beauregard to J. E. Montgomery, May 16, 1862, Beauregard Papers; *ORN,* 23:97, 104; William Y. Thompson, *E. M. Graham: North Louisianan* (Lafayette, La.: Center for Louisiana Studies, University of Southwestern Louisiana, 1984), 40–41.

55. Thomas Jordan to John Villepigue, May 19, 1862, Beauregard Papers; *St. Louis Missouri Republican,* May 21, 1862; *Cincinnati Gazette,* June 2, 1862.

56. Stephen V. Ash, *When the Yankees Came: Conflict and Chaos in the Occupied South, 1861–1865* (Chapel Hill: Univ. of North Carolina Press, 1995), 47–49; James A. Ramage, *Rebel Raider: The Life of General John Hunt Morgan* (Lexington: Univ. Press of Kentucky, 1986), 66; *Illustrated London News,* June 14, 1862; *Logansport [Ind.] Journal,* May 24, 1862; *ORN,* 23:53.

57. *ORN,* 23:53, 97; *St. Louis Missouri Republican,* June 3, 1862; Aurelius Lyman Voorhis, *Life and Times,* ed. Jerry Voorhis Sr. (New York: Vantage Press, 1976), 48–49; G. N. Fitch, G.O. 16, May 19, 1862, 43rd Indiana Infantry Records, RG 94, NA; G. N. Fitch to C. H. Dodge, May 17, 1862, and S. L. Phelps to Andrew Foote, May 17, 1862, Area File 5, RG 45, NA; *Cincinnati Commercial,* April 28, 1862.

58. *Mobile Advertiser and Register,* May 26, 1862; S. L. Phelps to Andrew Foote, May 21, 1862, Area File 5, RG 45, NA; *Cincinnati Commercial,* May 24, 1862; *ORN,* 23:101; *Memphis Argus,* May 28, 1862; Robertson, 150.

59. *OR,* 10 (pt. 1):897–898; J. R. Slack to Ann Slack, May 22, 1862, James R. Slack Papers, Indiana State Library, Indianapolis, Ind.

60. *OR,* 10 (pt. 1):898; Testimony, 56, Erwin File, Settled Cases of Southern Claims Commission, RG 217, NA; Isaac McMillan to his family, May 21–24, 1862, Isaac McMillan Papers, Indiana State Library, Indianapolis, Ind.; Joshua Fussell, *History of the Thirty-Fourth Regiment* (n.p.: Privately printed, n.d.), 13; *Logansport [Ind.] Journal,* May 31, 1862; Walke, 270.

61. Voorhis, 47; Walke, 271; *OR,* 10 (pt. 1):898.

62. Isaac McMillan to his family, May 21–25, 1862, McMillan Papers; S. L. Phelps to A. H. Foote, June 4, 1862, Area File 5, RG 45, NA.

63. Mark Lyons to Amelia Horsler, May 24, 1862, Lyons Papers.

64. Milligan, *Gunboats,* 70–73; Chester G. Hearn, *Ellet's Brigade: The Strangest Outfit of All* (Baton Rouge: Louisiana State Univ. Press, 2000), 2–14; Charles Ellet to Edwin Stanton, May 26, 1862, Charles Ellet Papers, University of Michigan Transportation Library, Ann Arbor, Mich.; *Cincinnati Gazette,* May 26, 1862; Davis, *Davis,* 232.

65. Charles Ellet to Ellie Ellet, May 28, 31 (quoted), 1862, Ellet Papers; *ORN,* 23:33.

66. William Harper to Lydia Harper, May 29, 1862, William Harper Papers, M0426, Indiana Historical Society, Indianapolis, Ind.; G. N. Fitch to Charles Davis, May 26, 1862, Area File 5, RG 45, NA; *Logansport [Ind.] Journal,* June 7, 1862.

67. *OR,* 10 (pt. 1):902.

68. *Logansport [Ind.] Journal,* June 7, 1862; Voorhis, 48–49; *Benton* Log, May 28, 31, 1862, RG 24, NA; *St. Louis Missouri Democrat,* June 4, 1862; George E. Currie, *Warfare along the Mississippi,* ed. Norman E. Clarke (Mt. Pleasant, Mich.: Clarke Historical Library, Central Michigan University, 1961), 41–43; *ORN,* 23:33–34.

69. Charles Ellet to Ellie Ellet, May 28, 29, 31, 1862, Ellet Papers; Currie, 41–43; Bell I. Wiley, *The Life of Billy Yank: The Common Soldier of the Union* (Baton Rouge: Louisiana State Univ. Press, 1952), 172.

70. *Memphis Appeal,* June 3, 1862; *OR,* 10 (pt. 2):579; Mark Lyons to Amelia Horsler, June 7, 1862, Lyons Papers; Thompson, *Graham,* 42; John P. Young, *The Seventh Tennessee Cavalry (Confederate): A History* (Nashville: Publishing House of the Methodist Episcopal Church, South, 1890), 31; Watkins Diary, June 3–4, 1862.

71. *ORN,* 23:37–43 (pp. 39, 41, 42 quoted).

72. Herbert P. Gambrell, "Rams versus Gunboats: A Landsman's Naval Exploits," *Southwest Review* 23 (October 1937): 63–64; Volunteers List, June 3, 1862, and Orders, June 3, 1862, Ellet Papers; *OR,* 10 (pt. 1):900.

73. Yost Diary, June 3, 1862; *OR,* 10 (pt. 1):900–901, 52 (pt. 1):39; Charles C. Coffin, *Four Years of Fighting* (Boston: Tichnor and Fields, 1866), 101; Barbiere, 213; S. L. Phelps to A. H. Foote, June 4, 1862, Area File 5, RG 45, NA.

74. *OR,* 10 (pt. 1):899; *Logansport [Ind.] Journal,* June 14, 1862.

75. Bringhurst and Swigart, 28; *Logansport [Ind.] Journal,* June 14, 1862; G. N. Fitch, G.O. 18, June 3, 1862, 43rd Indiana Infantry Records, RG 94, NA; Bearss, 68.

76. Edwin H. Sessel, "Our Evacuation of Fort Pillow," *Confederate Veteran* 6 (January 1898): 32; Delisdimier, 401; Moore, ed., *Rebellion Record,* 5:164–165; T. W. Blount, "Captain Thomas William Blount and His Memoirs," *Southwestern Historical Quarterly* 39 (July 1935): 8; Walke, 272; *ORN,* 23:49.

77. *Memphis Avalanche,* June 6, 1862; *OR,* 10 (pt. 1):901–902; *ORN,* 23:57.

78. *Benton* Log, June 4, 1862, RG 24, NA; *Illustrated London News,* July 19, 1862; *Waukegon [Ill.] Gazette,* June 14, 1862.

79. Yost Diary, June 5, 1862; *Cincinnati Gazette,* June 11, 1862; Voorhis, 50; *Benton* Log, June 5, 1862, RG 24, NA; Moore, ed., *Rebellion Record,* 5:166; *ORN,* 23:49, 51. Fitch claimed to have entered the fort first, but most witnesses held otherwise.

80. *St. Louis Missouri Democrat,* June 10, 1862; Davis, *Davis,* 237.

81. Voorhis, 50; *Logansport [Ind.] Journal,* June 14, 1862; Bringhurst and Swigart, 32; Glatthaar, "Common Soldier," 132.

82. *Rockville [Ill.] Parke County Republican,* June 25, 1862; *ORN,* 23:119, 684; *New York World,* June 11, 1862; *Cincinnati Gazette,* June 11, 1862; *Logansport [Ind.] Journal,* June 14, 1862; U.S. Navy Department, Historical Division, *Chronology,* 2:68.

83. Luraghi, 174–175; Musicant, 215–216.

84. Musicant, 216, 258; Bringhurst and Swigart, 44; Williams, *Beauregard,* chaps. 10–15; Monaghan, chaps. 6–8; Current, 4:1661.

85. *OR,* 10 (pt. 1):903.

86. Mark Lyons to Amelia Horsler, March 14, 1862, Lyons Papers; Bringhurst and Swigart, 29; Davis, *Davis,* 236.

CHAPTER THREE. MILITARY LIFE AT THE FORT

1. *Memphis Avalanche,* July 16, August 8, 1861; Scott, 99–100; Charles Aldrich, "Incidents Connected with the History of the Thirty-Second Iowa Infantry," *Iowa Journal of History and Politics* 4 (January 1906): 80; *Rushville [Ind.] Republican,* December 17, 1862; Charles Stewart to Julia Stewart, March 15, 1862, Stewart Papers; Williams, 46; *Butler Center [Iowa] Stars and Stripes,* February 25, 1863.

2. Thompson, *Graham,* 37; Robert C. Mainfort Jr. and Patricia E. Coats, eds., "Soldiering at Fort Pillow, 1862–1864: An Excerpt from the Civil War Memoirs of Addison Sleeth," *West Tennessee Historical Society Papers* 36 (1982): 86.

3. Daniel, 51–52; *Memphis Avalanche,* June 17, 1861; Mark Lyons to Amelia Horsler,

March 14, 1862, Lyons Papers; Charles Stewart to Julia Stewart, March 13, 1862, Stewart Papers; Poe, 11; Thompson, *Graham,* 37.

4. Daniel, 52; *Indianapolis State Journal,* September 27, 1862; Nicholas Hamer affidavit, February 17, 1888, Samuel Green Pension File, RG 15, NA.

5. *Logansport [Ind.] Journal,* May 3, 1862; Yost Diary, May 1, 1862; Testimony, 25–27, Erwin File, Settled Cases of Southern Claims Commission, RG 217, NA; Testimony, 1, 9–10, Lanier File, Congressional Jurisdiction Cases, RG 123, NA; *Nevada [Iowa] Republican Reveille,* January 29, 1863.

6. Robert C. Mainfort Jr., *Archaeological Investigations at Fort Pillow State Historic Area, 1976–1978* (Nashville: Division of Archaeology, 1980), 186; Testimony, 25–27, Erwin File, Settled Cases of Southern Claims Commission, RG 217, NA; Testimony, Lanier File, 10–11, 32 (quoted), Congressional Jurisdiction Cases, RG 123, NA; G. Dodge, S.O. 50, March 10, 1863, Orders by District of Columbus, RG 393, NA; E. H. Wolfe to Thomas H. Harris, July 27, 1863, LR by District of Columbus, RG 393, NA; George Adams File, Barred Claims of the Southern Claims Commission, RG 233, NA.

7. *New Era* Log, April 2, 5, 1864, RG 24, NA; Yost Diary, July 1, 1862; *Mason City [Iowa] Cerro Gordo Republican,* May 28, 1863; Mainfort and Coats, 77, 86; William Conner File, Barred Claims of the Southern Claims Commission, RG 233, NA.

8. E. H. Wolfe, S.O. 17, March 28, 1863, 52nd Indiana Infantry Records, RG 94, NA; Scott, 105; Mainfort and Coats, 86.

9. Wiley, *Johnny Reb,* 109–112; D. Winter to L. Polk, November 12, 1861, David Winter CSR (Engineers), RG 109, NA; *OR,* 10 (pt. 2):396; Mark Lyons to Amelia Horsler, April 15, 1862, Lyons Papers; Pacific Book Auction Galleries, Catalogue for October 20, 1994, Auction (San Francisco: Privately printed, 1994), Item #242; Philip D. Stephenson, *Civil War Memoir,* ed. Nathaniel C. Hughes Jr. (Conway, Ark.: UCA Press, 1995), 18.

10. Shingleton, 241; Barbiere, 57; Nancy D. Baird, ed., "There Is No Sunday in the Army: Civil War Letters of Lunsford P. Yandell, 1861–62," *Filson Club History Quarterly* 53 (October 1979): 319.

11. Robertson, 16, 97; *Logansport [Ind.] Journal,* May 10, 17, 1862; *Logansport [Ind.] Democratic Pharos,* May 21, 1862.

12. L. F. Booth to I. G. Kappner, March 6, 1864, LR by Fort Pickering, RG 393, NA; B. Swearingin to Mr. Finch, December 1, 1861, in possession of Tom Shouse; Poe, 12; J. M. Smith to L. Polk, November 15, 1861, J. M. Smith CSR (11th Arkansas Infantry), RG 109, NA; Wiley, *Johnny Reb,* 61–62; *Indianapolis State Journal,* September 27, 1862.

13. *Rushville [Ind.] Republican,* December 17, 1862; Mainfort and Coats, 77.

14. Testimony, 3, 6–8, 16, 26, Lanier File, Congressional Jurisdiction Cases of Southern Claims Commission, RG 123, NA; Aldrich, 83; *Nevada [Iowa] Republican Reveille,* March 12, 26, 1863; Will Kennedy to A. S. Kennedy, February 17, 1863, Will Kennedy Papers, Duke University Library, Durham, N.C.

15. William M. Mobley to Hannah Wylie, September 8, 1861, Wylie Papers; Testimony, 5, 13, Lanier File, Congressional Jurisdiction Cases of Southern Claims Commission, RG 123, NA; William T. Avery to his wife, January 25, 1862, Gordon/Avery Papers; Aldrich, 80.

16. S. L. Phelps to A. H. Foote, June 17, 1862, Area File 5, RG 45, NA; *New York Herald,* June 12, 1862; Mainfort, "Folk Art Map," 75; E. Wehler to John Hough, December 24, 1863, 178th New York Infantry Records, RG 94, NA.

17. Robertson, 152–153; E. H. Wolfe, S.O. 35, May 15, 1863, 52nd Indiana Infantry Records, RG 94, NA; A. Asboth, G.O. 4, January 21, 1863, General Orders of the District of Columbus, RG 393, NA; Mainfort, "Folk Art Map," 75.

18. Bearss, 154–156, 162; Milligan, ed., *Fresh-Water Navy,* 81; Mainfort and Coats, 89. No accounts of living conditions on Confederate warships at the fort have been found, but they probably mirrored basic arrangements on Federal ships.

19. Robertson, 148–152, 156; Wiley, *Johnny Reb,* 251–252; J. C. Tappan to L. Polk, September 28, 1861, L. Polk Papers, RG 109, NA; J. M. Smith to L. Polk, November 3, 1861, J. M. Smith CSR (11th Arkansas Infantry), RG 109, NA; Mainfort, "Folk Art Map," 75.

20. Robertson, 151; *Cincinnati Commercial,* May 3, 1862; *Logansport [Ind.] Journal,* May 24, 1862; *ORN,* 23:391; Scott, 102.

21. *Butler Center [Iowa] Stars and Stripes,* February 25, 1863; *Rushville [Ind.] Jacksonian,* April 15, 1863; John Scott, S.O. 57, May 16, 1863, 32nd Iowa Infantry Records, RG 393, NA; F. Moore to commanding officer, August 5, 1863, Co. C. Orders, 2nd Illinois Cavalry Records, RG 94, NA.

22. Ross Guffin, "A Night on the Mississippi," *Putnam's Magazine* 5 (April 1870): 424; Aldrich, 80; *Nevada [Iowa] Republican Reveille,* March 26, 1863.

23. *Cincinnati Commercial,* May 3, 1862; J. Ludlow to C. H. Davis, May 12, 1862, Area File 5, RG 45, NA; Mainfort, "Folk Art Map," 75.

24. Stephen B. Olney to W. A. Hammond, February 28, 1864, Stephen B. Olney File, Personal Papers of Physicians, RG 94, NA; J. M. Smith to L. Polk, November 15, 1861, J. M. Smith CSR (11th Arkansas Infantry), RG 109, NA; Aldrich, 13; Mainfort, "Folk Art Map," 75; *Rushville [Ind.] Republican,* December 28, 1862; Will Kennedy to A. S. Kennedy, February 17, 1863, Kennedy Papers.

25. Bearss, 157–158; *Logansport [Ind.] Democratic Pharos,* May 7, 21, 1862; *Rushville [Ind.] Jacksonian,* October 1, 1863; Robertson, 164.

26. Robertson, 147, 155–158; William M. Mobley to Hannah Wylie, September 8, 1861, Wylie Papers; Baird, 318.

27. William T. Avery to his wife, January 25, 1862, Gordon/Avery Papers; Robert S. Critchell, *Recollections of a Fire Insurance Man* (Chicago: Privately printed, 1909), 30–31; Mark Lyons to Amelia Horsler, March 14, 1862, Lyons Papers.

28. E. Wehler, G.O. 90, December 24, 1863, Co. C Orders, 178th New York Infantry Records, RG 94, NA; Lester L. Swift, ed., "Letters from a Sailor on a Tinclad," *Civil War History* 7 (March 1961): 51–52. Also see Wiley, *Billy Yank,* 45–47.

29. Robertson, 41; *Toledo Blade,* October 30, 1863; B. Swearingin to Mr. Finch, December 1, 1861, in possession of Tom Shouse; William W. Cherster, ed., "Diary of Captain Elisha Tompkin Hollis," *West Tennessee Historical Society Papers,* 39 (1985): 96; *Alton [Ill.] Democrat,* May 1, 1863.

30. Robertson, 183; Rushing, 9; Bragg, 17.

31. Robertson, 82–83, 94; Rushing, 9; Moore, *Rebellion Record,* 5:166; *Memphis Avalanche,* June 17, 1861; Critchell, 31; Bearss, 161.

32. Bringhurst and Swigart, 27; Milligan, ed., *Fresh-Water Navy,* 72; Pacific Book Auction Galleries, Item #242; Ross Guffin, S.O. 78, August 20, 1863, Co. C Orders, 2nd Illinois Cavalry Records, RG 94, NA; Robertson, 92; Stephenson, 18; Mainfort and Coats, 85.

33. Augustus C. Kean Memoir, Cabarrus-Slade Papers, Southern Historical Collection,

University of North Carolina Library, Chapel Hill, N.C.; Thompson, *Reminiscences*, 159; Mainfort and Coats, 89.

34. Bertram Wyatt-Brown, *Southern Honor: Ethics and Behavior in the Old South* (New York: Oxford Univ. Press, 1982), 364–365; Mark Lyons to Amelia Horsler, March 14, 1862, Lyons Papers; Riley P. Neely CSR (4th Tennessee Infantry), RG 109, NA; P. G. T. Beauregard to J. Winnard, March 15, 1862, Beauregard Papers.

35. A. Asboth to E. H. Wolfe, May 21, 1863, LS by District of Columbus, RG 393, NA; E. H. Wolfe to B. K. Logan, October 23, 1863, and W. T. Strickland to I. F. Quinby, October 2, 1862, 52nd Indiana Infantry Records, RG 94, NA; John P. T. Davis, Charges against Major W. T. Strickland, November 3, 1862, and W. T. Strickland to J. Lowell, November 22, 1862, William T. Strickland CSR (52nd Indiana Infantry), RG 94, NA; Frederick Dieke CSR (52nd Indiana Infantry), RG 94, NA; Indiana, *Report of the Adjutant General of the State of Indiana* (Indianapolis: Samuel M. Douglass, 1866), 5:512–516.

36. Scott, 407; E. H. Wolfe to A. Asboth, March 23, 1863, and endorsement, LR by District of Columbus, RG 393, NA; Fort Pillow Post Return for February 1864, Microcopy 617, NA.

37. William T. Avery to his wife, January 25, February 9, 1862, Gordon/Avery Papers.

38. Mainfort and Coats, 78, 81, 85; Reid Mitchell, *The Vacant Chair: The Northern Soldier Leaves Home* (New York: Oxford Univ. Press, 1993), 43–45, 49–50; William Harper to Lydia Harper, May 29, 1862, Harper Papers; Mark Lyons to Amelia Horsler, May 10, 1862, Lyons Papers; John Ryan Memoir, 5, Clarke Historical Library, Mt. Pleasant, Mich.

39. Seldon Hetzel CSR (178th New York Infantry), RG 94, NA; A. J. Smith, G.O. 56, April 27, 1863, G.O. 57, September 15, 1863, G.O. 58, September 21, 1863, G.O. 65, November 14, 1863, A. Asboth, G.O. 45, July 2, 1863, G.O. 46, July 21, 1863, G.O. 48, July 30, 1863, G.O. 50, August 3, 1863, Orders by District of Columbus, RG 393, NA.

40. Stephenson, 19–20; G. Fitch, Order 1, April 16, 1862, 46th Indiana Infantry Records, RG 393, NA.

41. Z. Main, G.O. 11, July 21, 1863, 52nd Indiana Infantry Records, RG 94, NA; E. Mix, S.O. 35, January 13, 1863, S.O. 36, January 19, 1863, 32nd Iowa Infantry Records, RG 94, NA; E. Wehler, G.O. 3, January 6, 1864, G.O. 8, January 16, 1864, 178th New York Infantry Records, RG 94, NA; Yost Diary, July 29, 1862.

42. John Y. Simon, ed., *The Papers of Ulysses S. Grant*, 26 vols. to date (Carbondale: Southern Illinois Univ. Press, 1979), 7:201; Mainfort and Coats, 88; Mainfort, *Archaeological Investigations*, 36–37, 98; R. Guffin, G.O. 3, January 7, 1864, 178th New York Infantry Records, RG 94, NA.

43. Rowland Stafford True, "Life Aboard a Gunboat: A First Person Account," *Civil War Times Illustrated* 9 (February 1971): 37–39.

44. Thompson, *Reminiscences*, 160–161; Mainfort and Coats, 83.

45. *Memphis Avalanche*, July 16, 1861; Thompson, *Graham*, 37–38; Mainfort and Coats, 83–85; William T. Avery to his wife, January 25, 1862, Gordon/Avery Papers.

46. Robertson, 79; entry for W. T. Avery to L. Polk, January 31, 1862, LR Register of L. Polk's Corps, RG 109; E. H. Wolfe to A. Asboth, February 7, 1863, LR by District of Columbus, RG 393, NA; entry for W. F. Bradford to R. P. Buckland, March 25, 1864, District of Memphis LR Register, 9:31, RG 393, NA; Stevenson, 60–61.

47. Charles Stewart to Julia Stewart, March 13, 1862, Stewart Papers; Thompson, *Graham*, 37; Mark Lyons to Amelia Horsler, April 15, 1862, Lyons Papers; E. H. Wolfe, G.O. 7, July 30, 1863, 52nd Indiana Infantry Records, RG 94, NA.

48. Mark Lyons to Amelia Horsler, March 31, April 15, 1862, Lyons Papers; William T. Avery to his wife, January 25, 1862, Gordon/Avery Papers; William B. Goodman and Manliff Malson files (MM65), Court Martial Cases, RG 153, NA.

49. Robinson, 102; Poe, 15; Thompson, *Graham,* 37–38; *Memphis Avalanche,* June 17, 1861; *Rushville [Ind.] Jacksonian,* April 15, 1863; Monthly Return for March 1864, Bradford Battalion Records, RG 94, NA.

50. Thompson, *Graham,* 37; Poe, 15; *Nevada [Iowa] Republican Reveille,* January 29, March 26, May 14, 1863; *Greensburg [Ind.] Decatur Republican,* January 22, 1863; *OR,* 32 (pt. 1): 530, 533.

51. Robertson, 108–109; Poe, 15; Bernard Schermerhorn to Josie Schermerhorn, April 14, May 4, 1862, Schermerhorn Papers; Will Kennedy to A. S. Kennedy, February 17, 1863, Kennedy Papers; *Memphis Avalanche,* August 8, 1861.

52. Mark Lyons to Amelia Horsler, April 15, 1862, Lyons Papers; *Mason City [Iowa] Cerro Gordo Republican,* May 28, 1863; Mitchell, *Vacant Chair,* 24–26.

53. Gerald F. Linderman, *Embattled Courage: The Experience of Combat in the American Civil War* (New York: Free Press, 1987), 241–243; Robertson, 61–64.

CHAPTER FOUR. THE FIRST FEDERAL GARRISON

1. *ORN,* 23:49, 145–146, 151, 255; Lauderdale County Court Minutes, vol. E, 88–93; Harrod C. Anderson Diary, June 1862, Louisiana State University Library, Baton Rouge, La.; Yost Diary, August 1, 1862; Watkins Diary, August 17, 1862; Egbert Thompson to C. H. Davis, June 12, 1862, Area 5 File, RG 45, NA.

2. Egbert Thompson to C. H. Davis, June 12, 1862, J. A. Winslow to Egbert Thompson, September 29, 1862, Area 5 File, RG 45, NA; *ORN,* 23:49, 152, 228–229, 390; Yost Memoir, 24–26; Yost Diary, June 14, 22, 23, July 9, 15–17, 25, August 2, 11, September 9, 1862; Watkins Diary, August 24, 1862.

3. Grimsley, *Hard Hand,* 95, 132; U.S. Congress, *The Statutes at Large, Treaties, and Proclamations of the United States of America,* ed. George P. Sanger (Boston: Little, Brown, 1863), 12:591; Cimprich, 37; *ORN,* 23:355–356; *OR,* 17 (pt. 2):153; Watkins Diary, August 17, 1862.

4. Simon, 6:335; *OR,* 17 (pt. 1):669, ser. 4, 1:1095; Ramage, 71; Mainfort and Coats, 82–83; Grimsley, *Hard Hand,* 16–17.

5. *Rushville [Ind.] Jacksonian,* September 17, 1862; *History of Rush County, Indiana* (Chicago: Brant and Fuller, 1888), 463; Noel Fisher, "'Prepare Them for My Coming': General William T. Sherman, Total War, and Pacification in West Tennessee," *Tennessee Historical Quarterly* 51 (summer 1992): 78; *OR,* 17 (pt. 2):205.

6. Yost Diary, August 21, 1862; *Greensburg [Ind.] Decatur Republican,* September 18, November 27, 1862; *Rushville [Ind.] Jacksonian,* September 17, 1862; Simon, 6:417; Cimprich, 37; Ash, 54; Grimsley, *Hard Hand,* 115.

7. Yost Diary, August, 26, 30, 1862.

8. Grimsley, *Hard Hand,* 118; Yost Diary, August 30, 1862; *OR,* 17 (pt. 2):261; *ORN,* 23:390–391, 420.

9. Swift, 54; Benjamin F. Cooling, *Fort Donelson's Legacy: War and Society in Kentucky and Tennessee, 1862–1863* (Knoxville: Univ. of Tennessee Press, 1997), 117; Ash, 68; Fisher, 83–84.

10. Richard E. Beringer et al., *Why the South Lost the Civil War* (Athens: Univ. of Geor-

gia Press, 1986), 172; Andrew J. Birtle, *U.S. Army Counterinsurgency and Contingency Operations Doctrine, 1860–1941* (Washington, D.C.: Center for Military History, 1998), 42–43; *OR,* 17 (pt. 2):211; *Rushville [Ind.] Republican,* October 1, December 17, 1862; *ORN,* 23:419, 24:172, 323–324, 445, 532, 658, 25:146–147, 179, 218–219, 336–337, 379–380, 427, 507, 562, 638, 692, 754.

11. Mainfort and Coats, 77; Testimony, 9, Lanier file, Congressional Jurisdiction Cases, RG 124, NA; *Rushville [Ind.] Republican,* October 1, 1862.

12. *OR,* 17 (pt. 2):215; Mainfort and Coats, 75; Watkins Diary, September 28, 1862; *Rushville [Ind.] Republican,* October 1, 1862; John W. Carroll, *Autobiography and Reminiscences* (Henderson, Tenn.: Privately printed, 1898), 26.

13. *Rushville [Ind.] Republican,* October 1, 1862; *OR,* 17 (pt. 1):146–147; *Greensburg [Ind.] Decatur Republican,* November 27, 1862, January 15, 1863; Grimsley, *Hard Hand,* 171–186.

14. *Rushville [Ind.] Republican,* October 1, 1862; Ash, 124; Watkins Diary, October 12, 1862; Indiana, *Report of the Adjutant General,* 5:532–548.

15. Testimony, 1, 4–5, 12–13, 21–23, 30, Lanier File, Congressional Jurisdiction Cases, RG 124, NA; *Logansport [Ind.] Journal,* June 7, 1862.

16. *Mason City [Iowa] Cerro Gordo Republican,* March 5, 1863; Watkins Diary, September 28, 1862; Testimony, 9, Lanier File, Congressional Jurisdiction Cases, RG 124, NA; E. H. Wolfe, S.O. 24, April 16, 1863, S.O. 63, June 16, 1863, 52nd Indiana Infantry Records, RG 94, NA; Ryan Memoir, 23.

17. U.S. Congress, *Statutes at Large,* 12:1267; Cimprich, 101; *Greensburg [Ind.] Decatur Republican,* November 27, 1862; List of Persons Taking an Oath of Allegiance to the United States, District of Columbus Provost Marshal Records, RG 393, NA; Birtle, 30.

18. Simon, 6:201, 333–334, 8:364–365, 9:243–244; G. M. Dodge, S.O. 27, October 12, 1862, Orders book for District of Columbus, RG 393, NA; Ryan Memoir, 3; McPherson, *Battle Cry,* 620–622.

19. Ash, 70; Watkins Diary, September 28, October 5, November 29, 1862; R. V. Richardson to G. W. Randolph, November 4, 1862, LR by the Confederate Secretary of War, RG 109, NA; *OR,* 17 (pt. 1):148; *Greensburg [Ind.] Decatur Republican,* January 15, 1863.

20. Tennessee, *Tennesseans in the Civil War: A Military History of Confederate and Union Units,* 2 vols. (Nashville: Tennessee Civil War Centennial Commission, 1964–1965), 1:80; R. V. Richardson to Jefferson Davis, November 3, 1862, LR by the Confederate Secretary of War, RG 109, NA; Simon, 6:240.

21. *Rushville [Ind.] Republican,* December 17, 1862; Mainfort and Coats, 76; Birtle, 44; W. T. Strickland to J. Lovell, November 27, 1862, LR by District of Columbus, RG 393, NA; Stephen Z. Starr, *The Union Cavalry in the Civil War,* 3 vols. (Baton Rouge: Louisiana State Univ. Press, 1979), 1:237–241; *OR,* 17 (pt. 2):517.

22. *Alton [Ill.] Democrat,* December 31, 1862; Aldrich, 75, 83; Moore, ed., *Rebellion Record,* vol. 8, poetry section, page 55; Brian Steel Wills, *A Battle from the Start: The Life of Nathan Bedford Forrest* (New York: HarperCollins, 1992), chaps. 1–4.

23. Aldrich, 78–80; John Scott to E. A. Carr, January 28, 1863, John Scott CSR (32nd Iowa Infantry), RG 94, NA; *OR,* 17 (pt. 2):494–495; John Scott to H. G. Curtis, April 29, 1863, 32nd Iowa Infantry Records, RG 94, NA; *Mason City [Iowa] Cerro Gordo Republican,* January 11, 1863; *Story City [Iowa] Herald,* March 9, 1922, 3.

24. E. H. Wolfe, G.O. 30, December 23, 1862, 52nd Indiana Infantry Records, RG 94, NA;

Scott, 85–91; U.S. Congress, *Alvin Hawkins,* 37th Cong., 3rd Sess., H. Doc. 46 (serial 1173), 2, 7–8.

25. *Alton [Ill.] Democrat,* December 31, 1862; *Rushville [Ind.] Republican,* January 28, 1863; *Story City [Iowa] Herald,* March 9, 1922, 3; Scott, 103–104.

26. Scott, 103; *Rushville [Ind.] Republican,* December 17, 1862; Ryan Memoir, 1; Mainfort, "Folk Art Map," 76; John Cimprich and Robert C. Mainfort Jr., eds., "Dr. Fitch's Report on the Fort Pillow Massacre," *Tennessee Historical Quarterly* 44 (spring 1985): 30; *ORN,* 26:219.

27. U.S. Congress, *Statutes at Large,* 12:1267. Lincoln decided to overlook the failure to hold congressional elections in Tennessee. See Cimprich, 101.

28. Cimprich, 19–22; *Philadelphia Press,* November 3, 1863 (quoted); Testimony, 3, William P. Posey File, Congressional Jurisdiction Cases, RG 123, NA; Testimony, 7, Shadrack Thomas File, Barred Cases of the Southern Claims Commission, RG 217, NA; Watkins Diary, December 5, 1862.

29. William Wood trial record, William Wood CSR (32nd Iowa Infantry), RG 94, NA; Sherman Hart to uncle, February 24, 1864, Historical Collectable Auctions, Catalogue for September 28, 2000, Auction (Burlington, N.C.: Privately printed, 2000), 41; Aldrich, 84.

30. John Scott to Lorenzo Thomas, April 2, 1863, 32nd Iowa Infantry Records, RG 94, NA; Scott, *Story,* 97, 100–102; Aldrich, 84; *Lawrenceburg [Ind.] Register,* July 3, 1863; Wiley, *Billy Yank,* 42–43.

31. *Rushville [Ind.] Jacksonian,* January 28, 1863, February 18, 1863; A. L. Towne to C. A. Towne, n.d., 1863, Albert Towne Papers, State Historical Society of Iowa, Iowa City, Iowa.

32. Historical Collectable Auctions Catalogue, 41; *Davenport Gazette,* January 17, 1863; *Greensburg [Ind.] Decatur Republican,* January 22, 1863; *Rushville [Ind.] Republican,* March 11, 1863.

33. *History of Rush County,* 459, 466–467, 765; *Biographical and Historical Memoirs of Story County, Iowa* (Chicago: Goodspeed Publishing Co., 1890), 415; Mitchell, *Vacant Chair,* 33; *Greensburg [Ind.] Decatur Republican,* July 9, 1863, August 13, 1863; *Nevada [Iowa] Republican Reveille,* March 12, (quoted), 26, April 23, 1863.

34. Barry Popchuck, ed., *Soldier Boy: The Civil War Letters of Charles O. Musser, 29th Iowa* (Iowa City: Univ. of Iowa Press, 1950), 92; *Nevada [Iowa] Republican Reveille,* March 26, 1863.

35. E. H. Wolfe, S.O. 3, February 11, 1863, 52nd Indiana Infantry Records, RG 94, NA; John Scott to District of Columbus adjutant, April 3, 1863, John Scott to T. H. Harris, May 12, 1863, 32nd Iowa Infantry Records, RG 94, NA.

36. Franklin Moore CSR (2nd Illinois Cavalry), RG 94; Ash, 63; Birtle, 42–43; *Lawrenceburg [Ind.] Register,* July 3, 1863; Will Kennedy to A. S. Kennedy, February 17, 1863, Kennedy Papers; Mainfort and Coats, 78, 80, 84–85; Ryan Memoir, 23; *OR,* 30 (pt. 3):655.

37. E. H. Wolfe to J. Lovell, January 9, 1863, LR by District of Columbus, RG 393, NA; *Butler Center [Iowa] Stars and Stripes,* January 21, 1863; *Nevada [Iowa] Republican Reveille,* January 29, 1863; List of Prisoners, District of Columbus, RG 393, NA; *Greensburg [Ind.] Decatur Republican,* January 22, 1863; Ryan Memoir, 2.

38. *Rushville [Ind.] Republican,* May 6, 1863; W. S. Calhoun et al. file (LL1048), Court Martial Cases, RG 153, NA; Albert Cushman CSR (12th Tennessee Cavalry, C.S.A.), RG 94, NA; Yost Diary, August 30, September 7, 1862.

39. *Rushville [Ind.] Republican,* March 11, 1863; Watkins Diary, February 8, 1863; S. A. Hurlbut, G.O. 152, November 17, 1863, General Orders of the 16th Army Corps, RG 393,

NA; Albert Cushman CSR (12th Tennessee Cavalry, C.S.A.), RG 109, NA; *Alton [Ill.] Democrat,* March 18, 1863; Ryan Memoir, 3–4; Will Kennedy to A. S. Kennedy, February 17, 1863, Kennedy Papers. For examples of areas with more guerrilla activity, see Daniel E. Sutherland, ed., *Guerrillas, Unionists, and Violence on the Confederate Home Front* (Fayetteville: Univ. of Arkansas Press, 1999).

40. Scott, 104–105; E. H. Wolfe to A. Asboth, February 28, 1863, LR by the District of Columbus, RG 393, NA; William Lieullen et al. file (LL1048), Court Martial Cases, RG 153, NA.

41. *Rushville [Ind.] Republican,* March 18, 1863, April 29, 1863; E. H. Wolfe to A. Asboth, March 11, April 4, 1863, LR by District of Columbus, RG 393, NA; Mainfort and Coats, 84.

42. E. H. Wolfe to W. L. Lathorp, July 8, 1863, E. H. Wolfe, S.O. 16, March 20, 1863, S.O. 20, April 1, 1863, 52nd Indiana Infantry Records, RG 94, NA; *Rushville [Ind.] Jacksonian,* April 15, 1863; John Adams CSR (52nd Indiana Infantry), RG 94, NA.

43. *Rushville [Ind.] Republican,* May 6, 20, 1863; Tennessee, *Tennesseans in the Civil War,* 1:38, 81; *Alton [Ill.] Democrat,* May 1, 1863.

44. Mainfort and Coats, 87.

45. E. H. Wolfe, S.O. 17, March 28, 1863, 52nd Indiana Infantry Records, RG 94, NA; Scott, 100.

46. Mainfort and Coats, 77, 84–85; *Greensburg [Ind.] Decatur Republican,* January 15, 1863; *Nevada [Iowa] Republican Reveille,* April 16, 1863; John P. Fairly file (MM1103), Court Martial Cases, RG 153, NA; Amos Collins to S. Hurlbut, March 19, 1863, LR Register for 16th Army Corps, vol. 4, RG 393, NA.

47. Mainfort and Coats, 84, 87, 90; Scott, 100–101.

48. E. H. Wolfe, S.O. 46, May 30, 1863, S.O. 69, June 25, 1863, 52nd Indiana Infantry Records, RG 94, NA; *ORN,* 23:619; A. L. Towne to C. A. Towne, n.d., 1863, Towne Papers; Hubert F. Peebles and Rufus Benson CSRs (32nd Iowa Infantry), RG 94, NA; Indiana, *Report of the Adjutant General of the State of Indiana* (Indianapolis: W. R. Holloway, 1865), 2:511–517.

49. Joseph T. Glatthaar, *Forged in Battle: The Civil War Alliance of Black Soldiers and White Officers* (New York: Free Press, 1990), 155; Ira Berlin, ed., *Freedom: A Documentary History of Emancipation, 1861–1867,* 4 vols. in 2 series to date (New York: Cambridge Univ. Press, 1982), ser. 2, 1:569, 583; *OR,* ser. 2, 5:797, 844, 940–941; Howard C. Westwood, "Captive Black Union Soldiers in Charleston—What to Do?" *Civil War History* 28 (March 1982): 39–41.

50. Cimprich, 53–59; E. H. Wolfe, G.O. 5, April 15, 1863, S.O. 54, June 8, 1863, S.O. 63, June 16, 1863, S.O. 69, June 25, 1863, S.O. 77, July 9, 1863, S.O. 112, August 31, 1863, S.O. 159, October 24, 1863, S.O. 174, November 3, 1863, 52nd Indiana Infantry Records, RG 94, NA; Wolfe to commanding officer, August 15, 1863, Co. C Orders, 2nd Illinois Cavalry Records, RG 94, NA; *Chicago Tribune,* November 30, 1863.

51. *Alton [Ill.] Democrat,* May 1, 29, 1863; S. A. Hurlbut to A. Asboth, May 27, 1863, LS by 16th Army Corps, RG 393, NA; Ryan Memoir, 5; E. H. Wolfe, S.O. 55, June 9, 1863, 52nd Indiana Infantry Records, RG 94, NA; *ORS,* 20:765.

52. *Lawrenceburg [Ind.] Register,* July 3, 1863; *Mason City [Iowa] Cerro Gordo Republican,* July 2, 1863; Charles Aldrich to commanding officer of the 2nd Missouri Artillery, May 12, 1863, 32nd Iowa Infantry Records, RG 94, NA; E. H. Wolfe, S.O. 66, June 19, 1863, 52nd Indiana Infantry Records, RG 94, NA.

53. E. H. Wolfe, S.O. 71, June 28, 1863, and E. H. Wolfe to Thomas H. Yeatman, October 8, 1863, 52nd Indiana Infantry Records, RG 94, NA; Trade Store Permits for December 1863,

Reports by the Assistant Special Agent at Memphis, RG 366, NA; Peter Casey to T. H. Yeatman, July 20, October 1, 1863, and Joseph B. Chandler to T. H. Yeatman, November 25, 1863, Reports of the Boards of Trade of the Memphis District, RG 366, NA; T. Stevens statement, n.d., 1863, LR by Assistant Special Agent at Memphis, RG 366, NA.

54. Guffin, 419; Mainfort and Coats, 88; E. H. Wolfe to Harris and Co., December 29, 1863, 52nd Indiana Infantry Records, RG 94, NA.

55. *Rushville [Ind.] Republican,* July 22, 29, 1863; A. Asboth, S.O. 169, July 9, 1863, Orders of District of Columbus, RG 393, NA.

56. Mainfort and Coats, 78–79; E. H. Wolfe to Henry Binmore, July 12, 1863, LR by the District of West Kentucky, RG 393, NA; E. H. Wolfe, G.O. 9, July 30, 1863, 52nd Indiana Infantry Records, RG 94, NA.

57. F. Moore to commanding officer of Co. C, July 29, 1863, Co. C Orders, 2nd Illinois Cavalry Records, RG 94, NA; A. Asboth to E. H. Wolfe, July 30, 1863, LS by District of Columbus, RG 393, NA; *OR,* 24 (pt. 2):687; Wills, 149–150; John U. Green affidavit, May 22, 1864, John U. Green CSR (12th Tennessee Cavalry, C.S.A.), RG 109, NA; unpaginated testimony, Thomas C. Coppedge File, and testimony, 4, Robert Medlin File, Settled Case Files for the Southern Claims Commission, RG 217, NA.

58. F. Moore to commanding officer of Co. C, August 21, 30, September 27, 1863, Co. C orders, 2nd Illinois Cavalry Records, RG 94, NA; *OR,* 24 (pt. 2):687, 30 (pt. 2):655; Nathaniel C. Hughes et al., *Brigadier General Tyree H. Bell, C.S.A.: Forrest's Fighting Lieutenant* (Knoxville: Univ. of Tennessee Press, 2004), 88; Mainfort and Coats, 20; *Rushville [Ind.] Republican,* September 23, 1863.

59. *Rushville [Ind.] Jacksonian,* September 23, 1863; *Rushville [Ind.] Republican,* October 28, November 4, 1863; E. H. Wolfe, S.O. 145, October 8, 1864, 52nd Indiana Infantry Records, RG 94, NA.

60. E. H. Wolfe to B. K. Logan, October 23, 1863, S.O. 157, October 23, 1863, 52nd Indiana Infantry Records, RG 94, NA; *Toledo Blade,* October 30, 1863; Ryan Memoir, 23; William R. Roberts to Charles M. Adams, August 6, 1863, LR by District of Columbus, RG 393, NA; William H. Lea affidavit, October 19, 1865, William Lea petition, November 17, 1865, and Albert Lea answer, December 16, 1865, Affidavits and Statements Filed with the Memphis Provost Marshall of Freedmen, RG 105, NA.

61. Ash, 100–104, 192; Eliza Smith to a sister, April 24, 1864, in John L. Kimbrough, "Through the Lines: West Tennessee to North Carolina," http://www.jlkstamps.com/long/letter.htm, accessed 2003; LeRoy P. Graf and Ralph W. Haskins, eds., *The Papers of Andrew Johnson* (Knoxville: Univ. of Tennessee Press, 1983), 6:648–650; Mainfort and Coats, 80–81; Company G Morning Book, October 29–31, 1863, 52nd Indiana Infantry Records, RG 94, NA; E. H. Wolfe to commanding officer, November 7, 1863, Company B Orders, 2nd Illinois Cavalry Records, RG 94, NA.

62. Case brief, March 26, 1881, William P. Posey File, Congressional Jurisdiction Cases, RG 123, NA; Paul H. Bergeron, ed., *The Papers of Andrew Johnson* (Knoxville: Univ. of Tennessee Press, 1996), 13:348, 447; Mainfort and Coats, 87; E. H. Wolfe to J. Hough, October 21, 1863, and E. H. Wolfe, S.O. 161, October 25, 1863, 52nd Indiana Infantry Records, RG 94, NA.

63. E. H. Wolfe, S.O. 64, June 17, 1863, S.O. 188, December 1, 1863, 52nd Indiana Infantry Records, RG 94, NA; Mainfort and Coats, 74, 76; A. Asboth, S.O. 123, May 25, 1863, Orders of District of Columbus, RG 393, NA.

64. Henry George, *History of the 3d, 7th, 8th, and 12th Kentucky C.S.A.* (Louisville: C. T. Dearing Printing Company, 1911), 60, 69; Carroll, 26; *OR,* 31 (pt. 1):572; William Faulkner to ?, n.d., William Faulkner CSR (12th Kentucky Cavalry, C.S.A.), RG 94, NA.

65. Wills, 149–150; Christopher S. Dwyer, "Raiding Strategy: As Applied by the Western Confederate Cavalry in the American Civil War," *Journal of Military History* 63 (April 1999): 263–267; E. H. Wolfe to John Hough, November 20, 1863, 52nd Indiana Infantry Records, RG 94, NA.

66. Mainfort and Coats, 77–78; Wills, 150.

67. *OR,* 31 (pt. 1):572; J. Hough to E. H. Wolfe, November 25, 1863, LS by District of Columbus, RG 393, NA; *ORS,* 47:695–696; Edward Wehler, G.O. 2 and 3, January 6, 1864, 178th New York Infantry Records, RG 94, NA; Wills, *Battle,* 150; William Faulkner to ?, n.d., Faulkner CSR (12th Kentucky Cavalry C.S.A.), RG 94, NA; E. H. Wolfe to T. H. Harris, January 2, 1864, LR by 16th Army Corps, RG 393, NA.

68. Mainfort and Coats, 89; Guffin, 419–424; *Indianapolis Journal,* January 18, 1864.

69. *OR,* 32 (pt. 1):179; *ORN,* 25:540.

70. S. A. Hurlbut, S.O. 11, January 11, 1864, S.O. of 16th Army Corps, RG 393, NA; S. A. Hurlbut to E. H. Wolfe, January 17, 1864, LS by 16th Army Corps, RG 393, NA; C. B. Revelle to J. M. Tomeny, March 8, 1864, LR by Assistant Special Agent at Memphis, RG 366, NA; P. T. Morgan to J. M. Tomeny, March 17, 1864, Fragmentary Papers of Assistant Special Agent at Memphis, RG 366, NA; E. H. Wolfe, S.O. 15, January 18, 1864, S.O. 19, January 21, 1864, 52nd Indiana Infantry Records, RG 94, NA; *ORS,* 47:696, 17:465; *New Era* Log, January 31, 1864, RG 24, NA.

CHAPTER FIVE. THE LAST GARRISON AND THE MASSACRE

1. *New Era* Log, February 8, 1864, RG 24, NA; Cimprich and Mainfort, eds., "Dr. Fitch's Report," 29; *OR,* 32 (pt. 1):538; Charles L. Lufkin, "'Not Heard from since April 12, 1864': The Thirteenth Tennessee Cavalry, U.S.A.," *Tennessee Historical Quarterly* 45 (summer 1986): 138–139. As another cavalry regiment had already been designated the 13th, Bradford's unit later was renamed the 14th.

2. Cimprich, 92; I. G. Kappner to L. Methundy, February 20, 1864, LS by Fort Pickering, RG 393, NA; *OR,* 32 (pt. 2):311 (quoted); *ORS,* 77:269; Ash, 120–122.

3. U.S. Congress, *Fort Pillow Massacre,* 38th Cong., 1st Sess., H. Doc. 65. (serial 1206), 65, 97; R. P. Buckland to S. A. Hurlbut, January 29, 1864, LS by the District of Memphis, RG 393, NA; *OR,* 32 (pt. 2):311; T. H. Yeatman to S. A. Hurlbut, January 23, 1864, and endorsement, LR by Assistant Special Agent at Memphis, RG 366, NA; S. A. Hurlbut, S.O. 37, January 27, 1864, S.O. of 16th Army Corps, RG 393, NA; S. A. Hurlbut, G.O. 11, January 18, 1864, G.O. of 16th Army Corps, RG 393, NA. Hurlbut's adjutant later claimed that Bradford requested an assignment to Fort Pillow.

4. Cimprich and Mainfort, eds., "Dr. Fitch's Report," 29–30; George Bodnia, ed., "Fort Pillow 'Massacre': Observations of a Minnesotan," *Minnesota History* 43 (spring 1973): 187–188; *St. Louis Missouri Democrat,* April 22, 1864; Contract between E. B. Benton and Coy Horton et al., March 30, 1864, Contracts–Memphis, West Tennessee, Tennessee Records, RG 105, NA; Cimprich, 68–69; Regimental Returns for February and March 1864, Bradford Battalion Records, RG 94, NA; Thomas McClure, "The Fort Pillow Massacre," in Ward Edwards, *Lion-*

Hearted Luke, or, the Plan to Capture Mosby: A Story of Perilous Adventure in the Rebellion (New York: Novelist, 1884), 21–22. Benton's surviving contract only lists fourteen contrabands hired in Memphis, but he might have hired more out of the Fort Pillow camp.

5. *OR,* 16 (pt. 2):159, 32 (pt. 1):559; Tennessee, *Tennesseans in the Civil War,* 1:353; Neal Clark and John C. Taylor Pension Files (Bradford's 13th Tennessee Cavalry Battalion), RG 15, NA; Lufkin, 138; Tennessee, *Report of the Adjutant General of the State of Tennessee of the Military Forces of the State from 1861 to 1866* (Nashville: S. C. Mercer, 1866), 646; *Cincinnati Gazette,* April 22, 1864; Wiley G. Poston to Caroline Poston, February 26, 1864, copy at Fort Pillow State Historic Area Museum, Henning, Tenn..

6. R. P. Buckland to William Bradford, February 24, 27, March 22, 1864, LS by District of Memphis, RG 393, NA; P. T. Morgan to J. M. Tomeny, March 17, 1864, Fragmentary Papers of Assistant Special Agent at Memphis, RG 366, NA; Graf, ed., *Papers of Andrew Johnson,* 7:178; John C. Barr and John H. Porter CSRs (Bradford's 13th Tennessee Cavalry Battalion), RG 94, NA; Cimprich and Mainfort, eds., "Dr. Fitch's Report," 27, 30; *ORS,* 65:621; William Bradford to R. P. Buckland, March 23, 25, 1864, LR Register, District of Memphis, RG 393, NA.

7. James Alsobrook File, Barred Claims of the Southern Claims Commission, RG 233, NA; *New Era* Log, February 21, 23–28, March 15–17, 1864, RG 24, NA; Wiley G. Poston to Caroline Poston, February 26, 1864, Fort Pillow museum.

8. Wills, 152, 169, 171; *OR,* 32 (pt. 3):362.

9. Wills, 171, 174, 176; Wiley, *Johnny Reb,* 115, 289.

10. Wills, 75–76, 176–177; William S. Fitzgerald, "We Will Always Stand by You," *Civil War Times Illustrated* 32 (November/December 1993): 71.

11. Richard L. Fuchs, *An Unerring Fire: The Massacre at Fort Pillow* (Rutherford, N.J.: Farleigh Dickinson Univ. Press, 1994), 101; *OR,* 32 (pt. 1):556, 610; Thomas D. Witt to G. W. Cutter, March 15, 1863, Lionel Booth CSR (1st Missouri Light Artillery), RG 94, NA; Glatthaar, *Forged in Battle,* 39.

12. *OR,* 32 (pt. 1):608, 610, 32 (pt. 3):176–177, 547; Carl A. Lamberg to J. H. Harris, April 12, 1864, LR by 2nd U.S.C.L.A., RG 94, NA.

13. *OR,* 32 (pt. 3):177; Cimprich and Mainfort, eds., "Dr. Fitch's Report," 29; U.S. Congress, *Fort Pillow Massacre,* 3; *ORS,* 77:270, 459–462; Joseph Key Pension File (11th U.S.C.H.A.–New), RG 15, NA; *Harper's Weekly,* May 7, 1864, 302. The problematic story in *Harper's Weekly* has Tyler expressing views typical of black soldiers but contains a number of factual errors on other matters.

14. Cimprich, 84, 90–92; Cimprich and Mainfort, eds., "Dr. Fitch's Report," 29–30.

15. U.S. Congress, *Fort Pillow Massacre,* 25; CSRs for Bradford's 13th Tennessee Cavalry Battalion, 11th U.S.C.H.A.–New, and 2nd U.S.C.L.A., RG 94, NA; Samuel Green deposition, March 30, 1887, Samuel Green Pension File (11th U.S.C.H.A.–New), RG 15, NA; Carl A. Lamberg to J. H. Harris, April 12, 1864, LR by the 2nd U.S.C.L.A., RG 94, NA.

16. Cimprich and Mainfort, eds., "Dr. Fitch's Report," 29; John Cimprich and Robert C. Mainfort Jr., eds., "Fort Pillow Revisited: New Evidence about an Old Controversy," *Civil War History* 28 (December 1982): 298; Fuchs, 99; Mainfort, *Archaeological Investigations,* 13, 28; *OR,* 32 (pt. 1):538, 560, 596, 614.

17. U.S. Navy Department, Historical Division, *Dictionary of American Naval Fighting Ships* (Washington, D.C.: GPO, 1970), 5:55; *New Era* Log, April 8–10, 1864, RG 24, NA; *ORN,* 26:219. Fuchs, 112, rejects testimony about a plan for the *New Era* to cover a Federal retreat as

just bragging, but I am not entirely convinced. There was at least a plan for signaling directions from the fort to the gunboat.

18. U.S. Congress, *Fort Pillow Massacre,* 71; *New Era* Log, April 10, 1864, RG 24, NA; L. F. Booth to Stephen Hurlbut, April 3, 1864, and W. F. Bradford to R. P. Buckland, April 10, 1864, LR Register of the 16th Army Corps, RG 393, NA. See *OR,* ser. 2, 7:345, for the later claim by a woman caught smuggling military supplies that she warned Booth of the coming attack. Much of her testimony is questionable.

19. *OR,* 32 (pt. 1):608, 612, 32 (pt. 3):117, 751; James C. Alsobrook File, Barred Claims of the Southern Claims Commission, RG 233, NA; James Christenberg CSR (Bradford's 13th Tennessee Cavalry Battalion), RG 94, NA; Lufkin, 141. Robert Selph Henry, *"First With the Most" Forrest* (New York: Bobbs-Merrill Company, 1944), 245, and Lonnie E. Maness, "The Fort Pillow Massacre: Fact or Fiction," *Tennessee Historical Quarterly* 45 (winter 1986): 297, refer to a meeting between Forrest and his subordinate commanders to plan the attack, but no primary source mentions such a consultation.

20. Wills, 8–16, 157, 169–170.

21. Ibid., 178; *ORS,* 32:353, 586; *OR,* 32 (pt. 1):608, 32 (pt. 3):754–755, 864–865. McDonald's Battalion later became part of the 3rd Tennessee Cavalry. Redesignations later made Russell's regiment into the 20th Tennessee Cavalry, Wilson's into the 21st Tennessee Cavalry, and Barteau's into the 22nd Tennessee Cavalry.

22. Cimprich and Mainfort, eds., "Fort Pillow Revisited," 298; Alex M. Jones to Sally J. Jones, April 15, 1864, Jones-Black Family Papers, University of Memphis Library; *Memphis Appeal,* May 13, 1864; Cherster, 96; W. R. Dyer Diary, April 11, 1864, TSLA. Wisdom's unit later merged into the 18th Tennessee Cavalry.

23. *New Era* Log, April 12, 1864, RG 24, NA; *OR,* 32 (pt. 1):538, 621; Cimprich and Mainfort, eds., "Fort Pillow Revisited," 298; Lois D. Bejach, ed., "The Journal of a Civil War 'Commando'–DeWitt Clinton Fort," *West Tennessee Historical Society Papers* 2 (1948): 19; Alex M. Jones to Sally J. Jones, April 15, 1864, Jones-Black Family Papers; Cimprich and Mainfort, eds., "Dr. Fitch's Report," 30. The earliest account of an unnamed civilian guide for the opening attack appeared in Thomas Jordan and J. P. Pryor, *The Campaigns of Lieut. Gen. N. B. Forrest, and of Forrest's Cavalry* (New York: Blelock and Company, 1868), 425. A local tradition recounted in Theodore A. Mills, "Fort Pillow" (1931 typescript in John Cimprich's possession), 6, 10, and Frances T. Wakefield and Emma S. Turner, "Fort Pillow," in *Lauderdale County from Earliest Times,* ed. Kate J. Peters (Ripley, Tenn.: Sugar Hill Lauderdale County Library, 1957), 23–24, says the guide was John P. Laney, but, unlike Chalmers's battle report, has the Confederate entrance occurring near the Ripley Road gate. John A. Wyeth, *The Life of General Nathan Bedford Forrest* (New York: Harper and Brothers, 1899), 339, declared William J. Shaw the guide but probably read too much into Shaw's affidavit.

24. *OR,* 32 (pt. 1):536, 538, 621; Cimprich and Mainfort, eds., "Dr. Fitch's Report," 30; *St. Louis Missouri Democrat,* April 22, 1864. A newly discovered, unpublished account of the battle by Tyree H. Bell (not seen by this author) apparently has a unique version of many of the event's details. See Hughes et al., *Bell,* 119–125.

25. *OR,* 32 (pt.1):520, 534–535, 538, 559, 613–614, 621; *New Era* Log, April 12, 1864, RG 24, NA; Richard R. Hancock, *Hancock's Diary* (Nashville: Bramdon Printing Company, 1887), 354–355; U.S. Congress, *Fort Pillow Massacre,* 41, 86; *ORN,* 26:220; *Memphis Appeal,* May 2, 1864.

26. *OR,* 32 (pt. 1):538, 613–614 (quoted); Green deposition, March 30, 1887, Samuel Green Pension File (11th U.S.C.I.–New), RG 15, NA; Mainfort, *Archaeological Investigations,* 4, 23, 28; Bodnia, 188.

27. *OR,* 32 (pt. 1):520, 528, 566–567; U.S. Congress, *Fort Pillow Massacre,* 30, 82, 120; Bodnia, 188–189; *New Era* Log, April 12, 1864, RG 24, NA.

28. Cimprich and Mainfort, eds., "Dr. Fitch's Report," 30, 36; McClure, 22; *OR,* 32 (pt. 1):538, 559; *New Era* Log, April 12, 1864, RG 24, NA.

29. *OR,* 32 (pt. 1):610, 614, 559–560, 621; Jordan and Pryor, 429–430; Charles W. Anderson, "The True Story of Fort Pillow," *Confederate Veteran* 3 (November 1895): 322–324; *Memphis Appeal,* May 2, 1864; *Mobile Advertiser and Register,* April 26, 1864.

30. *OR,* 32 (pt. 1):538, 559–560, 596; *ORN,* 26:219; Jordan and Pryor, 430; Noah A. Trudeau, *Like Men of War: Black Troops in the Civil War, 1862–1865* (Boston: Little, Brown, 1998), 160. A letter in *OR,* 32 (pt. 1):610–611, seems to imply that Forrest had no artillery with him, but the *New Era*'s Log, April 12, 1864, RG 24, NA, a letter in the May 13, 1864, *Memphis Appeal,* and the battery's record of events in *ORS,* 32:586–587, clearly state otherwise. These records also contradict the 1895 memory in Anderson, "True Story," 322, that the Confederates did not fire their artillery.

31. *OR,* 32 (pt. 1):596, 614–615, 621; Bodnia, 188. Historians have followed Jordan and Pryor, 432–433, and Anderson, "True Story," 323, in locating the downriver detachment's move during the subsequent truce. Similarly, they have accepted Wyeth, 345, in placing the Barteau detachment's move at the same time. However, firsthand accounts vary widely on the timing of these actions. A letter in the May 9, 1864, *Memphis Appeal* and Hancock, 355–356, put both detachments in place before the truce. Another letter in the *Memphis Appeal* (May 2, 1864) seems to have them taking their positions after the truce as part of the final preparation, although this could not apply to Anderson's group because it fired on the steamboats during the truce.

32. *OR,* 32 (pt. 1):596, 614; Jordan and Pryor, 432. Because no standardized time system existed then, accounts give different times for the truce and final charge. This study uses the times given in *New Era* Log, April 12, 1864, RG 24, NA, which likely were recorded closer to the event than the others.

33. Cimprich and Mainfort, eds., "Dr. Fitch's Report," 31; Cimprich and Mainfort, eds., "Fort Pillow Revisited," 299, 301.

34. Bodnia, 188; U.S. Congress, *Fort Pillow Massacre,* 124, 127; *OR,* 32 (pt. 1):572–573, 615; *ORN,* 26:220.

35. *OR,* 32 (pt. 1):525–527, 530–531, 569; U.S. Congress, *Fort Pillow Massacre,* 51; Bodnia, 188; Carroll, 28–29.

36. *OR,* 32 (pt. 1):538, 561, 594–595, 614; Cimprich and Mainfort, eds., "Dr. Fitch's Report," 38; *ORS,* 65:62; *Chicago Tribune,* April 21, 1864; *New Era* Log, April 12, 1864.

37. Jordan and Pryor, 436; *OR,* 32 (pt. 1):561, 615; *New Era* Log, April 12, 1864, RG 24, NA; *Memphis Appeal,* May 2, 1864; Carroll, 29; Bodnia, 188.

38. Bodnia, 188; Daniel Van Horn Pension File (Bradford's 13th Tennessee Cavalry Battalion), RG 15, NA.

39. Wills, 157–158, 169, 171, 176–177; Hughes et al., *Bell,* 87, 101. Ronald K. Huch, "Fort Pillow Massacre: The Aftermath of Paducah," *Illinois State Historical Society Journal* 66 (spring 1973): 70, argues that frustration from not beating the black troops at Paducah caused the Fort Pillow massacre, but Bell's Brigade and Forrest's escort (the only troops at both battles)

were only lightly engaged at Paducah, and most members' accounts do not even mention the black troops there. In a brief skirmish at Moscow on December 4, 1863, Colonel "Black" Bob McCulloch led a charge, not including any of his men at Fort Pillow, against a force including black troops, but Confederate accounts again do not mention the blacks. See Dyer Diary, March 24, 1864; Cherster, 96; *Memphis Appeal,* May 13, 1864; *OR,* 31 (pt. 1):583–585, 590.

40. Cimprich and Mainfort, eds., "Fort Pillow Revisited," 301; Mark Grimsley, "Race in the Civil War," *North and South* 4 (March 2001): 40; U.S. Congress, *Fort Pillow Massacre,* 22, 27, 34, 43; *OR,* 32 (pt. 1):532; Bodnia, 188; Tennessee, *Tennesseans in the Civil War,* 1:56, 93–94, 97, 99, 102–103.

41. Cimprich and Mainfort, eds., "Fort Pillow Revisited," 299, 301.

42. William Witherspoon, *Reminiscences of a Scout, Spy, and Soldier of Forrest's Cavalry* (Jackson, Tenn.: McCowat-Mercer Printing Company, 1910), 57; *Memphis Appeal,* June 14, 1864; Bodnia, 188; U.S. Congress, *Fort Pillow Massacre,* 29, 54–59; *OR,* 32 (pt. 1):519–520, 523, 537. Hospital registers do not mention bayonet wounds, but visitors to the fort on April 13 claimed to observe such wounds on some of the dead.

43. Achilles V. Clark CSR (20th Tennessee Cavalry), RG 109, NA; Cimprich and Mainfort, eds., "Fort Pillow Revisited," 299, 301; *OR,* 32 (pt. 1):525, 531–532, 536; *Memphis Appeal,* May 13, 1864; Anderson, 323, 325–326.

44. Bodnia, 188–189; U.S. Congress, *Fort Pillow Massacre,* 17, 19, 32, 34–37, 39, 54, 82, 121; Cimprich and Mainfort, eds., "Dr. Fitch's Report," 36; *OR,* 32 (pt. 1):523, 525, 529, 531–532, 536–537, 539; U.S. War Department, *Medical and Surgical History of the Rebellion,* 12 vols. (Washington, D.C.: GPO, 1870), 7:19.

45. Cimprich and Mainfort, eds., "Fort Pillow Revisited," 301–302; *OR,* 32 (pt. 1):525, 539; Cimprich and Mainfort, eds., "Dr. Fitch's Report," 36; excerpt from *Cairo News,* April 16, 1864, in *Philadelphia Inquirer,* April 24, 1864; *St. Louis Missouri Democrat,* April 22, 1864.

46. Cimprich and Mainfort, eds., "Dr. Fitch's Report," 31, 36.

47. Ibid., 36–37.

48. *OR,* 32 (pt. 1):609, 615; *ORN,* 26:224–225; *St. Louis Union,* April 6, 1864; Jordan and Pryor, 440; Cimprich and Mainfort, eds., "Fort Pillow Revisited," 300; C. Fitch, "Capture of Fort Pillow–Vindication of General Chalmers by a Federal Officer," *Southern Historical Society Papers* 7 (September 1879): 440–441. One Federal in *OR,* 32 (pt. 1):527, said he saw a field officer, possibly James R. Chalmers, order the killing of a contraband boy, but the general denied this in *Congressional Record,* 46th Cong., 1st Sess., 1125 (May 7, 1879).

49. U.S. Congress, *Fort Pillow Massacre,* 18, 21, 26–27, 30, 34, 40, 44–47; Cimprich and Mainfort, eds., "Fort Pillow Revisited," 299; David J. Cole, "'Shooting Niggers Sir': Confederate Mistreatment of Union Black Soldiers at the Battle of Olustee," in *Black Flag Over Dixie: Racial Atrocities and Reprisals in the Civil War,* ed. Gregory J. W. Urwin (Carbondale: Southern Illinois Univ. Press, 2004), 74–77; Jack Hurst, *Nathan Bedford Forrest: A Biography* (New York: Knopf, 1993), 177; Fuchs, 12; Green deposition, March 30, 1887, Samuel Green Pension File (11th U.S.C.I.–New), RG 15, NA. For Federal reports of smaller scale massacres, not yet confirmed by Confederate evidence, in March 1864, see Noah A. Trudeau, "Proven Themselves in Every Respect to Be Men: Black Cavalry in the Civil War," in *Black Soldiers in Blue: African American Troops in the Civil War Era,* ed. John David Smith (Chapel Hill: Univ. of North Carolina Press, 2002), 291–293. Without explanation, Arthur W. Bergeron Jr., "The Battle of Olustee," in Smith, 144, claims that incident only involved a few unnecessary deaths.

50. *OR,* 32 (pt. 1):615–616; *ORN,* 26:220; Cimprich and Mainfort, eds., "Dr. Fitch's Report," 37; *Memphis Appeal,* June 23, 1864; Cimprich and Mainfort, eds., "Fort Pillow Revisited," 300.

51. Cimprich and Mainfort, eds., "Dr. Fitch's Report," 38; U.S. Congress, *Fort Pillow Massacre,* 20, 29, 82; Hughes et al., *Bell,* 126; Wyeth, 380.

52. Cimprich and Mainfort, eds., "Fort Pillow Revisited," 300; Cimprich and Mainfort, eds., "Dr. Fitch's Report," 37–38; *Mobile Advertiser and Register,* April 26, 1864; Bodnia, 190; *OR,* 32 (pt. 1):557, 610, 616; Jordan and Pryor, 440–443; *St. Louis Missouri Democrat,* April 16, 1864.

53. *OR,* 32 (pt. 1):610, 616, 622; Dyer Diary, April 12, 1864; Jordan and Pryor, 441; Glatthaar, *Forged in Battle,* 156; Cimprich and Mainfort, eds., "Fort Pillow Revisited," 295–300, 304. Calculated by units, rather than race, the death tolls are 29–34 percent for white units and 63 percent for black units. For the compilation of Table 7, see Appendix B.

CHAPTER SIX. THE MASSACRE'S AFTERMATH

1. *St. Louis Missouri Democrat,* April 16, 1864; U.S. Navy Department, Historical Division, *Chronology,* 6:506; *ORN,* 26:222–225; *OR,* 32 (pt. 1):555.

2. Jordan and Pryor, 443; *Springfield Illinois State Journal,* April 18, 1864; *OR,* 32 (pt. 3):777, 32 (pt. 1):532, 534–535, 562; U.S. Congress, *Fort Pillow Massacre,* 26, 37, 40, 43, 45, 50, 94.

3. *New York Times,* May 3, 1864; *St. Louis Missouri Democrat,* April 16, 1864; Jordan and Pryor, 443; *ORN,* 26:222; *OR,* 32 (pt. 1):526.

4. *OR,* 32 (pt. 1):598; *ORN,* 26:220, 222, 225; Cimprich and Mainfort, eds., "Dr. Fitch's Report," 39; List of Paroled Prisoners, April 13, 1864, Letters from Squadron Officers (1863–64), vol. 31, RG 24, NA; *St. Louis Missouri Democrat,* April 16, 1864.

5. *ORN,* 26:223, 226, 231; *New York Times,* May 3, 1864; *St. Louis Missouri Democrat,* April 16, 1864; *St. Louis Union,* April 16, 1864; *OR,* 32 (pt. 1):558, 563–565, 568–569, 571.

6. *St. Louis Union,* April 16, 1864; *St. Louis Missouri Democrat,* April 16, 1864 (quoted); Cimprich and Mainfort, "Dr. Fitch's Report," 39. Anderson, "True Story," 325, stated that the Federal officers with whom he drank were punished for it, but no corroborating evidence has been found.

7. *ORN,* 26:220, 223, 234; *New Era* Log, April 13, 1864, RG 24, NA; *Cincinnati Commercial,* April 20, 1864; *St. Louis Missouri Democrat,* April 16, 1864; Steven L. Roca, "Presence and Precedents: The USS *Red Rover* during the American Civil War, 1861–1865" *Civil War History* 44 (June 1998): 102–103; Jordan and Pryor, 454.

8. Jordan and Pryor, 454; Green deposition, March 30, 1887, Samuel Green Pension File 11th U.S.C.I.–New), RG 15, NA; *OR,* 32 (pt. 3):798.

9. *OR,* 32 (pt. 1):557, 589, 592; Wyeth, 361. Jordan and Pryor, 455, states that, after Bradford unsuccessfully attempted an escape, he was killed by soldiers with grudges against him. Henry, 269, and Maness, "Fort Pillow Massacre," 309, claim that Bradford died during an escape attempt.

10. *New Era* Log, April 14–15, 1864; *Moose* and *Hastings* Logs, April 14–16, 1864, RG 24, NA; *ORN,* 26:215, 218, 220; Illinois Hospital Register #125, 10–11, RG 94, NA; *OR,* 32 (pt. 1):555, 32 (pt. 3):381.

11. *New Era* Log, April 23–26, June 20–August 18, 1864, RG 24, NA; A. Conner Memo, April 26, 1864, and James P. Patrick to Lizzie Booth, April 28, 1864, Lionel Booth CSR (11th U.S.C.I.–New), RG 94, NA; *ORN,* 26:480, 555, 731, 750, 27:56, 100, 144.

12. *St. Louis Union,* April 14, 1864; *St. Louis Missouri Democrat,* April 15, 1864; *Cincinnati Commercial,* April 20, 1864; *Chicago Tribune,* April 21, 1864.

13. *St. Louis Union,* April 16, 23 (supplement), 1864; *Cincinnati Commercial,* April 20, 1864; *ORN,* 26:225–226; *Springfield Illinois State Journal,* April 18, 1864; *New York Times,* May 3, 1864; *St. Louis Missouri Democrat,* April 16, 1864. Letters to the two St. Louis papers are similar enough to indicate that the writers either visited the fort together or were the same person.

14. *St. Louis Missouri Democrat,* April 16, 1864.

15. *Cincinnati Gazette,* April 15, 16, 18, 22, 1864; *Springfield Illinois State Journal,* April 16, 18, 1864; *Philadelphia Press* excerpt in *Boston Liberator,* April 22, 1864; *New York Tribune,* April 15, 23, 1864; *Chicago Tribune,* April 16, 1864; *St. Louis Missouri Democrat,* April 18, 1864.

16. *Cincinnati Commercial,* April 18, 1864; *Washington National Intelligencer,* May 7, 1864; *Boston Journal,* April 15, 1864.

17. *Portland [Maine] Advertiser* excerpt in *Boston Liberator,* May 13, 1864; *Chicago Times,* April 16, 1864; *New York World,* April 16, 1864; *St. Louis Westliche Post* excerpt in *St. Louis Missouri Republican,* April 17, 1864; *Springfield Illinois State Journal,* April 16, 1864.

18. *New York National Antislavery Standard,* August 6, 1864; *Boston Liberator,* May 6, 13, June 3, 1864; *Philadelphia Christian Recorder,* April 23, 30, 1864; *New York Anglo African,* May 28, 1864.

19. *Harper's Weekly,* April 30, 1864, 284; *Frank Leslie's Illustrated Newspaper,* May 7, 1864, 97; Alice Fahs, *The Imagined Civil War: Popular Literature of the North and South, 1861–1865* (Chapel Hill: Univ. of North Carolina Press, 2001), 154, 166; W. Fletcher Thompson Jr., *The Image of War: The Pictorial Reporting of the American Civil War* (New York: Thomas Yoseloff, 1960), 172–173.

20. Charles and James E. Haynes, "The Massacre at Fort Pillow" (songsheets) (Chicago: H. M. Higgins, 1864); Moore, ed., *Rebellion Record,* vol. 8, poetry section, page 40; James T. Ayers, *The Diary of James T. Ayers: Civil War Recruiter,* ed. John H. Franklin (Springfield: Illinois State Historical Society, 1947), 18–19.

21. *OR,* 32 (pt. 1):558, 563–572; *ORN,* 26:220, 222; Cimprich and Mainfort, eds., "Fort Pillow Revisited," 303.

22. Bodnia, 188–189; *St. Louis Missouri Democrat,* April 22, 1864; *Chicago Tribune,* April 22, 1864; OR, 32 (pt. 1):555, 32 (pt. 3):381.

23. *OR,* 32 (pt. 3):210, 362, 366–367, 381–382, 411; Cimprich, 87, 92.

24. *OR,* 32 (pt. 3):405–406; U.S. Congress, *Fort Pillow Massacre,* 67; T. H. Harris to T. J. Jackson, April 28, 1864, T. H. Harris to S. A. Hurlbut, April 29, 1864, F. Hastings to T. H. Harris, April 30, 1864, W. Wollbrecht to T. H. Harris, April 30, 1864, Tom J. Jackson to T. H. Harris, April 28, 1864, and Lizzie Booth to T. H. Harris, April 28, 1864, Thomas J. Jackson CSR, RG 94, NA.

25. Cimprich and Mainfort, eds., "Fort Pillow Revisited," 297–301; Maness, "Fort Pillow Massacre," 293, 295; *OR,* ser. 1, 32 (pt. 1):610, 621; Dyer Diary, April 12, 1864, TSLA. Maness believes his riverbank argument also discredits the "Marion" and "Memphis" letters, which will be discussed later in this chapter.

26. Cimprich and Mainfort, eds., "Fort Pillow Revisited," 297, 299.

27. Alex M. Jones to Sally J. Jones, April 15, 1864, Jones-Black Family Papers; *OR*, 32 (pt. 1):623; Cimprich and Mainfort, eds., "Fort Pillow Revisited," 300.

28. *OR*, 32 (pt. 1):610, 612; Fitch, "Capture of Fort Pillow," 440; *ORN*, 26:224–225. A number of early sources used the word "retreat" but then clearly described flight.

29. *OR*, 32 (pt. 1):610, ser. 2, 7:155; L. T. Lindsay to R. McCulloch, April 19, 1864, J. Chalmers Papers, RG 109, NA; U.S. Congress, *Fort Pillow Massacre*, 94, 96; CSRs for Bradford's 13th Tennessee Cavalry Battalion, 2nd U.S.C.L.A., and 11th U.S.C.I. (New), RG 94, NA; Pension Files for members of Bradford's 13th Tennessee Cavalry Battalion, 2nd U.S.C.L.A., and 11th U.S.C.I. (New), RG 15, NA.

30. Gregory J. W. Urwin, "'We Cannot Treat Negroes . . . as Prisoners of War': Racial Atrocities and Reprisals in Civil War Arkansas," *Civil War History* 42 (September 1996): 195–201; Anne J. Bailey, "Was There a Massacre at Poison Spring?" *Military History of the Southwest* 20 (fall 1990): 164.

31. Jordan and Thomas, 142–191; Bailey, 167.

32. Cimprich and Mainfort, eds., "Fort Pillow Revisited," 296–297, 304 (this version incorrectly transcribed the number of "Marion's" regiment); *Mobile Advertiser and Register,* April 26, 1864; *Memphis Appeal,* April 18, 21, 27, 1864; *Atlanta Intelligencer,* May 4, 1864; Ward W. Briggs Jr., ed., *Soldier and Scholar: Basil Lanneau Gildersleeve and the Civil War* (Charlottesville: Univ. Press of Virginia, 1998), 303. For another reaction to early newspaper reports somewhat like Gildersleeve's, see Daniel E. Sutherland, ed., *A Very Violent Rebel: The Civil War Diary of Ellen Renshaw House* (Knoxville: Univ. of Tennessee Press, 1996), 130.

33. *OR*, 32 (pt. 3):381, 32 (pt. 1):518–540, 558, 563–565, 569–572.

34. *OR*, 32 (pt. 1):518–519.

35. *Congressional Globe,* 38 Cong., 1 Sess., 1662–1665, 1673 (April 16, 1864), 1744 (April 18, 1864), 1842 (April 21, 1864); U.S. Congress, *Fort Pillow Massacre*, 1; Bruce Tap, *Over Lincoln's Shoulder: The Committee on the Conduct of the War* (Lawrence: Univ. of Kansas Press, 1998), 29; Roy P. Basler, ed., *The Collected Works of Abraham Lincoln* (New Brunswick, N.J.: Rutgers Univ. Press, 1953), 7:303.

36. U.S. Congress, *Fort Pillow Massacre*, 8–123; *OR*, 32 (pt. 1):519–540.

37. Bergeron, ed., *Papers of Andrew Johnson,* 11:484; U.S. Congress, *Fort Pillow Massacre*, 15–45 (pp. 15 and 18 quoted); Fuchs, 105.

38. Cimprich and Mainfort, eds., "Dr. Fitch's Report," 27–28, 30–37.

39. Maness, "Fort Pillow Massacre," 294–295; *New Era* Log, April 12, 1864, RG 24, NA; 28–39; U.S. Congress, *Fort Pillow Massacre*, 26, 46, 50; *OR*, ser. 1, 32 (pt. 1):616; Illinois Hospital Register, 125:9, RG 94, NA; *St. Louis Missouri Democrat,* April 22, 1864.

40. *OR*, ser. 1, 32 (pt. 1):535, 562; *ORN*, 26:222; Cimprich and Mainfort, eds., "Dr. Fitch's Report," 38; Maness, "The Fort Pillow Massacre," 295; *St. Louis Missouri Democrat,* April 22, 1864.

41. Gideon Welles, *Diary,* 2nd ed., ed. Howard K. Beale (New York: Houghton Mifflin, 1960), 2:23–25; Basler, ed., *Works of Lincoln,* 7:328; Edward Bates, *Diary,* ed. Howard K. Beale (Washington, D.C.: GPO, 1933), 365; Tap, 200; *OR*, ser. 2, 7:113.

42. Tap, 202–203; U.S. Congress, *Fort Pillow Massacre*, 2–7 (pp. 2, 5, and 6 quoted). T. Harry Williams, "Benjamin F. Wade and the Atrocity Propaganda of the Civil War," *Ohio State Archeological and Historical Quarterly* 48 (January 1939): 43, speculated that the committee

also intended the report to convert public opinion to a more radical reconstruction program, an interpretation endorsed by Tap, 197–198, 208, and Derek W. Frisby, "'Remember Fort Pillow!': Politics, Atrocity Propaganda, and the Evolution of Hard War," in *Black Flag Over Dixie: Racial Atrocities and Reprisals in the Civil War.* ed. Gregory J. W. Urwin (Carbondale: Southern Illinois Univ. Press, 2004), 107. However, the report never explicitly makes such a connection.

43. U.S. Congress, *Fort Pillow Massacre,* 43, 46, 48, 51, 84, 86; Carroll, 28–29; *Memphis Appeal,* May 2, 1864; *Mobile Advertiser and Register,* April 26, 1864; Fuchs, 93; Jordan and Pryor, 433.

44. Illinois Hospital Register #125, 9, RG 94, NA; *New Era* Log, April 13, 1864; RG 24, NA; U.S. Congress, *Fort Pillow Massacre,* 21, 25–26, 47; Bodnia, 188; *OR,* 32 (pt. 1):525, 527, 537, 567, 616; "List of Internments, 1866," Fort Pillow File, Consolidated Correspondence, RG 92, NA. Although the *New Era*'s log says that the woman buried was black, testimony in U.S. Congress, *Fort Pillow Massacre,* 90, states that she was white. When the army tried to consolidate burials at the fort in 1866, workers could not relocate her. They found only one female, who came from the earlier Federal graveyard and had a marker stating she died in 1863.

45. U.S. Congress, *Fort Pillow Massacre,* 14, 18, 87, 95; *OR,* 32 (pt. 1):522; Cimprich and Mainfort, eds., "Fort Pillow Revisited," 303; *Memphis Appeal,* June 14, 1864.

46. U.S. Congress, *Fort Pillow Massacre,* 27, 30–31, 40; *OR,* 32 (pt. 1):522, 530, 533, 563.

47. U.S. Congress, *Fort Pillow Massacre,* 30. Frisby, 113–115, takes an opposing view.

48. Basler, ed., *Works of Lincoln,* 7:345–346; John G. Nicolay and John Hay, *Abraham Lincoln: A History* (New York: Century, 1890), 6:483–484. A different interpretation appears in T. Harry Williams, *Lincoln and the Radicals* (Madison: Univ. of Wisconsin Press, 1941), 348, and Frisby, 125.

49. *Memphis Appeal,* May 2, 1864.

50. *OR,* 32 (pt. 3):822, 32 (pt. 1):597, 615; Wills, 15, 36. In Bejack, 19, DeWitt Clinton Fort gauged the time of shooting after the charge at thirty minutes.

51. *OR,* 32 (pt. 1):597, 621–622; *Mobile Advertiser and Appeal,* May 7, 1864.

52. *Memphis Appeal,* May 13, 1864.

53. *Charleston Mercury,* April 21, May 2, 3, 1864; *Mobile Advertiser and Register,* May 6, 1864; *Atlanta Intelligencer,* May 8, 1864.

54. *OR,* 32 (pt. 1):617, 619; Dudley Taylor Cornish, *The Sable Arm: Negro Troops in the Union Army, 1861–1865* (New York: Longmans, Green, 1956), 177–178; Bergeron, "Olustee," 144–145; Tap, 206.

55. Bryce Suderow, "The Battle of the Crater: The Civil War's Worst Massacre," *Civil War History* 43 (September 1997): 220–224; Urwin, "We Cannot," 209–210. William Marvel, *The Battles for Saltville* (Lynchburg, Va.: H. E. Howard, 1992), 145–148, and Thomas D. Mays, *The Saltville Massacre* (Fort Worth, Tex.: McWhiney Foundation Press, 1995), 58–72, sharply disagree on the number killed at the incident and its significance.

56. *Congressional Globe,* 38th Cong., 1st Sess. (June 15, 1864), 2988; U.S. Congress, *Statutes at Large,* 12:129; Glatthaar, *Forged in Battle,* 179.

57. Roy P. Basler, "And for His Widow and His Orphan," *Quarterly Journal of the Library of Congress* 27 (October 1970): 292–294; Roy P. Basler, ed., *The Collected Works of Abraham Lincoln: Supplement* (Westport, Conn.: Greenwood Press, 1974), 243; U.S. Congress, *Statutes at Large,* 13:389.

58. *OR,* 32 (pt. 3):464.

59. *Philadelphia Inquirer,* April 29, 1864; *Memphis Bulletin,* April 28, 1864. Mack J. Leaming, who had raised the flags during the battle, claimed in an October 22, 1864, letter to C. C. Washburn that the flag belonged to the Bradford Battalion (Andrew Johnson Papers, Library of Congress).

60. Wills, 199–200, 213–215; G. A. Hanson, *Minor Incidents of the Late War* (Bartow, Fla.: Sessions, Barker and Kilpatrick, Publishers, 1887), 74–75; William C. Davis, *Lone Star Rising: The Revolutionary Birth of the Texas Republic* (New York: Free Press, 2004), 248; *OR,* 32 (pt. 3):819; Kenneth Bancroft Moore, "Fort Pillow, Forrest, and the United States Colored Troops in 1864," *Tennessee Historical Quarterly* 54 (summer 1995): 113.

61. *OR,* 32 (pt. 1):586–587, 589–591, 593, 600–601; Moore, "Fort Pillow," 119–121. Washburne believed that all of his black troops had taken an oath to give no quarter, but no corroborating evidence exists.

62. Suderow, 222; Edwin S. Redkey, ed., *A Grand Army of Black Men: Letters from African-American Soldiers in the Union Army, 1861–1865* (New York: Cambridge Univ. Press, 1992), 68, 99, 273; Trudeau, *Like Men of War,* 268–269; R. J. M. Blackett, ed., *Thomas Morris Chester, Black Civil War Correspondent: His Dispatches from the Virginia Front* (Baton Rouge: Louisiana State Univ. Press, 1989), 262.

63. John F. Brobst, *Well Mary: Civil War Letters of a Wisconsin Volunteer,* ed. Margaret B. Roth (Madison: Univ. of Wisconsin Press, 1960), 56–57; Glatthaar, *Forged in Battle,* 157–158; Charles Harvey Brewster, *When This Cruel War Is Over: Civil War Letters,* ed. David W. Blight (Amherst: Univ. of Massachusetts Press, 1992), 304; Harry F. Jackson and Thomas F. O'Donnell, eds., *Back Home in Oneida: Herman Clarke and His Letters* (Syracuse, N.Y.: Syracuse Univ. Press, 1965), 142; Urwin, "We Cannot," 207; Robert H. Strong, *A Yankee Private's Civil War,* ed. Ashley Haley (Chicago: Henry Regnery Company, 1961), 15–16.

64. Humphey H. Hood to Benjamin Hood, May 3, 1864, Benjamin Hood Papers, Illinois State Historical Society, Springfield, Ill.; Keith P. Wilson, *Campfires of Freedom: The Camp Life of Black Soldiers during the Civil War* (Kent, Ohio: Kent State Univ. Press, 2002), 79; Versalle F. Washington, *Eagles on Their Buttons: A Black Regiment in the Civil War* (Columbia: Univ. of Missouri Press, 1999), 40; J. H. Meteer to Caleb Mills, April 18, 1864, Caleb Mills Papers, Indiana Historical Society, Indianapolis, Ind.; Tap, 207.

65. Grimsley, *Hard Hand,* 18; Brigham D. Madsen, *The Shoshoni Frontier and the Bear River Massacre* (Salt Lake City: Univ. of Utah Press, 1983), 20, 143, 192–199; Stan Hoig, *The Sand Creek Massacre* (Norman: Univ. of Oklahoma Press, 1961), vii–viii, 69, 129, 161–170.

66. Mark Grimsley, "'Rebels' and 'Redskins': U.S. Military Conduct toward White Southerners and Native Americans in Comparative Perspective," in *Civilians in the Path of War,* ed. Mark Grimsley and Clifford J. Rogers (Lincoln: Univ. of Nebraska Press, 2002), 154–155; Mark Grimsley, "Union Soldiers and the Persistence of Restraint in the Civil War" (unpublished essay, copy in John Cimprich's possession), passim; Trudeau, *Like Men of War,* 58–59, 88, 100–102; Suderow, 220; Urwin, "We Cannot," 210; Hoig, 170; Michael Fellman, "At the Nihilist Edge: Reflections on Guerrilla Warfare during the American Civil War," in *On the Road to Total War: The American Civil War and the German Wars of Unification, 1861–1871,* ed. Stig Forster and Jorg Nagler (New York: Cambridge Univ. Press, 1997), 522–531. For massacres of Southern unionist civilians by Confederates, see Stanley S. McGowen, "Battle or Massacre?: The Incident on the Nueces, August 10, 1862," *Southwestern Historical Quarterly* 104 (July 2001):

80–86; Jonathan D. Sarris, "Anatomy of an Atrocity: The Madden Branch Massacre and Guerrilla Warfare in North Georgia, 1861–1865," *Georgia Historical Quarterly* 77 (winter 1993): 684, 705; Philip S. Paludan, *Victims: A True Story of the Civil War* (Knoxville: Univ. of Tennessee Press, 1981), 97.

67. *OR,* ser. 2, 7:703, 1010.

CHAPTER SEVEN. PUBLIC MEMORY AND FORT PILLOW

1. Wakefield and Turner, 32; *Memphis Argus,* September 10, 1865; Mainfort, *Archaeological Investigations,* 89.

2. Mainfort, *Archaeological Investigations,* 88–90; Lists of Remains of Federal Dead Exhumed at Fort Pillow, 1866 and 1867, Cemetery Reports–Fort Pillow, RG 92, NA; *Memphis Commercial Appeal,* February 20, 1949, IV-3; G. Kurt Piehler, *Remembering War the American Way* (Washington, D.C.: Smithsonian Institution Press, 1995), 51. Cemetery officials disagreed with the number of bodies found in 1866. Mainfort, *Archaeological Investigations,* 186, 190, notes that his 1976–1978 digs found a few bits of human bone remaining in the fort's south trench.

3. Michael Kammen, *Mystic Chords of Memory: The Transformation of Tradition in American Culture* (New York: Knopf, 1991), 9–10.

4. For a few of the many examples, see William M. Thayer, *A Youth's History of the Rebellion,* 3 vols. (New York: J. Miller, 1865), 3:289–305; Benson J. Lossing, *Pictorial History of the Civil War in the U.S.A.,* 3 vols. (Philadelphia: G. W. Childs, 1866), 3:245; J. T. Headley, *The Great Rebellion: A History of the Civil War in the U.S.,* 2 vols. (Hartford, Conn.: American Pub. Co., 1866), 2:296; Robert Tomes, *The War with the South,* 3 vols. (New York: Virtue and Yorston, 1867), 3:321; George W. Williams, *History of the Negro Race in America, 1619–1880,* 2 vols. (New York: G. P. Putnam's Sons, 1883), 2:359–375.

5. Willard Glazier, *Battles for the Union* (Hartford, Conn.: Dustin, Gilman and Co., 1878), 345–346; Henry H. Lloyd, *Battle History of the Great Rebellion,* 4 vols. (New York: H. H. Lloyd, 1865), 4:291; Lieutenant Keene, *Black Cudjo, or, the Contraband Spy: A Thrilling Story of the Fort Pillow Massacre* (New York: Novelist, 1883), 2–3, 13, 17–18.

6. C. Fitch, "Capture of Fort Pillow," 440–441; McClure, 22; *Washington National Tribune,* February 9, 1888. Also see an unpublished account, Samuel Green Pension File (11th U.S.C.I.–New), RG 15, NA

7. William T. Sherman, *Memoirs* (New York: D. Appleton and Company, 1875), 2:12–13.

8. Fuchs, 105; Edward A. Pollard, *Southern History of the War* (New York: C. B. Richardson, 1866), 3:252.

9. Moore, ed., *Rebellion Record,* vol. 8, poetry section, page 55; Jordan and Pryor, 439–440; N. B. Forrest to C. A. White, November 16, 1868, Forrest (Nathan Bedford) Papers, 1866–1868, Pearce Civil War Collection, Navarro College, Corsicana, Tex..

10. Bergeron, ed., *Papers of Andrew Johnson,* 11:484–485; *Memphis Post,* December 27–28, 1866; *Congressional Record,* 46th Cong., 1st Sess., 1129 (May 7, 1879); Wills, 334–342.

11. Wills, 342–343; Jordan and Pryor, viii; Charles R. Wilson, *Baptized in Blood: The Religion of the Lost Cause, 1865–1920* (Athens: Univ. of Georgia Press, 1980), 7; Iwona Irwin-Zarecka, *Frames of Remembrance: The Dynamics of Collective Memory* (New Brunswick, N.J.: Transaction Publishers, 1994), 80.

12. Jordan and Pryor, 422, 432–434, 442–443; Robert H. Cartmell Diary, January–April 1864, TSLA; *Memphis Appeal,* June 23, 1864; Wilson, *Baptized in Blood,* 46–47; *OR,* 32 (pt. 1):608, 612, 614. The only antagonistic act charged against African American troops in the biography was that of having "indulged in provoking, impudent jeers" during the truce, an allegation mentioned in two previous Confederate sources that blamed the entire garrison rather than singling out blacks. See Cimprich and Mainfort, eds., "Fort Pillow Revisited," 299, 301.

13. An unverifiable but believable 1864 letter, posted at John L. Kimbrough, "Through the Lines: West Tennessee to North Carolina," http://www.jlkstamps.com/long/letter.htm, accessed 2003, states that only Forrest's capture of Fort Pillow ended the Federals' mistreatment of civilians, but the most specific example given clearly referred to the much more active garrison of 1863.

14. Jordan and Pryor, 439–440; Mitchell, *Soldiers,* 30, 218; Wiley, *Billy Yank,* 349–350; Wiley, *Johnny Reb,* 313; McPherson, *For Cause and Comrades,* 53.

15. *Mobile Advertiser and Register,* April 26, 1864; Cimprich and Mainfort, eds., "Fort Pillow Revisited," 301–302; *OR,* 32 (pt. 1):597; *Memphis Appeal,* May 13, 1864.

16. Bodnia, 189; Cimprich and Mainfort, eds., "Fort Pillow Revisited," 305.

17. Jordan and Pryor, 444–448, 704; Roll 896, Miscellaneous Rolls and Related Records of Federal Prisoners of War, 1861–65, RG 249, NA. As noted in Grimsley, *Hard Hand,* 14, no treaties establishing binding rules of warfare existed until the twentieth century.

18. Jordan and Pryor, 439, 444, 449; *OR,* 32 (pt. 1):597, 612, 615; Cimprich and Mainfort, eds., "Fort Pillow Revisited," 301–302; excerpt from *Cairo News* in *Philadelphia Inquirer,* April 24, 1864. Seven of the 18 officers at or above the rank of sergeant in black units and 14 to 17 of the 37 to 41 officers above that rank in white units died in the incident.

19. Jordan and Pryor, 432–433, 440, 448, 450–453; Wilson, *Baptized in Blood,* 100, 139–143; Fuchs, 13.

20. Anderson, "True Story," 323, 325; Thomas F. Berry, *Four Years with Morgan and Forrest* (Oklahoma City, Okla.: Harlow-Ratliff Company, 1914), 270–271; Theodore F. Brewer, "Storming of Fort Pillow," *Confederate Veteran,* 33 (December 1925): 459, 478; Carroll, 28–29; *Congressional Globe,* 46th Cong., 1st Sess., 1125–1128 (May 7, 1879); James Chalmers, "Forrest and His Campaigns," *Southern Historical Society Papers* 7 (October 1879): 470; James Dinkins, *Personal Recollections and Experiences in the Confederate Army* (Cincinnati: Robert Clarke Company, 1897), 150–154 [same version in James Dinkins, "Capture of Fort Pillow," *Confederate Veteran* 33 (December 1925): 461–462]; Thomas D. Duncan, *Recollections* (Nashville: McQuiddy Printing Company, 1922), 134–135; Hancock, 351, 360, 367; Hanson, 72. Also see a memoir not published until much later, Bejack, 19–20.

21. *Congressional Globe,* 46th Cong., 1st Sess., 1125 (May 7, 1879); Chalmers, "Forrest," 470.

22. Hanson, 72; Berry, 269–271; Dinkins, 152–154. For another version of Hanson's story, supposedly remembered from a conversation with Forrest, see Dabney Herndon Maury, *Recollections of a Virginian in the Mexican, Indian, and Civil Wars* (New York: Charles Scribner's Sons, 1894), 217.

23. Carroll, 29; Hancock, 361; Berry, 220–221; Duncan, 134; Witherspoon, 66.

24. Wyeth, v, 361, 367–368, 371, 382; Nicolay and Hay, 6:483–484; Henry, 268.

25. Wyeth, 382–390.

26. Ibid.; Cimprich and Mainfort, "Fort Pillow Revisited," 305.

27. Wyeth, 382–390 (pp. 384 and 385 quoted); Hughes et al., *Bell*, x, 126, 256–257 (quoted).

28. Ibid., vii, 349, 350, 355 (quoted), 367–371, 629, 653; Wilson, *Baptized in Blood*, 39–43; Gaines M. Foster, *Ghosts of the Confederacy: Defeat, the Lost Cause, and the Emergence of the New South, 1865–1913* (New York: Oxford Univ. Press, 1987), 5, 126.

29. Herman Hattaway, *General Stephen D. Lee* (Jackson: Univ. Press of Mississippi, 1976), 222–223; Foster, 126; David W. Blight, *Race and Reunion: The Civil War in American Memory*, (Cambridge, Mass.: Harvard Univ. Press, 2001), 381; James Harvey Mathes, *General Forrest*, ed. James Grant Wilson (New York: D. Appleton and Company, 1902), v, 223–224.

30. James F. Rhodes, *History of the United States from the Compromise of 1850* (New York: Macmillan, 1904), 5:512–513; Blight, 357–359.

31. Blight, 386–388; John W. Burgess, *The Civil War and the Constitution* (New York: Scribner's Sons, 1901), 2:236; James K. Hosmer, *The American Civil War* (New York: Harper and Brothers, 1908), 2:111; Carter G. Woodson, *The Negro in Our History* (Washington, D.C.: Associated Publishers, 1922), 376; Foster, 184.

32. Foster, 6; "A Gift to the Commander-in-Chief" *Confederate Veteran* 34 (July 1926): 278.

33. Foster, 129–131, 273; Court Carney, "The Contested Image of Nathan Bedford Forrest," *Journal of Southern History* 67 (August 2001): 602; *Memphis Commercial Appeal*, August 14, 1908; "Site of Fort Pillow in Mississippi River," *Confederate Veteran* 16 (December 1908): 625; *Ripley [Tenn.] News*, September 25, 1908; Wakefield and Turner, 32.

34. Mills, 6, 8–12; *Jackson [Tenn.] Sun*, August 19, 1934.

35. Irwin-Zarecka, 62, 74; James G. Randall, *The Civil War and Reconstruction* (Boston: D. C. Heath and Co., 1931), 507; Arthur C. Cole, *The Irrepressible Conflict, 1850–1865* (New York: Macmillan, 1934), 320; W. E. Burghardt Du Bois, *Black Reconstruction* (New York: Russell and Russell, 1935), 114–115; John H. Franklin, *From Slavery to Freedom: A History of American Negroes* (New York: McGraw-Hill, 1947), 289; Benjamin Quarles, *The Negro in the Civil War* (Boston: Little, Brown, 1953), 206.

36. Williams, *Lincoln and the Radicals*, 434–435; E. Merton Coulter, *The Confederate States of America, 1861–1865* (Baton Rouge: Louisiana State Univ. Press, 1950), 264, 340.

37. Eric William Shepherd, *Bedford Forrest: The Confederacy's Greatest Cavalryman* (New York: Dial Press, 1930), 170–172; Andrew Nelson Lytle, *Bedford Forrest and His Critter Company* (New York: Milton, Balch and Company, 1931), 279–280; Carney, 618–619, 630; Henry, 259–264.

38. John L. Jordan, "Was There a Massacre at Fort Pillow?" *Tennessee Historical Quarterly* 6 (June 1947): 99–100, 113–114, 131–132, 191 (pp. 100 and 131 quoted); John Cimprich and Robert C. Mainfort Jr., "The Fort Pillow Massacre: A Statistical Note," *Journal of American History* 76 (December 1989): 832–833.

39. Cornish, 174–175. Also following World War II, Frank Yerby's novel *Foxes of Harrow* (New York: Dial Press, 1946), 520–521, presented the incident briefly as an ugly racist massacre but incorrectly portrayed the garrison as making a formal surrender first.

40. Albert Castel, "The Fort Pillow Massacre: A Fresh Examination of the Evidence," *Civil War History* 4 (March 1958): 38, 41, 43, 45, 47–50; Cimprich and Mainfort, "Fort Pillow Massacre," 833.

41. John Bodnar, *Remaking America: Public Memory, Commemoration, and Patriotism in the Twentieth Century* (Princeton, N.J.: Princeton Univ. Press, 1992), 208–210; Perry Lentz, *The Falling Hills* (New York: Scribner, 1967), esp. 4–5, 145, 214, 362, 366, 408, 434, 437.

42. James Sherburne, *The Way to Fort Pillow* (Boston: Houghton Mifflin, 1972), esp. 206, 208, 222–226, 239, 242–243, 249.

43. *Memphis Commercial Appeal,* 1973 clipping, Fort Pillow Historical Area Museum; "Fort Pillow Historical Trail and Trek" (handout from 1970s), Fort Pillow Vertical File, Memphis and Shelby County Library; Tennessee Department of Conservation, "Master Plan Report: Fort Pillow State Historic Area" (typescript, 1975), 34–36, Fort Pillow Historical Area Museum, Henning, Tenn.; Mainfort, *Archaeological Investigations,* 1, 77; Tom Shouse, interview by John Cimprich, Henning, Tenn., July 10, 1997.

44. Cimprich and Mainfort, "Fort Pillow Massacre," 833; Bodnia, 186–190; Cimprich and Mainfort, eds., "Fort Pillow Revisited," 293–306; Cimprich and Mainfort, eds., "Dr. Fitch's Report," 27–39; Robert B. Toplin, "Ken Burns' *The Civil War* as an Interpretation of History," in *Ken Burns' "The Civil War": The Historians Respond,* ed. Robert B. Toplin (New York: Oxford Univ. Press, 1996), 29–31; *Memphis Commercial Appeal,* November 20, 1975, 3 (quoted), November 30, 1975, 7; Shouse interview.

45. Mainfort, *Archaeological Investigations,* 1, 77–78, 132, 191.

46. Wills, 380; Carney, 625–630; *Memphis Press Scimitar,* May 25, 1982, A-1.

47. Maness, "Fort Pillow Massacre," 287–315. His essay was reprinted in Lonnie E. Maness, *An Untutored Genius: The Military Career of General Nathan Bedford Forrest* (Oxford, Miss.: Guild Bindery Press, 1990). Roy Morris Jr., "Fort Pillow: Massacre or Madness?" *America's Civil War* 13 (November 2000): 32, takes a similar view. Several recent studies of racial incidents during the Civil War accept that unnecessary killing occurred but try to minimize the extent. See Frisby, 110–126, Marvell, 145–148, Bergeron, "Olustee," 144.

48. Joyce Hansen, *Which Way Freedom?* (New York: Walker, 1986), esp. 23, 117.

49. Gregory J. Macaluso, *The Fort Pillow Massacre: The Reason Why* (New York: Vantage, 1989), 9–16, 49–53.

50. Shouse interview.

51. Toplin, 20, 25, 27.

52. Cimprich and Mainfort, "Fort Pillow Massacre," 830–837; Wills, 185–193. Also see Hurst, 171–177; Hughes et al., *Bell,* 128–130.

53. Fuchs, 12, 103, 136. James D. Lockett, "The Lynching Massacre of Black and White Soldiers at Fort Pillow, Tennessee, April 12, 1864," *Western Journal of Black Studies* 22 (summer 1998): 87–91, and John Gauss, *Black Flag! Black Flag!: The Battle at Fort Pillow* (Lanham, Md.: Univ. Press of America, 2003), 130–173, express similar views.

APPENDIX B. COMPILING DATA FOR TABLE 7

1. Cimprich and Mainfort, "Fort Pillow Massacre," 836–837.

2. *OR,* 32 (pt. 1):556; 11th U.S.C.I. (New) CSRs, 2nd U.S.C.L.A. CSRs, George C. Thomas CSR (7th Kansas Cavalry), John T. Young CSR (24th Missouri Infantry), and A. J. W. Thompson CSR (32nd Iowa Infantry), RG 94, NA; Roll 896, Miscellaneous Rolls and Related Records of Federal Prisoners of War, 1861–65, RG 249, NA; Charles Fitch file, Personal Papers of Physicians, RG 94, NA. The 6th U.S.C.H.A. recruited one new member at Fort Pillow, George

Shaw, who therefore did not appear in regimental records but was in U.S. Congress, *Fort Pillow Massacre*, 25, and Illinois Hospital Register #125, 10, RG 94, NA. After the incident the 6th was absorbed by the 11th U.S.C.I. (New).

3. Bradford's 13th Tennessee Cavalry Battalion Return, April 8, 1864, Muster Rolls, RG 94, NA; Bradford's 13th Tennessee Cavalry Battalion, CSRs, RG 94, NA; George Dunn, Francis M. Peck, Thomas Ruffins, and Henry I. Wilkins CSRs (14th Tennessee Cavalry, U.S.A.), RG 94, NA; John F. Ray, Berry I. Rogers, William J. Stephens, James M. Christenburg, James Clark, John H. Copher, and William F. Price CSRs (6th Tennessee Cavalry, U.S.A.); Henry E. Williams Medical Cards (Bradford's 13th Tennessee Cavalry Battalion), RG 94, NA; Cimprich and Mainfort, eds., "Dr. Fitch's Report," 29. After the incident the unionist state government renamed Bradford's Battalion as the 14th Tennessee Cavalry and later merged it into the 6th Tennessee Cavalry.

4. H. W. Holloway CSR (2nd Illinois Cavalry), RG 94, NA; Andrew M. Baker CSR (52nd Indiana Infantry), RG 94, NA; *OR*, 32 (pt. 1): 520, 528, 567; U.S. Congress, *Fort Pillow Massacre*, 30, 82, 120; Bodnia, 188–189. If new evidence showed that the civilian combatants belonged to the enrolled militia, they would deserve inclusion.

5. Robert Blaylock, Henry M. Brock, Carroll A. Callison, Elam V. Cashion, Michael Click, Marcus Cloys, George W. Crawford, Miles M. Deason, Daniel M. Floyd, John B. Johnson, Franklin A. Keys, William Mauldin, James Mitchell, William A. Nicholson, James A. Tally, and Matthew C. Wiggs Pension Files (13th Tennessee Cavalry), RG 15, NA; Tennessee Hospital Register #588, 19, and Illinois Hospital Register, 125:5–6, 9–11, RG 94, NA; List of Wounded Received aboard *Silver Cloud,* April 13, 1864, Letters from Squadron Officers, vol. 31, RG 24, NA; 6th U.S.C.H.A. return, May 10, 1864, Muster Rolls, RG 94, NA; *St. Louis Missouri Democrat,* April 16, 1864; Jordan and Pryor, 704; *OR*, 32 (pt. 1): 510, 562; U.S. Congress, *Fort Pillow Massacre*, 13, 32–33.

Bibliography

MANUSCRIPT COLLECTIONS

Alabama Department of Archives and History, Montgomery, Ala.
Mark Lyons Papers.
Charles S. Stewart Papers.

Clarke Historical Library, Mt. Pleasant, Mich.
John Ryan Memoir.

Duke University Library, Durham, N.C.
Braxton Bragg Papers.
Jeremy F. Gilmer Papers.
David B. Harris Papers.
Thomas Jordan Papers.
Will Kennedy Papers.
Daniel Ruggles Papers.
William Wylie Papers.

Fort Pillow State Historical Area Museum, Henning, Tenn.
Cornelia Anderson Watkins Diary.
Wiley G. Poston Letter.
Tennessee Department of Conservation, "Master Plan Report: Fort Pillow State Historic Area" (typescript, 1975).

Historical Society of Pennsylvania, Philadelphia, Pa.
Gratz Collection.

Illinois State Historical Society, Springfield, Ill.
Benjamin Hood Papers.
George R. Yost, "A Brief History of the U.S. Gunboat *Cairo* of the Mississippi Squadron."
George R. Yost Diary.

Indiana Historical Society, Indianapolis, Ind.
Caleb Mills Papers.
William Harper Papers.
Bernard Schermerhorn Papers.

Indiana State Library, Indianapolis, Ind.
Charles B. Lasselle Papers.
Isaac McMillan Papers.
Augustus G. Sinks Memoir.
James R. Slack Papers.

Library of Congress, Washington, D.C.
P. G. T. Beauregard Papers.
Braxton Bragg Papers.
Andrew Johnson Papers.
Leonidas Polk Papers.

Louisiana State University Library, Baton Rouge, La.
Harrod C. Anderson Diary.

Memphis and Shelby County Public Library, Memphis, Tenn.
Fort Pillow Vertical File.
Goodman Papers.

National Archives, Washington, D.C.
Microcopy 617: Post Returns.
RG 15: Records of the Veterans Administration.
RG 24: Naval Records.
RG 29: Census Bureau Records, 1860.
RG 45: Naval Records Collection of the Office of Naval Records and Library.
RG 92: Quartermaster General's Office Records.
RG 94: Adjutant General's Office Records.
RG 105: Records of the Bureau of Refugees, Freedmen, and Abandoned Land.
RG 109: Confederate Records.
RG 123: Court of Claims Records.
RG 217: Records of the Accounting Officers of the Department of the Treasury.
RG 233: Records of the House of Representatives.
RG 366: Civil War Special Agencies of the Treasury Department.
RG 393: Army Continental Commands, 1821–1920.

Naval Historical Center, Washington D.C.
George R. Yost Memoir.

Navarro College Library, Corsicana, Tex.
Pearce Civil War Collection, Forrest (Nathan Bedford) Papers, 1866–1868.

Privately Owned Documents
James U. Ledsinger Letter.
Theodore A. Mills, "Fort Pillow" (typescript, n.d.).
B. Swearingin Letter.

Southern Historical Collection, University of North Carolina Library, Chapel Hill, N.C.
Cabarrus-Slade Papers.
John Houston Bills Diary.

State Historical Society of Iowa, Iowa City, Iowa
Hugh Johnson Papers.
Albert Town Papers.

Tennessee State Library and Archives, Nashville, Tenn.
Army of Tennessee Papers.
Robert H. Cartmell Diaries.
Confederate Collection.
James C. Edenton Diary.
Gordon/Avery Family Papers.
Lauderdale County Court Minutes, vols. D and E.
Lauderdale County Deed Register, vol. I.

University of Memphis Library, Memphis, Tenn.
Fort Pillow Papers.
Jones-Black Family Papers.

University of Michigan Transportation Library, Ann Arbor, Mich.
Charles Ellet Papers.

Vigo County Public Library, Terre Haute, Ind.
John S. Pickard Diary.

NEWSPAPERS

Alton [Ill.] Democrat, 1862–1863.

Atlanta Intelligencer, 1864.

Boston Journal, 1862, 1864.

Boston Liberator, 1864.

Butler Center [Iowa] Stars and Stripes, 1863.

Charleston Mercury, 1864.

Chicago Times, 1862–1864.

Chicago Tribune, 1862–1864.

Cincinnati Commercial, 1862, 1864.

Cincinnati Gazette, 1862–1864.

Cincinnati Times, 1862, 1864.

Davenport Gazette, 1863.

Frank Leslie's Illustrated Newspaper, 1862, 1864.

Greensburg [Ind.] Decatur Republican, 1862.

Harper's Weekly, 1862, 1864.

Humboldt [Tenn.] Chronicle, 1862.

Illustrated London News, 1862.

Indianapolis State Journal, 1862, 1864.

Jackson [Tenn.] Sun, 1934.

Lawrenceburg [Ind.] Register, 1863.

Logansport [Ind.] Democratic Pharos, 1862.

Logansport [Ind.] Journal, 1862.

Mason City [Iowa] Cerro Gordo Republican, 1863.

Memphis Appeal, 1861–1864.

Memphis Argus, 1861–1862, 1865.

Memphis Avalanche, 1861–1862.

Memphis Bulletin, 1862–1864.

Memphis Commercial Appeal, 1908, 1973, 1975.

Memphis Post, 1866.

Memphis Press Scimitar, 1982.

Mobile Advertiser and Register, 1862, 1864.

Nevada [Iowa] Republican Reveille, 1863.

New York Anglo African, 1864.

New York Herald, 1862.

New York National Antislavery Standard, 1864.

New York Times, 1862–1864, 1999.

New York Tribune, 1862–1864.

New York World, 1862, 1864.

Peoria Transcript, 1862.

Philadelphia Christian Recorder, 1864.

Philadelphia Inquirer, 1864.

Philadelphia Press, 1862–1864.

Ripley [Tenn.] News, 1908.

Rockville [Ill.] Parke County Republican, 1862–1864.

Rushville [Ind.] Jacksonian, 1862–1864.

Rushville [Ind.] Republican, 1862–1864.

St. Louis Missouri Democrat, 1862–1864.

St. Louis Missouri Republican, 1862–1864.

St. Louis Union, 1864.

Springfield Illinois State Journal, 1863–1864.

Story City [Iowa] Herald, 1922.

Toledo Blade, 1863.

Washington National Intelligencer, 1864.

Washington National Tribune, 1888.

Waukegan [Ill.] Gazette, 1862.

PUBLISHED PRIMARY SOURCES

"A Gift to the Commander-in-Chief." *Confederate Veteran* 34 (July 1926): 278.

Aldrich, Charles. "Incidents Connected with the History of the Thirty-Second Iowa Infantry." *Iowa Journal of History and Politics* 4 (January 1906): 70–85.

Anderson, Charles W. "The True Story of Fort Pillow." *Confederate Veteran* 3 (November 1895): 322–326.

Anderson, John Q., ed. *Brokenburn: The Journal of Kate Stone.* Baton Rouge: Louisiana State Univ. Press, 1995.

Atkinson, J. H., ed. "A Civil War Letter of Captain Elliot Fletcher, Jr." *Arkansas Historical Quarterly* 22 (spring 1963): 49–54.

Ayers, James T. *The Diary of James T. Ayers: Civil War Recruiter.* Edited by John H. Franklin. Springfield: Illinois State Historical Society, 1947.

Baird, Nancy, ed. "There Is No Sunday in the Army: Civil War Letters of Lunsford P. Yandell, 1861–62." *Filson Club History Quarterly* 53 (October 1979): 317–327.

Baker, Alpheus. "Island No. 10." *Southern Bivouac* 1 (October 1882): 54–62.

Barbiere, Joe. *Scraps from the Prison Table at Camp Chase and Johnson's Island.* Doylestown, Pa.: W. W. H. Davis, 1868.

Basler, Roy P., ed. *The Collected Works of Abraham Lincoln.* 9 vols. New Brunswick, N.J.: Rutgers Univ. Press, 1953–1955.

——, ed. *The Collected Works of Abraham Lincoln: Supplement.* Westport, Conn.: Greenwood Press, 1974.

Bates, Edward. *Diary.* Edited by Howard K. Beale. Washington, D.C.: GPO, 1933.

Bejach, Lois D., ed. "The Journal of a Civil War 'Commando'–DeWitt Clinton Fort." *West Tennessee Historical Society Papers* 2 (1948): 5–32.

Berlin, Ira, ed. *Freedom: A Documentary History of Emancipation, 1861–1867.* 4 vols. in 2 series to date. New York: Cambridge Univ. Press, 1982–.

Berry, Thomas F. *Four Years with Morgan and Forrest.* Oklahoma City: Harlow-Ratliff Company, 1914.

Blackett, R. J. M., ed. *Thomas Morris Chester, Black Civil War Correspondent: His Dispatches from the Virginia Front.* Baton Rouge: Louisiana State Univ. Press, 1989.

Blount, T. W. "Captain Thomas William Blount and His Memoirs." *Southwestern Historical Quarterly* 39 (July 1935): 1–13.

Bodnia, George, ed. "Fort Pillow 'Massacre': Observations of a Minnesotan." *Minnesota History* 43 (spring 1973): 186–190.

Bolton, George W. *"In Defense of My Country."* Edited by Sue L. Eakin and Morgan Peoples. Bernice, La.: Privately printed, 1983.

Bragg, Junius N. *Letters of a Confederate Surgeon, 1861–1865.* Edited by Helen B. Gaugan. Camden, Ark.: Privately printed, 1960.

Brewer, Theodore F. "Storming of Fort Pillow." *Confederate Veteran* 33 (December 1925): 459, 478.

Brewster, Charles Harvey. *When This Cruel War Is Over: Civil War Letters.* Edited by David W. Blight. Amherst: Univ. of Massachusetts Press, 1992.

Briggs, Ward W., Jr., ed. *Soldier and Scholar: Basil Lanneau Gildersleeve and the Civil War.* Charlottesville: Univ. Press of Virginia, 1998.

Bringhurst, Thomas H., and Frank Swigart. *History of the Forty-Sixth Regiment Indiana Volunteer Infantry.* Logansport, Ind.: Press of Wilson, Humphreys and Company, 1888.

Brobst, John. *Well Mary: Civil War Letters of a Wisconsin Volunteer.* Edited by Margaret B. Roth. Madison: Univ. of Wisconsin Press, 1960.

Browne, Junius H. *Four Years in Secessia.* Chicago: George and C. W. Sherwood, 1865.

Bryner, Cloyd. *Bugle Echoes: The Story of Illinois 47th.* Springfield, Ill.: Phillips Bros., 1905.

Callender, Eliot. "What a Boy Saw on the Mississippi." In *Military Essays and Recollections,* vol. 1. Chicago: Military Order of the Loyal Legion, Illinois Commandary, 1891.

Campbell, John Q. *The Union Must Stand.* Edited by Mark Grimsly and Todd D. Miller. Knoxville: Univ. of Tennessee Press, 2000.

Carroll, John W. *Autobiography and Reminiscences.* Henderson, Tenn.: Privately printed, 1898.

Cavins, Aden G. *War Letters.* Evansville, Ind.: Rosenthal-Kuebbler Printing Co., 1907.

Chalmers, James R. "Forrest and His Campaigns." *Southern Historical Society Papers* 7 (October 1879): 451–486.

Cherster, William W., ed. "Diary of Captain Elisha Tompkin Hollis." *West Tennessee Historical Society Papers* 39 (1985): 82–118.

Cimprich, John, and Robert C. Mainfort Jr., eds. "Dr. Fitch's Report on the Fort Pillow Massacre." *Tennessee Historical Quarterly* 44 (spring 1985): 27–39.

——, eds. "Fort Pillow Revisited: New Evidence about an Old Controversy." *Civil War History* 28 (December 1982): 293–306.

Coffin, Charles C. *Four Years of Fighting.* Boston: Tichnor and Fields, 1866.

Critchell, Robert S. *Recollections of a Fire Insurance Man.* Chicago: Privately printed, 1909.

Currie, George E. *Warfare along the Mississippi.* Edited by Norman E. Clarke. Mt. Pleasant, Mich.: Clarke Historical Library, Central Michigan University, 1961.

Delisdimier, L. T. "Cruise of the Steamer Price." In *The Confederate Soldier in the Civil War, 1861–1865,* edited by Benjamin LaBree. Louisville: Courier Journal Job-Printing Co., 1895.

Dinkins, James. "Capture of Fort Pillow." *Confederate Veteran* 33 (December 1925): 461–462.

——. *Personal Recollections and Experiences in the Confederate Army.* Cincinnati: Robert Clarke Company, 1897.

Duncan, Thomas D. *Recollections.* Nashville: McQuiddy Printing Company, 1922.

Edwards, Richard. *St. Louis Directory.* St. Louis: Southern Pub. Co., 1860.

Fitch, C. "Capture of Fort Pillow–Vindication of General Chalmers by a Federal Officer." *Southern Historical Society Papers* 7 (September 1879): 439–441.

Fussel, Joshua. *History of the Thirty-Fourth Regiment.* N.p.: Privately printed, n.d.

Gambrell, Herbert P. "Rams versus Gunboats: A Landsman's Naval Exploits." *Southwest Review* 23 (October 1937): 46–78.

George, Henry. *History of the 3rd, 7th, 8th, and 12th Kentucky CSA.* Louisville: C. T. Dearing Printing Company, 1911.

Graf, Leroy P., Ralph Haskins, and Paul Bergeron, eds. *The Papers of Andrew Johnson.* 16 volumes. Knoxville: Univ. of Tennessee Press, 1967–2000.

Grimes, Absalom C. "Diary." *Confederate Veteran* 22 (December 1914): 549–551.

Guffin, Ross. "A Night on the Mississippi." *Putnam's Magazine* 5 (April 1870): 419–424. Reprinted in Diffley, Kathleen, ed. *To Live and Die: Collected Stories of the Civil War, 1861–1876.* Durham, N.C.: Duke Univ. Press, 2002.

Hancock, Richard R. *Hancock's Diary.* Nashville: Bramdon Printing Company, 1887.

Hanson, G. A. *Minor Incidents of the Late War.* Bartow, Fla.: Sessions, Barker, and Kilpatrick, Publishers, 1887.

Haynes, Charles, and James E. Haynes. "The Massacre of Fort Pillow." [Song-sheets.] Chicago: H. M. Higgins, 1864.

Hewett, Janet, ed. *Supplement to the Official Records of the Union and Confederate Armies.* 100 vols. Wilmington, N.C.: Broadfoot, 1994–2001.

Indiana. *Report of the Adjutant General of the State of Indiana.* 10 vols. Indianapolis: Various publishers, 1865–1869.

Jackson, Harry F., and Thomas F. O'Donnell, eds. *Back Home in Oneida: Herman Clarke and His Letters.* Syracuse, N.Y.: Syracuse Univ. Press, 1965.

Kimbrough, John L. "Through the Lines: West Tennessee to North Carolina." http://www.jlkstamps.com/long/letter.htm, accessed 2003.

Knox, Thomas W. *Campfire and Cotton Field.* New York: Blelock and Company, 1865.

Law, J. G. "Diary of a Confederate Soldier." *Southern Historical Society Papers* 10 (August, September, December 1882): 882, 378–381, 564–569.

Mainfort, Robert C., Jr., and Patricia E. Coats, eds. "Soldiering at Fort Pillow, 1862–1864: An Excerpt from the Civil War Memoirs of Addison Sleeth." *West Tennessee Historical Society Papers* 36 (1982): 72–90.

Maury, Dabney Herndon. *Recollections of a Virginian in the Mexican, Indian, and Civil Wars.* New York: Charles Scribner's Sons, 1894.

McClure, Thomas W. "The Fort Pillow Massacre." In Ward Edwards, *Lion-Hearted Luke, or, the Plan to Capture Mosby: A Story of Perilous Adventure in the Rebellion.* New York: Novelist, 1884.

McLean, William E. *The Forty-Third Regiment of Indiana Volunteers.* Terre Haute, Ind.: C. W. Brown, 1902.

Milligan, John D., ed. *From the Fresh-Water Navy: 1861–64.* Annapolis, Md.: Naval Institute Press, 1970.

Moore, Frank, ed. *The Rebellion Record: A Diary of American Events.* 11 vols. New York: D. Van Nostrand, 1861–1868.

Partin, Robert. "A Confederate Sergeant's Report to His Wife during the Bombardment of Fort Pillow." *Tennessee Historical Quarterly* 15 (September 1956): 243–252.

Poe, James T. *The Raving Foe.* Edited by J. C. Poe. Eastland, Tex.: Longhorn Press, 1967.

Popchock, Barry, ed. *Soldier Boy: The Civil War Letters of Charles O. Musser, 29th Iowa.* Iowa City: Univ. of Iowa Press, 1995.

Read, C. W. "Reminiscences of the Confederate States Navy." *Southern Historical Society Papers* 1 (May 1876): 331–362.

Redkey, Edwin S., ed. *A Grand Army of Black Men: Letters from African-American Soldiers in the Union Army, 1861–1865.* New York: Cambridge Univ. Press, 1992.

Russell, William H. *My Diary North and South.* Edited by Fletcher Pratt. New York: Harper and Row, 1965.

Scott, John. *Story of the Thirty-Second Iowa Infantry Volunteers.* Nevada, Iowa: Privately printed, 1896.

Sessel, Edwin H. "Our Evacuation of Fort Pillow." *Confederate Veteran* 6 (January 1898): 32.

Sherman, William T. *Memoirs.* 2 vols. New York: D. Appleton and Company, 1875.

Shingleton, Royce, ed. "'With Loyalty and Honor as a Patriot': Recollections of a Confederate Soldier." *Alabama Historical Quarterly* 33 (fall/winter 1971): 240–263.

Simon, John Y., ed. *The Papers of Ulysses S. Grant.* 26 vols. to date. Carbondale: Southern Illinois Univ. Press, 1967–.

"Site of Fort Pillow in Mississippi River." *Confederate Veteran* 16 (December 1908): 625.

Stephenson, Philip D. *Civil War Memoir.* Edited by Nathaniel C. Hughes Jr. Conway, Ark.: UCA Press, 1995.

Stevenson, William G. *Thirteen Months in the Rebel Army.* New York: A. S. Barnes and Burr, 1862.

Strong, Robert H. *A Yankee Private's Civil War.* Edited by Ashley Haley. Chicago: Henry Regnery Company, 1961.

Sutherland, Daniel E., ed. *A Very Violent Rebel: The Civil War Diary of Ellen Renshaw House.* Knoxville: Univ. of Tennessee Press, 1996.

Swift, Lester L., ed. "Letters from a Sailor on a Tinclad." *Civil War History* 7 (March 1961): 48–62.

Tennessee. *Report of the Adjutant General of the State of Tennessee of the Military Forces of the State from 1861–1866.* Nashville: S. C. Mercer, 1866.

"Thomas Joseph Payne, Captain (C.S.A.)." http://www.mindspring.com/~jogt/surnames/paynetj.htm, accessed 2003.

Thompson, Meriwether Jefferson "Jeff." *The Civil War Reminiscences of General M. Jeff Thompson.* Edited by Donal J. Stanton et al. Dayton, Ohio: Morningside Press, 1988.

Trudeau, Noah A., ed. *Voices of the 55th: Letters from the 55th Massachusetts Volunteers, 1861–1865.* Dayton, Ohio: Morningside Press, 1996.

True, Rowland Stafford. "Life aboard a Gunboat: A First Person Account." *Civil War Times Illustrated* 9 (February 1971): 36–43.

U.S. Congress. *Alvin Hawkins.* 37th Cong., 3rd Sess., H. Doc. 46 (serial 1173).

——. *Congressional Globe.* 38th Cong.

——. *Congressional Record.* 46th Cong.

——. *Fort Pillow Massacre.* 38th Cong., 1st Sess., H. Doc. 65 (serial 1206).

——. *The Statutes at Large, Treaties, and Proclamations of the United States of America,* vols. 12–13. Edited by George P. Sanger. Boston: Little, Brown, 1863–1865.

U.S. Department of the Interior. Census Office. *Eighth Census of the United States, 1860.* 4 vols. Washington, D.C.: GPO, 1864.

U.S. Navy Department. *Official Records of the Union and Confederate Navies in the War of the Rebellion.* 31 vols. Washington, D.C.: GPO, 1894–1927.

U.S. War Department, *Medical and Surgical History of the Rebellion.* 12 vols. Washington, D.C.: GPO, 1870.

——. *The War of the Rebellion: A Compilation of the Official Records of the Union and Confederate Armies.* 131 vols. Washington, D.C.: GPO, 1880–1901.

Voorhis, Aurelius Lyman. *Life and Times.* Edited by Jerry Voorhis Sr. New York: Vantage Press, 1976.

Walke, Henry. *Naval Scenes and Reminiscences of the Civil War.* New York: F. R. Reed and Company, 1877.

——. "The Western Flotilla at Fort Donelson, Island Number Ten, Fort Pillow, and Memphis." In Robert U. Johnson and Clarence C. Buel, eds. *Battles and Leaders of the Civil War,* vol. 1. New York: Century Co., 1887.

Washington, Versalle F. *Eagles on Their Buttons: A Black Regiment in the Civil War.* Columbia: Univ. of Missouri Press, 1999.

Wells, Gideon. *Diary,* 2nd ed. Edited by Howard K. Beale. 3 vols. New York: Houghton Mifflin, 1960.

Williams, James M. *From That Terrible Field: Civil War Letters.* Edited by John K. Fulmer. Tuscaloosa: Univ. of Alabama Press, 1981.

Wilson, Ephraim A. *Memories of the War.* Cleveland: W. M. Bayne Printing Company, 1893.

Witherspoon, William. *Reminiscences of a Scout, Spy, and Soldier of Forrest's Cavalry.* Jackson, Tenn.: McCowat-Mercer Printing Company, 1910.

Young, John P. *The Seventh Tennessee Cavalry (Confederate): A History.* Nashville: Publishing House of the Methodist Episcopal Church, South, 1890.

SECONDARY SOURCES

Ambrose, Stephen E. *Citizen Soldiers.* New York: Simon and Schuster, 1997.

Ash, Stephen V. *When the Yankees Came: Conflict and Chaos in the Occupied South, 1861–1865.* Chapel Hill: Univ. of North Carolina Press, 1995.

Bailey, Anne J. "Was There a Massacre at Poison Spring?" *Military History of the Southwest* 20 (fall 1990): 156–168.

Basler, Roy P. "And for His Widow and His Orphan." *Quarterly Journal of the Library of Congress* 27 (October 1970): 291–294.

Bearss, Edwin C. *Hardluck Ironclad: The Sinking and Salvage of the Cairo,* 2nd ed. Baton Rouge: Louisiana State Univ. Press, 1980.

Bergeron, Arthur W., Jr. *Guide to Louisiana Confederate Military Units, 1861–1865.* Baton Rouge: Louisiana State Univ. Press, 1989.

Beringer, Richard E., et al. *Why the South Lost the Civil War*. Athens: Univ. of Georgia Press, 1986.

Biographical and Historical Memoirs of Story County, Iowa. Chicago: Goodspeed Publishing Co., 1890.

Birtle, Andrew J. *U.S. Army Counterinsurgency and Contingency Operations Doctrine, 1860–1941*. Washington, D.C.: Center for Military History, 1998.

Blight, David W. *Race and Reunion: The Civil War in American Memory*. Cambridge, Mass.: Harvard Univ. Press, 2001.

Boatner, Mark M., III. *Encyclopedia of the American Revolution*, 2nd ed. New York: Stackpole Press, 1994.

Bodnar, John. *Remaking America: Public Memory, Commemoration, and Patriotism in the Twentieth Century*. Princeton: Princeton Univ. Press, 1991.

Burgess, John W. *The Civil War and the Constitution*. 2 vols. New York: Scribner's Sons, 1901.

Carney, Court. "The Contested Image of Nathan Bedford Forrest." *Journal of Southern History* 67 (August 2001): 601–630.

Castel, Albert. "Fort Pillow: Victory or Massacre." *American History Illustrated* 9 (April 1974): 4–10, 46–48.

——. "The Fort Pillow Massacre: A Fresh Examination of the Evidence." *Civil War History* 4 (March 1958): 37–50.

Cimprich, John. *Slavery's End in Tennessee, 1861–1865*. Tuscaloosa: Univ. of Alabama Press, 1985.

Cimprich, John, and Robert C. Mainfort Jr. "The Fort Pillow Massacre: A Statistical Note." *Journal of American History* 76 (December 1989): 830–837.

Cole, Arthur C. *The Irrepressible Conflict, 1850–1856*. New York: Macmillan, 1934.

Cooling, Benjamin F. *Fort Donelson's Legacy: War and Society in Kentucky and Tennessee, 1862–1863*. Knoxville: Univ. of Tennessee Press, 1997.

——. *Forts Henry and Donelson: The Key to the Confederate Heartland*. Knoxville: Univ. of Tennessee Press, 1987.

Cornish, Dudley Taylor. *The Sable Arm: Negro Troops in the Union Army, 1861–1865*. New York: Longmans, Green, 1956.

Coulter, E. Merton. *The Confederate States of America, 1861–1865*. Baton Rouge: Louisiana State Univ. Press, 1950.

Cullum, George W. *Biographical Register of the Officers and Graduates of the U.S. Military Academy*, 3rd. ed. 3 vols. Boston: Houghton Mifflin, 1891.

Current, Richard N., ed. *Encyclopedia of the Confederacy*. 4 vols. New York: Simon and Schuster, 1993.

Daniel, Larry J. *Soldiering in the Army of Tennessee: A Portrait of Life in a Confederate Army*. Chapel Hill: Univ. of North Carolina Press, 1991.

Daniel, Larry J., and Lynn Bock. *Island No. 10: Struggle for the Mississippi Valley*. Tuscaloosa: Univ. of Alabama Press, 1996.

Davis, Charles H. *Life of Charles Henry Davis, Rear Admiral, 1807–1877.* Boston: Houghton Mifflin, 1899.

Davis, William C. *Lone Star Rising: The Revolutionary Birth of the Texas Republic.* New York: Free Press, 2004.

———. "The Massacre at Saltville." *Civil War Times Illustrated* 9 (February 1971): 4–11, 43–48.

Du Bois, W. E. Burghardt. *Black Reconstruction.* New York: Russell and Russell, 1935.

Dwyer, Christopher S. "Raiding Strategy: As Applied by the Western Confederate Cavalry in the American Civil War." *Journal of Military History* 63 (April 1999): 263–281.

Fahs, Alice. *The Imagined Civil War: Popular Literature of the North and South, 1861–1865.* Chapel Hill: Univ. of North Carolina Press, 2001.

Fellman, Michael. "At the Nihilist Edge: Reflections on Guerrilla Warfare during the American Civil War." In *On the Road to Total War: The American Civil War and the German Wars of Unification, 1861–1871,* edited by Stig Forster and Jorg Nagler. New York: Cambridge Univ. Press, 1997.

Fisher, Noel. "'Prepare Them for My Coming': General William T. Sherman, Total War, and Pacification in West Tennessee." *Tennessee Historical Quarterly* 51 (summer 1992): 75–86.

Fitzgerald, William S. "We Will Always Stand by You." *Civil War Times Illustrated* 32 (November/December 1993): 71–72, 88–90.

Foos, Paul. *A Short, Offhand, Killing Affair: Soldiers and Social Conflict during the Mexican-American War.* Chapel Hill: Univ. of North Carolina Press, 2002.

Foster, Gaines M. *Ghosts of the Confederacy: Defeat, the Lost Cause, and the Emergence of the New South, 1865–1913.* New York: Oxford Univ. Press, 1987.

Fowler, William M., Jr. *Under Two Flags: The American Navy in the Civil War.* New York: Norton, 1990.

Franklin, John H. *From Slavery to Freedom: A History of American Negroes.* New York: McGraw-Hill, 1947.

Fuchs, Richard L. *An Unerring Fire: The Massacre at Fort Pillow.* Rutherford, N.J.: Farleigh Dickinson Univ. Press, 1994.

Gauss, John. *Black Flag! Black Flag!: The Battle at Fort Pillow.* Lanham, Md.: Univ. Press of America, 2003.

Gillespie, Michael L. "The Novel Experiment: Cotton-Clads and Steamboatmen." *Civil War Times Illustrated* 22 (December 1983): 34–39.

Glatthaar, Joseph T. "The Common Soldier of the Civil War." In *New Perspectives on the Civil War: Myths and Realities of the National Conflict,* edited by John Y. Simon and Michael E. Stevens. Madison, Wisc.: Madison House, 1998.

———. *Forged in Battle: The Civil War Alliance of Black Soldiers and White Officers.* New York: Free Press, 1990.

Glazier, Willard. *Battles for the Union*. Hartford, Conn.: Duston, Gilman and Co., 1878.

Gosnell, H. Allen. *Guns on the Western Waters: The Story of the River Gunboats in the Civil War*. Baton Rouge: Louisiana State Univ. Press, 1949.

Grimsley, Mark. *The Hard Hand of War: Union Military Policy toward Southern Civilians, 1861–1865*. New York: Cambridge Univ. Press, 1995.

——. "Race in the Civil War." *North and South* 4 (March 2001): 36–55.

——. "'Rebels' and 'Redskins': U.S. Military Conduct toward White Southerners and Native Americans in Comparative Perspective." In *Civilians in the Path of War,* edited by Mark Grimsley and Clifford J. Rogers. Lincoln: Univ. of Nebraska Press, 2002.

——. "Union Soldiers and the Persistence of Restraint in the Civil War" (unpublished essay, copy in John Cimprich's possession).

Hattaway, Herman. *General Stephen D. Lee*. Jackson: Univ. Press of Mississippi, 1976.

Hattaway, Herman, and Archer Jones. *How the North Won: A Military History of the Civil War*. Urbana: Univ. of Illinois Press, 1983.

Headley, J. T. *The Great Rebellion: A History of the Civil War in the U.S.* 2 vols. Hartford, Conn.: American Pub. Co., 1866.

Hearn, Chester G. *Ellet's Brigade: The Strangest Outfit of All*. Baton Rouge: Louisiana State Univ. Press, 2000.

Henry, Robert Selph. *"First With the Most" Forrest*. New York: Bobbs-Merrill Company, 1944.

History of Rush County, Indiana. Chicago: Brant and Fuller, 1888.

Hoig, Stan. *The Sand Creek Massacre*. Norman: Univ. of Oklahoma Press, 1961.

Hoppin, James Mason. *Life of Andrew Hull Foote*. New York: Harper and Brothers, 1874.

Hosmer, James K. *The American Civil War*. 2 vols. New York: Harper and Brothers, 1908.

Huch, Ronald K. "Fort Pillow Massacre: The Aftermath of Paducah," *Illinois State Historical Society Journal* 66 (spring 1973): 62–70.

Hughes, Nathaniel C., Jr. *The Battle of Belmont: Grant Strikes South*. Chapel Hill: Univ. of North Carolina Press, 1991.

Hughes, Nathaniel C., Jr., et al. *Brigadier General Tyree H. Bell, C.S.A.: Forrest's Fighting Lieutenant*. Knoxville: Univ. of Tennessee Press, 2004.

Hughes, Nathaniel C., Jr., and Roy P. Stonesifer Jr. *The Life and Wars of Gideon J. Pillow*. Chapel Hill: Univ. of North Carolina, 1993.

Hurst, Jack. *Nathan Bedford Forrest: A Biography*. New York: Knopf, 1993.

Irwin-Zarecka, Iwana. *Frames of Remembrance: The Dynamics of Collective Memory*. New Brunswick, N.J.: Transaction Publishers, 1994.

Johnston, William Preston. *The Life of Gen. Albert Sidney Johnston*. New York: D. Appleton and Company, 1878.

Jordan, John L. "Was There a Massacre at Fort Pillow?" *Tennessee Historical Quarterly* 6 (June 1947): 99–133.

Jordan, Thomas, and J. P. Pryor. *The Campaigns of Lieut. Gen. N. B. Forrest, and of Forrest's Cavalry.* New York: Blelock and Company, 1868.

Jordan, Weymouth T., and Gerald W. Thomas. "Massacre at Plymouth: April 20, 1864." *North Carolina Historical Review* 72 (April 1995): 125–197.

Kammen, Michael. *Mystic Chords of Memory: The Transformation of Tradition in American Culture.* New York: Knopf, 1991.

Lewis, Gene D. *Charles Elliot, Jr.: The Engineer as Individualist, 1810–1862.* Urbana: Univ. of Illinois Press, 1968.

Linderman, Gerald F. *Embattled Courage: The Experience of Combat in the American Civil War.* New York: Free Press, 1987.

———. *The World Within War: America's Combat Experience in World War II.* New York: Free Press, 1997.

Lloyd, Henry H. *Battle History of the Great Rebellion.* 4 vols. New York: H. H. Lloyd, 1865.

Lockett, James D. "The Lynching Massacre of Black and White Soldiers at Fort Pillow, Tennessee, April 12, 1864." *Western Journal of Black Studies* 22 (summer 1998): 84–93.

Lossing, Benson J. *Pictorial History of the Civil War in the U.S.A.* 3 vols. Philadelphia: G. W. Childs, 1866–1868.

Lovett, Bobby L. "The West Tennessee Colored Troops in Civil War Combat." *West Tennessee Historical Society Papers* 34 (1980): 53–70.

Lufkin, Charles L. "'Not Heard from since April 12, 1864': The Thirteenth Tennessee Calvary, U.S.A." *Tennessee Historical Quarterly* 45 (summer 1986): 133–151.

Luraghi, Raimondo. *A History of the Confederate Navy.* Translated by Paolo E. Coletta. Annapolis, Md.: Naval Institute Press, 1996.

Lytle, Andrew Nelson. *Bedford Forest and His Critter Company.* New York: Milton, Balch and Company, 1931.

Macaluso, Gregory J. *The Fort Pillow Massacre: The Reason Why.* New York: Vantage, 1989.

Madsen, Brigham D. *The Shoshoni Frontier and the Bear River Massacre.* Salt Lake City: Univ. of Utah Press, 1985.

Mainfort, Robert C., Jr. "A Folk Art Map of Fort Pillow." *West Tennessee Historical Society Papers* 40 (1986): 73–78.

———. *Archaeological Investigations at Fort Pillow State Historic Area, 1976–1978.* Nashville: Division of Archaeology, 1980.

Maness, Lonnie E. "The Fort Pillow Massacre: Fact or Fiction." *Tennessee Historical Quarterly* 45 (winter 1986): 287–315.

———. "Fort Pillow under Confederate and Union Control." *West Tennessee Historical Society Papers* 38 (1984): 84–98.

——. *An Untutored Genius: The Military Career of General Nathan Bedford Forest.* Oxford, Miss.: Guild Bindery Press, 1990.

Marvel, William. *The Battles for Saltville.* Lynchburg, Va.: H. E. Howard, 1992.

Mathes, James Harvey. *General Forrest.* Edited by James Grant Wilson. New York: D. Appleton and Company, 1902.

Mays, Thomas D. *The Saltville Massacre.* Fort Worth, Tex.: McWhiney Foundation Press, 1995.

McGowen, Stanley S. "Battle or Massacre?: The Incident on the Nueces, August 10, 1862." *Southwestern Historical Quarterly* 104 (July 2000): 65–86.

McPherson, James M. *Battle Cry of Freedom: The Civil War Era.* New York: Oxford Univ. Press, 1988.

——. *For Cause and Comrades: Why Men Fought in the Civil War.* New York: Oxford Univ. Press, 1997.

Milligan, John D. *Gunboats Down the Mississippi.* Annapolis, Md.: Naval Institute Press, 1965.

Mitchell, Reid. *Civil War Soldiers.* New York: Viking Press, 1988.

——. *The Vacant Chair: The Northern Soldier Leaves Home.* New York: Oxford Univ. Press, 1993.

Monaghan, Jay. *Swamp Fox of the Confederacy: The Life and Military Service of M. Jeff Thompson.* Tuscaloosa, Ala.: Confederate Publishing Company, 1956.

Moore, Kenneth Bancroft. "Fort Pillow, Forrest, and the United States Colored Troops in 1864." *Tennessee Historical Quarterly* 54 (summer 1995): 112–123.

Morris, Roy, Jr. "Fort Pillow: Massacre or Madness?" *America's Civil War* 13 (November 2000): 26–32.

Musicant, Ivan. *Divided Waters: The Naval History of the Civil War.* New York: Harper-Collins, 1995.

Nicolay, John G., and John Hay. *Abraham Lincoln: A History.* 10 vols. New York: Century, 1890.

O'Brien, Sean Michael. *In Bitterness and In Tears: Andrew Jackson's Destruction of the Creeks and Seminoles.* Westport, Conn.: Praeger, 2003.

Olson, James S., and Randy Roberts. *My Lai: A Brief History with Documents.* Boston: Bedford Books, 1998.

Paludan, Phillip S. *Victims: A True Story of the Civil War.* Knoxville: Univ. of Tennessee Press, 1981.

Piehler, G. Kurt. *Remembering War the American Way.* Washington, D.C.: Smithsonian Institution Press, 1995.

Pollard, Edward A. *Southern History of the War.* 3 vols. New York: C. B. Richardson, 1866.

Quarles, Benjamin. *The Negro in the Civil War.* Boston: Little, Brown, 1953.

Ramage, James A. *Rebel Raider: The Life of John Hunt Morgan.* Lexington: Univ. Press of Kentucky, 1986.

Randall, James G. *The Civil War and Reconstruction*. Boston: D. C. Heath and Co., 1931.

Rhodes, James F. *History of the United States from the Compromise of 1850*. 10 vols. New York: Macmillan, 1904.

Robertson, James I., Jr. *Soldiers Blue and Gray*. Columbia: Univ. of South Carolina Press, 1988.

Robinson, Armstead Louis. *Bitter Fruits of Bondage: The Demise of Slavery and the Collapse of the Confederacy, 1861–1865*. Charlottesville: Univ. of Virginia Press, 2005.

Roca, Steven L. "Presence and Precedents: The USS *Red Rover* during the American Civil War, 1861–1865." *Civil War History* 44 (June 1998): 91–110.

Roman, Alfred. *The Military Operations of General Beauregard*. 2 vols. New York: Harper and Brothers, 1884.

Rushing, Anthony C. *Ranks of Honor: A Regimental History of the 11th Arkansas Infantry Regiment and Poe's Cavalry Battalion C.S.A., 1861–1865*. Little Rock, Ark.: Eagle Press, 1990.

Sarris, Jonathan D. "Anatomy of an Atrocity: The Madden Branch Massacre and Guerrilla Warfare in North Georgia, 1861–1865." *Georgia Historical Quarterly* 77 (winter 1993): 679–710.

Sheppard, Eric William. *Bedford Forrest: The Confederacy's Greatest Cavalryman*. New York: Dial Press, 1930.

Silverstone, Paul. *Warships of the Civil War Navies*. Annapolis, Md.: Naval Institute Press, 1989.

Slagle, Jay. *Ironclad Captain: Seth Ledyard Phelps and the U.S. Navy, 1841–1864*. Kent, Ohio: Kent State Univ. Press, 1996.

Smith, John David, ed. *Black Soldiers in Blue: African American Troops in the Civil War Era*. Chapel Hill: Univ. of North Carolina Press, 2002.

Starr, Stephen Z. *The Union Cavalry in the Civil War*. 3 vols. Baton Rouge: Louisiana State Univ. Press, 1979.

Sudrow, Bryce. "The Battle of the Crater: The Civil War's Worst Massacre." *Civil War History* 43 (September 1997): 219–224.

Sutherland, Daniel E., ed. *Guerrillas, Unionists, and Violence on the Confederate Home Front*. Fayetteville: Univ. of Arkansas Press, 1999.

Symonds, Craig L. *Stonewall of the West: Patrick Cleburne and the Civil War*. Lawrence: Univ. of Kansas Press, 1997.

Tap, Bruce. *Over Lincoln's Shoulder: The Committee on the Conduct of the War*. Lawrence: Univ. of Kansas Press. 1998.

Tennessee. *Tennesseans in the Civil War: A Military History of Confederate and Union Units*. 2 vols. Nashville: Tennessee Civil War Centennial Commission, 1964–1965.

Thayer, William M. *A Youth's History of the Rebellion*. 3 vols. New York: J. Miller, 1865.

Thompson, W. Fletcher, Jr. *The Image of War: The Pictorial Reporting of the American Civil War.* New York: Thomas Yoseloff, 1960.

Thompson, William Y. *E. M. Graham: North Louisianian.* Lafayette, La.: Center for Louisiana Studies, University of Southwestern Louisiana, 1984.

Tomes, Robert. *The War with the South.* 3 vols. New York: Virtue and Yorston, 1867.

Toplin, Robert B., ed. *Ken Burns' "The Civil War": The Historians Respond.* New York: Oxford Univ. Press, 1996.

Trudeau, Noah A. "'Kill the Last Damn One of Them': The Fort Pillow Massacre." In *With My Face to the Enemy: Perspectives on the Civil War,* edited by Robert Cowly. New York: G. P. Putnam's Sons, 2001.

——. *Like Men of War: Black Troops in the Civil War, 1862–1865.* Boston: Little, Brown, 1998.

Tucker, Spencer C. *Andrew Foote: Civil War Admiral on Western Waters.* Annapolis, Md.: Naval Institute Press, 2000.

Urwin, Gregory J. W., ed. *Black Flag Over Dixie: Racial Atrocities and Reprisals in the Civil War.* Carbondale: Southern Illinois Univ. Press, 2004.

——. "'We Cannot Treat Negroes . . . as Prisoners of War': Racial Atrocities and Reprisals in Civil War Arkansas," *Civil War History* 42 (September 1996): 193–210.

U.S. Navy Department, Historical Division. *Civil War Naval Chronology.* 6 vols. Washington, D.C.: GPO, 1961–1966.

——. *Dictionary of American Naval Fighting Ships.* 8 vols. Washington, D.C.: GPO, 1970.

Utley, Robert M., and Wilcomb E. Washburn. *Indian Wars,* 2nd ed. New York: American Heritage, 1985.

Wakefield, Frances T., and Emma S. Turner. "Fort Pillow." In *Lauderdale County from Earliest Times,* edited by Kate J. Peters. Ripley, Tenn.: Sugar Hill Lauderdale County Library, 1957.

Westwood, Howard C. "Captive Black Union Soldiers in Charleston–What to Do?" *Civil War History* 28 (March 1982): 28–44.

Wiley, Bell I. *The Life of Billy Yank: The Common Soldier of the Union.* Baton Rouge: Louisiana State Univ. Press, 1952.

——. *The Life of Johnny Reb: The Common Soldier of the Confederacy.* Baton Rouge: Louisiana State Univ. Press, 1943.

Williams, George W. *History of the Negro Race in America, 1619–1880.* 2 vols. New York: G. P. Putnam's Sons, 1883.

Williams, T. Harry. "Benjamin F. Wade and the Atrocity Propaganda of the Civil War." *Ohio State Archeological and Historical Quarterly* 48 (January 1939): 35–43.

——. *Lincoln and the Radicals.* Madison: Univ. of Wisconsin Press, 1941.

———. *P. G. T. Beauregard: Napoleon in Gray.* Baton Rouge: Louisiana State Univ. Press, 1955.

Wills, Brian Steel. *A Battle from the Start: The Life of Nathan Bedford Forrest.* New York: HarperCollins, 1992.

Wilson, Charles R. *Baptized in Blood: The Religion of the Lost Cause, 1865–1920.* Athens: Univ. of Georgia Press, 1980.

Wilson, Keith P. *Campfires of Freedom: The Camp Life of Black Soldiers during the Civil War.* Kent, Ohio: Kent State Univ. Press, 2002.

Woodson, Carter G. *The Negro in Our History.* Washington, D.C.: Associated Publishers, 1922.

Wyatt-Brown, Bertram. *Southern Honor: Ethics and Behavior in the Old South.* New York: Oxford Univ. Press, 1982.

Wyeth, John A. *The Life of General Nathan Bedford Forrest.* New York: Harper and Brothers, 1899.

NOVELS

Hansen, Joyce. *Which Way Freedom?* New York: Walker, 1986.

Keene, Lieutenant. *Black Cudjo, or, the Contraband Spy: A Thrilling Story of the Fort Pillow Massacre.* New York: Novelist, 1883.

Lentz, Perry. *The Falling Hills.* New York: Scribner, 1967.

Sherburne, James. *The Way to Fort Pillow.* Boston: Houghton Mifflin, 1972.

Yerby, Frank. *Foxes of Harrow.* New York: Dial Press, 1946.

OTHER SOURCES

Historical Collectible Auctions. Catalogue for September 28, 2000, Auction. Burlington, N.C.: Privately printed, 2000.

Pacific Book Auction Galleries. Catalogue for October 20, 1994, Auction. San Francisco: Privately printed, 1994.

Shouse, Tom. Interview by John Cimprich, Henning, Tenn., July 10, 1997.